AF699973

THE MYTH OF DIALECTICS

The Myth of Dialectics

Reinterpreting the Marx–Hegel Relation

John Rosenthal
Assistant Professor of Philosophy
Colorado College
Colorado, USA

First published in Great Britain 1998 by
MACMILLAN PRESS LTD
Houndmills, Basingstoke, Hampshire RG21 6XS and London
Companies and representatives throughout the world

A catalogue record for this book is available from the British Library.

ISBN 0–333–69442–2

First published in the United States of America 1998 by
ST. MARTIN'S PRESS, INC.,
Scholarly and Reference Division,
175 Fifth Avenue, New York, N.Y. 10010

ISBN 0–312–17600–7

Library of Congress Cataloging-in-Publication Data
Rosenthal, John, 1961–
The myth of dialectics : reinterpreting the Marx–Hegel relation /
John Rosenthal.
p. cm.
Includes bibliographical references and index.
ISBN 0–312–17600–7
1. Value. 2. Money. 3. Logic. 4. Marxian economics. 5. Marx, Karl, 1818–1883. 6. Hegel, Georg Wilhelm Friedrich, 1770–1831. I. Title.
HB201.R83 1997
338.5'21—DC21 97–8402
CIP

© John Rosenthal 1998

All rights reserved. No reproduction, copy or transmission of this publication may be made without written permission.

No paragraph of this publication may be reproduced, copied or transmitted save with written permission or in accordance with the provisions of the Copyright, Designs and Patents Act 1988, or under the terms of any licence permitting limited copying issued by the Copyright Licensing Agency, 90 Tottenham Court Road, London W1P 9HE.

Any person who does any unauthorised act in relation to this publication may be liable to criminal prosecution and civil claims for damages.

The author has asserted his right to be identified as the author of this work in accordance with the Copyright, Designs and Patents Act 1988.

This book is printed on paper suitable for recycling and made from fully managed and sustained forest sources.

10 9 8 7 6 5 4 3 2 1
07 06 05 04 03 02 01 00 99 98

Printed in Great Britain by
The Ipswich Book Company Ltd
Ipswich, Suffolk

Contents

Preface

This volume might appear to have an esoteric theme and indeed it does: the 'Marx–Hegel relation' and the mysteries of 'dialectics' which are commonly supposed to comprise its core. It also, however, has a thoroughly mundane theme: money and the distinctive mode of sociality, viz. 'the market' or commodity-exchange, of which money is the indispensable instrument. My reasons for coming to the latter theme by way of the tortuous detour of the former have to do no doubt with such biographical accidents as induce an individual to train in philosophy, but also, on the 'macro' level, with some recent developments in intellectual history and, more specifically, in the history of 'Marxism'.

In light of the collapse of the Communist regimes of Eastern Europe and the widespread and increasingly aggressive rejection of Marx's theoretical legacy which accompanied the latter, one of the more surprising intellectual developments of recent years has been a certain revival in academic circles of specifically *Hegelian* Marxism. At least inasmuch as the Anglo-American context is concerned, the impulse for this 'return to Hegel' among Marxist scholars can be supposed to have derived in large measure from a somewhat earlier event of a quite different order: namely, the emergence in the mid-1980s of an alleged 'analytical' reformulation of Marx, employing the methodological tools of modern neoclassical economics. This 'reformulation' of Marx quickly revealed itself in the work of its most prominent exponents, John Roemer and Jon Elster, likewise to represent an outright rejection (albeit of ostensibly socialist inspiration) of almost everything customarily associated with him, and thus demanded a response from more traditionally-minded Marxists. Among the latter, many knew of no better way to counter Elster's and Roemer's assault on the Marxian canon than to cite Lenin's aphorism to the effect that: 'It is impossible to understand Marx's *Capital*, and especially its first chapter, without having studied the whole of Hegel's *Logic*.'

The defenders of Marx could be assured that their opponents would not await any mystical illumination which required so strict a discipline. Substantive debate between the two camps thus being largely precluded, they turned to the task of commentary and the disclosure of 'correspondences' between the Marxian and Hegelian corpora: 'correspondences' which often seemed to be imbued with a sort of cabbalistic significance – since their social-analytical import too often remained unclarified. In any case, henceforth the recapturing of Marx's original insights was once again supposed to depend upon a correct appreciation of his 'dialectical method'.

In *The Myth of Dialectics*, I have wanted to chart a kind of theoretical 'third way' which avoids the alternative of 'analytical' or Hegelian Marxism. I have wanted to establish that, yes, there is something more (indeed much more) to Marx's political economy than what can be grasped with the tools of neoclassical economics, but, no, that something more is not 'dialectics'. It is, I suggest, the Marxian theory of value. The latter has been widely misconstrued as a peculiar theory of *price-formation*: a 'labour theory of value', distinguishable from that of Ricardo only, say, by its greater refinement or even just the unnecessary abstruseness of its Hegeloid trappings. But I argue that Marx's theory is in fact *sui generis* and that its object is not (or at least not in the first instance) the system of prices, but rather the *form of value* itself which the coalescence of any determinate price-system presupposes. Inasmuch as it must gain existence as something really distinct from the particular goods whose value gets not only expressed *in it* but also precisely incarnated *by it*, this value-form of the commodity is, namely, the *money-form*. Apart from the latter, all the various value-phenomena discernible in the circulation sphere of a capitalist economy – prices, wages, profits, and so on – would lack the very medium of their existence.

Marx's so-called 'value theory' is, then, from the outset a theory of *money* and a theory of money, I am suggesting, in a unique sense which finds no exact parallel in either neoclassical economics or classical political economy. It is indeed remarkable that this is so often overlooked and that Marx gets attributed a 'value theory' on the Ricardian pattern. For Marx himself was unequivocal in identifying the lack of any analysis of the value-form – even as some monetary unit had continually to be employed in the manner of a *numéraire* for *other* theoretical purposes – as the 'fundamental deficiency' of classical political economy. Thus, for example, in the *Theories of Surplus Value*, he dismisses the section of Ricardo's *Principles* on the 'Measure of Value' as 'without anything significant. The connection between value, its immanent measure through labour-time and the necessity for an *external* measure of the value of commodities is not grasped, not even raised as a question'. Later on in the same text, he remarks more succinctly: 'Ricardo misjudges the importance of the market, because he does not understand the nature of money'.

Now, it is precisely in the development of his value theory – and indeed, as Lenin's remark suggests, most notably in the very first chapter of *Capital*, volume I – that Marx makes systematic use of linguistic formulae bearing a distinctly Hegelian stamp. Hence the more acute of the 'new' Hegelian Marxists have quite rightly placed special emphasis upon it. I will argue here, however, that the presence of such apparently Hegelian formulae in the discourse of *Capital* has absolutely *nothing* to do with any adoption on Marx's part of a 'dialectical method'. Inasmuch as the scientific legitimacy of Marx's analysis is concerned, this is all to the good: since, as I will try to show in some detail, the 'method' which Hegel's own exposition tends most characteristically to follow, is not in fact *logical* in character at all, but rather *para*logical. As for the particular part of Hegel's system which bears the title of 'logic' (and which is after a fashion 'identical' with the whole of the system), this represents a kind of esoteric philosophy with deep roots in Christian mysticism. The formulae most closely associated with Hegelian 'dialectic' – concerning, for instance, the 'unity' and/or 'identity' of opposites and the 'reality' of contradiction which is supposed to follow therefrom – are, in their original Hegelian context, unintelligible apart from this mystical background.

It so happens, however, that the very object of Marx's value theory exhibits a structure which lends itself to being grasped in such formulae as when applied to 'first-order' physical reality, as they are in Hegel's usage, have an unmistakably idealist connotation. Herein, I suggest, lies the whole paradox and mystery of the 'Marx–Hegel relation': that Marx is able to make a rational scientific application precisely of Hegel's *mysticism*. He is able to do so because money is, in effect, with respect to commodities just such an 'existent universal' as the Christ is supposed to be with respect to Christians: it is nothing other than the universality implicit to all commodities as 'exchange-values' existing *alongside* them in the form of some particular commodity or 'use-value'. More precisely, this is so just for the historically primordial form of money, viz. commodity-money. I will try to show, however, that inasmuch as the formal peculiarities of the money-commodity are impressed upon it by virtue of the economic functions which it is called upon to discharge, so too must such peculiarities be reflected in any more sophisticated sort of monetary device as well.

The 'metaphysical subtleties' of money pose a problem which economic theory in the usual sense – for which the availability of a monetary unit in which to express value magnitudes is for the most part just a stroke of luck or theoretical contrivance – does not bother much to address: namely, why in fact is there money at all? Why do the diverse elements of the social product acquire a mysterious 'value objectivity' which has to be not only in principle but *really* distinct from their 'first order' objectivity as physical things? The solution to this problem is not to be found in any special intricacy of Hegelian 'logic', but rather in certain special requirements of commodity exchange. In examining the specificity of the exchange system here, I will try to show that what circulates among persons in the objective form of money is in substance nothing other than control over definite portions of the total labour requisite to social production. Since the overwhelming majority of the world's population now find their practical working lives subjected to the anonymous dictates of the market, an effort to understand the social meaning of the money-form will not, I hope, seem entirely without relevance.

JOHN ROSENTHAL
London

Acknowledgements

I would like first of all to express my gratitude to the late Reiner Schürmann. I am sure Reiner did not share my enthusiasm for Marx. But he had no interest or stake in promoting ideological conformity and hence was prepared to lend his support to a project based strictly upon his judgment of its intellectual merits. In a more general academic environment which is not always very conducive to the sort of scholarship which this work represents, he helped create the niche within which I was able to pursue it and I will always be very grateful for that.

I first happened upon many of the basic ideas which would eventually issue in this book while attending seminars on Hegel given by Rüdiger Bubner. I don't know that Professor Bubner would agree with much that is contained in these pages. But I am very grateful for the opportunity which he provided me to study Hegel (and also the 'young' Marx) in an unbiased setting, and grateful too for the solicitude which he showed for my intellectual development at that time and after.

I would like to thank Ross Thomson for being a broad-minded enough economist to take an interest in this project and for the many helpful comments he offered at various stages in its development. I have to thank Ross too for exhibiting an apparently above-average memory for banal events and the honesty to use it – which qualities did, strangely enough, prove crucial at one juncture in the institutional history of this document.

I would also like to express my gratitude to two other economists, Salimmulah Khan and Robert J. King, for their readiness to transgress disciplinary boundaries and to let them be transgressed – which made for many enjoyable and productive discussions with both. My conversations with Salim on the history of money were especially helpful to me as I was composing the last part of the book. Needless to say, any errors I have made in utilizing his suggestions are entirely of my own devising.

During a brief period at the University of Massachusetts at Amherst, I had the good fortune to get to know and to study with Robert Ackermann. Bob's criticisms of a very early draft of the first part of this work helped me to break my dependence upon the Althusserian account of 'historicism' and to develop what I hope is a more nuanced account of my own. I want to thank him in particular for that and more generally for all the guidance and encouragement he has provided over the years.

Finally, I owe a special debt of gratitude to Wal Suchting. We have never met. But the old-fashioned philosophical correspondence and exchange of texts which we have conducted over the last several years has been for me at any rate a continual source of enlightenment and amusement. Wal's detailed criticisms of my dissertation exposed all the hollow spots in that text and provided me great impetus to rethink and refine my arguments as I converted the latter into the present volume. I cannot be sure that he will find that his criticisms have been effectively met and indeed I am sure in certain places that they have not been. Nonetheless, I am also sure that this book is significantly better for his having made them. (*Note*: Wal Suchting died in January 1997. The preceding words were written in December 1996. They were written to be read by Wal and I leave them as is. Wal knew all the details of the difficult period of gestation of this volume and his interest and encouragement and insight helped me enormously to focus on the task at hand and bring it to completion. I am very sorry that he is not here to see the outcome.)

Key to Abbreviations and Bibliographical Note

In citing Marx's writings, I have in general provided simultaneous references to both an acceptable English translation, where available, and the standard German edition of his works, namely, the *Marx–Engels Werke*. Abbreviations used are as follows:

MEW = *Marx–Engels Werke* (Berlin: Dietz, 1956–).
MEGA = *Marx–Engels Gesamtausgabe* (Berlin: Dietz, 1972–).
C = *Capital*, volumes I, II, III (London: Penguin/New Books, 1976–81); *Das Kapital*, in *MEW*, volumes 23, 24, 25.
CHDS = *Critique of Hegel's Doctrine of the State*, in Karl Marx, *Early Writings* (New York: Vintage, 1975); *Kritik des Hegelschen Staatsrechts*, in *MEW*, vol. 1.
CPE = *A Contribution to the Critique of Political Economy* (New York: International, 1970); *Zur Kritik der Politischen Ökonomie*, in *MEW*, vol. 13.
EPM = *The Economic & Philosophic Manuscripts of 1844* (New York: International, 1964); *Ökonomische und philosophische Manuscripte*, in *MEW*, Ergänzungsband, Erster Teil.
GI = Karl Marx and Frederick Engels, *The German Ideology* (New York: International, 1970); *Die deutsche Ideologie*, in *MEW*, vol. 3.
Gr. = *Grundrisse* (London: Penguin/New Left Books, 1973); *MEW*, vol. 42.
Res. = 'Results of the Immediate Production Process', which appears as an appendix to the Penguin edition of *Capital*, vol. I; *Resultate des unmittelbaren Produktionsprozesses* (Frankfurt: Verlag Neue Kritik, 1969).

In each dual reference, the page numbers from the German edition will follow those from the English separated by a slash. As they appear here, the English versions of extracts from Marx's German-language texts typically involve modifications of my own. Sometimes these are of such a substantial sort as to amount, in effect, to new translations and sometimes I have indeed simply re-translated the passages from scratch. I have not bothered to flag such departures from the cited

English editions, since, in any case, I have taken the German original as my standard throughout.

Marx's *The Poverty of Philosophy* was originally composed by him in French. The abbreviation used in citing it here and bibliographical data are as follows:

PP = *The Poverty of Philosophy* (New York: International, 1963); *Misère de la philosophie* (Paris: Editions Sociales, 1977).

All translations of cited passages from this text are my own. Page references to the English edition are merely provided as a convenience to the reader.

In citing Hegel's *Science of Logic*, I have followed the same practice as that described for the Marx texts. Otherwise in citing Hegel, I have simply availed myself of the convenience of referring to paragraph numbers rather than pages of specific editions. The *Zusätze* or 'additions' to Hegel's principal texts – these having been compiled from lecture notes taken by his students – are indicated by an 'add.'. Except where otherwise noted, the German editions which I have used are included in G.W.F. Hegel, *Werke in zwanzig Bänden* (Frankfurt am Main: Suhrkamp, 1969–). Abbreviations are as follows:

En. = *Enzyklopädie der philosophischen Wissenschaften im Grundrisse* (1830) (Hamburg: Felix Meiner, 1969).
En.L = 'Encyclopedia *Logic*', i.e. the first part of the *Enzyklopädie*, titled *Wissenschaft der Logik*, in *Werke*, vol. 8.
Phen. = *The Phenomenology of Spirit*, trans. A.V. Miller (Oxford: Oxford University Press, 1977); *Phänomenologie des Geistes*, in *Werke*, vol. 3.
Ph.R = *The Philosophy of Right*, trans. T.M. Knox (Oxford: Clarendon Press, 1952); *Grundlinien der Philosophie des Rechts*, ed. Helmut Reichelt (Frankfurt am Main: Ullstein, 1972).
SL = *Science of Logic*, trans. A.V. Miller (London: Allen & Unwin, 1969); *Wissenschaft der Logik*, erster & zweiter Teile, in *Werke*, vols. 5 & 6.

In the intitial stages of preparation of this volume, I conferred the nineteenth-century translation of Hegel's 'Encyclopedia *Logic*' by W. Wallace (*The Logic of Hegel* [Oxford/New York: Clarendon Press, 1975]) and, more recently, the new translation by T.F Geraets, W.A. Suchting and H.S. Harris (*The Encyclopedia Logic* [Indianapolis: Hackett, 1991]). The English renderings of passages cited from this text here are, however, my own re-translations from the German. Translations from the other parts of the *Encyclopädie* are likewise mine. Otherwise, the citations of Hegel follow the given English translations, though with frequent and sometimes substantial modifications of my own.

Part I

Marx's *Capital* and the Myth of 'Dialectics'

1 'Rigmarole' or 'Method'?

The persistence of a 'certain Hegelian phraseology' in the discourse of Marx's *Capital* has been much remarked upon. For professional economists of what we could call a broadly neoclassical inspiration, it has been a source of constant annoyance, a 'metaphysical' residue worthy only of ridicule and contempt, at best an irrelevance and at worst an obstacle to serious scientific inquiry. The special target of abuse for Marx's critics among the economists has been his theory of value, as developed at the very outset of the first volume of *Capital*. Even if other aspects of Marx's economics deserved (at least ostensibly) more studied consideration, the attitude toward his value-theory has been one of simple dismissal, and such lack of engagement could always be justified by summarizing everything which the critics found most distasteful and inaccessible about the theory under the epithet of 'Hegelianism'. In more recent times, self-styled 'analytical Marxists' – who are, much like the aspiring Romanian entrepreneur I met not long ago, Marxist '*dans leurs coeurs*', but stridently neoclassical in their theoretical practice and indeed openly *anti*-Marxist in their estimations of most everything usually associated with Marx – have followed the same sort of procedure in claiming to have developed a 'Marxian theory of exploitation' on the basis of the postulates of general equilibrium analysis: hence a 'Marxian theory of exploitation' which has been 'liberated' from the Marxian theory of value. As is customary in this sort of discourse, the charge of 'Hegelianism' is offered as all the justification which is needed for not entering into the intricacies of the latter theory, and thus placing oneself at risk of discovering what it is about.

Indeed, it is typically assumed by Marx's critics that they already know what his theory of value is about – or, at any rate, what it ought to be about: viz. the actual ratios at which commodities exchange or, more precisely, the uniform expression of their exchangeability, viz. *price*. Marx's theory of value is supposed, in short, to fulfil the role of a theory of price-formation. Once this supposition is admitted, it is natural enough to conclude, following Böhm-Bawerk's famous critique, that the theory as set out at the start of volume I of *Capital* stands in contradiction to Marx's theory of prices of production as developed in volume III (which is supposed to be, as Joan Robinson once put it, just 'everyone's theory'[1]). Virtually the *only* passage from volume I which ever gets discussed in such treatments (and Böhm-Bawerk here too set the precedent) is that in which Marx deduces from an equation representing the value equivalence of two commodities in exchange ('for example, 1 quarter wheat = 1 cwt. iron') that abstract labour must constitute that in respect to which this equivalence is established: the famous 'third thing, which is in and for itself neither the one nor the other' (*C*I, 127–8/51–2). The attentiveness with which even just this passage gets considered, however, can be gauged by the glib observation which represents the customary response to it: namely, that Marx's deduction is obviously mistaken, since the equivalence in question could just as well be established between rather the 'utilities' of the compared commodities – this after the citation of a passage whose final paragraph begins, 'If then we disregard the use-value of commodities . . .'![2] In any event, by focusing thus upon Marx's deduction of the so-called 'substance' of value, such readings manage to overlook the fact that the greater part of Marx's initial value analysis is dedicated to what he himself called a 'genetic' derivation of the value-*form*. With respect to this value-form analysis, allusions to 'rigmarole', 'Hegelian mumbo-jumbo', and so on, are normally presented as sufficient to make all discussion superfluous.

In contrast (though I want in fact to suggest that this prima facie contrast expresses a more fundamental uniformity), those few professional economists who claim allegiance to the Marxian theory of value have taken up the epithet of 'Hegelianism' and recast it as a commendation. For 'Marxists' in the discipline (in other words, for 'Marxists' *simplex*, being neither 'neo-' nor 'analytical'), certain Hegelian residues in Marx's analysis have even served to suggest a criterion for the *greater* scientificity of his (alleged) procedure as against that of his opponents. Thus the accusation levelled at Marx by the neoclassicals to the effect that his theory of value is unnecessarily burdened with 'metaphysical' entities has been turned back against them. If the neoclassicals insist upon the phenomenal form of economic experience – for example, the system of relative prices – the 'Marxists' respond by pointing to the seemingly well-known fact that it is the task of science to rend the veil of such immediate 'appearances' in order to get at the 'essences' revealed in them: for instance, the very system of values which the neoclassicals eschew as irrelevant. It may seem odd that social scientists of professed 'materialist' convictions would choose to employ a rhetoric which in Hegel's usage was designed precisely to affirm what he himself identified as the basic hypothesis of *idealism*: viz. that concerning the *irreality* of the objects of sensuous perception or, in other words, *of the material world*.[3] Nonetheless, the frequency with which pronouncements of this tenor emanate from the 'Marxist' camp in the economic debates is impossible to ignore.[4]

Such an unexpected outpouring of sympathy for the Hegelian conception of philosophical science from within economics has not, however, typically had the consequence that what was discarded as 'metaphysical' irrelevance by the neoclassicals has been reclaimed as theoretical foundation by the 'Marxists'. If the Hegelian formulae put to work in Marx's value theory do not present an obstacle to the 'Marxist' in the discipline, this is more often than not simply a question of having *gotten around them* in a less overtly hostile manner than one's neoclassical (or 'neo-Ricardian' or 'post-Keynesian') colleagues. It may not be necessary to excise the first chapter of *Capital*, viz. the chapter on the commodity or the value-form as such, in order to make Marx palatable. And it may even be possible to invest the essence/appearance couplet with a more modern set of connotations by asserting the primacy of values as the 'intrinsic regulators' of prices – though in practice this connection most often gets forgotten when the time comes to discuss the dynamics of capitalist competition through which prices are actually set, and hence the promised causal relation tends to get degraded to something more in the order of a statistical correlation. But, in any event, if, in response to the neoclassical challenge, the significance of Marx's theory of value is only defended by arguing for the superiority of 'labour-values' as predictors of market prices – if, in other words, we defend Marx's theory from the charge that it is an unsound theory of price-formation by arguing that it is indeed a sound theory of price-formation – then it is not only the first *chapter* of *Capital* which will have been bypassed, but in effect the greater part of the first *two volumes*. The analyses of which these volumes consist are, after all, expressly predicated upon the counterfactual assumption that prices do not deviate from values at all: that they are 'the same', or at least the ones are directly proportional to the others.[5] Just as surely as the attacks of his detractors, such defences of Marx clearly elude the question of the object and objectives of his theory of value – which is to say, for the most part, they elude his theory of value.[6]

Nonetheless, despite the glibness of the references to Hegel which tend to decorate the economists' disagreements with respect to Marx, such allusions do at least direct us to what is a real problem: namely and crudely, that of determining just what exactly, if anything, is 'Hegelian' about Marx's theoretical discourse in *Capital*. This particular problem can, of course, only be resolved on the condition that we address in turn the question of what is in general distinctive about a 'Hegelian' style of exposition as opposed to any other – what is, in effect, 'Hegelian' about Hegel. I hope it will be appreciated, at any rate when we come to treat this problem in greater detail, that it is not a simple matter of intellectual 'influences'. It pertains rather to the logical structure of Marx's analysis, and, hence, ultimately bears upon the legitimacy of the latter. In this regard, incidentally, Marx's detractors among the economists have tended to show greater insight than his supporters: since the former, as noted, have applied the epithet of 'Hegelianism' in order to absolve themselves of the obligation of engaging the details of his value-theoretical analysis, thus, at least in a backhanded manner, acknowledging that the aptness of this description will depend upon certain logical peculiarities which that argument exhibits. For his neoclassical critics, there is something about the logic of Marx's value theory which they find exotic – and in an off-putting fashion, of course. Before we have finished, I hope to be able to specify just what this 'something' is; to show how it relates to the exotic qualities of so-called 'Hegelian logic'; and, finally and most importantly, to demonstrate in what way this logically 'exotic' aspect of Marx's analysis might be justified by the *objectively* (or *onto*logically) bizarre constitution of the economic phenomena it is designed to grasp.

2 Marx on the 'Marx–Hegel Relation'

2.1 THE 'FAMOUS QUOTATIONS'

For the moment, let us stay with the crude formulation of our problem and simply pose the question: what exactly is 'Hegelian' in the discourse of *Capital*? Now, it could be suspected that a philosopher might be of some use here. And indeed for academic philosophers, the Hegelian legacy in *Capital* has been a matter of great concern: it has been their very, so to speak, professional justification for considering *Capital* – and, more often than not, also their alibi for not considering it too closely. The prolonged debate in the philosophical literature over the so-called 'Marx–Hegel relation' has hinged upon the respective conceptions of 'dialectical method' elaborated by the two authors and supposedly adhered to in their works. In the oft-cited 1873 'Afterword' to the second German edition of *Capital*, Marx himself lent his authority to such an orientation by all at once: proclaiming 'his' 'dialectical method' the 'direct opposite' of Hegel's; stressing that he had, nonetheless, acknowledged himself to be a 'pupil' of 'that great thinker'; criticizing the 'mystification' to which 'the dialectic' is subject in Hegel's treatment; yet praising Hegel as regardless 'the first to present its general forms of motion in a comprehensive and conscious manner'; and glibly dismissing his own utilization of a Hegelian 'mode of expression' – *namely*, 'here and there in the chapter on value theory' – as mere 'coquetry' (*C*I, 102–3/27).

Such 'famous quotations' (as Althusser baptized them) have been the lifeblood of much of the philosophical discussion on Marx's later political-economic writings. Yet, cast in the form of a pure commentary on 'method' as such, they tell us very little. Indeed, they tell us nothing at all about the specific character of Marx's political economy and very little even about the substance of Marx's alleged 'relation' to his philosophical predecessor – aside, that is, from the not uninteresting fact that Marx's own subjective estimation of Hegel was obviously both highly ambivalent and in its ambivalence a source of no little irritation for him.[1] If the 'relation' in question is, however, supposed to be a *theoretical* one, then clearly its content will have to depend upon the character of Marx's political economy, as well as that of whatever aspect or aspects of the Hegelian theoretical corpus might be supposed to have contributed to the development of the latter. In this respect, in fact only that remark which appears precisely to *diminish* the significance of Hegel – the coy allusion to 'coquetry' – would seem to offer anything promising.

This is also the site of what has become perhaps the most heavily commented mixed metaphor in at least the modern history of philosophy and the human sciences: the 'famous quotation' in which Marx observes that in Hegel '[the dialectic] is standing on its head', and hence that 'it must be inverted, in order to discover the rational kernel within the mystical shell'. We will have before too long (see chapter 7 below) to say something about the nature and viability of both this inversion and the extraction which is supposed somehow to result from it. But, in itself, the 'inversion/extraction' metaphor is not much more helpful than the dizzying series of conflicting pronouncements concerning Hegel which precede it and which, apparently, it is meant to summarize. What Marx says then in elaborating upon this metaphor, however, suggests more concretely the character of the theoretical results which the extracted 'rational kernel' of 'the dialectic' is supposed to yield. Thus he writes:

> In its mystified form, the dialectic became the fashion in Germany, because it seemed to transfigure and glorify what exists. In its rational form it is a scandal and an abomination to the bourgeoisie and its doctrinaire spokesmen, because it includes in its positive understanding of what exists a simultaneous understanding of its negation, its inevitable destruction; it grasps every form which has come into existence in fluid movement, and therefore grasps it according to its transient side as well; it does not let itself be impressed by anything and is in its very essence critical and revolutionary. (103/27–8)

Here, then, we have at last a statement, albeit a rather overwrought statement, which purports to tell us something about just what Marx's 'dialectical method' is: or, more exactly, which purports to tell us what this method – hypostatized into an independent subject as 'the dialectic' – *does*.

Without committing ourselves to the position that any of what Marx says in this passage has a very clearly determinable meaning – the following chapter will be devoted to the task of showing that most of it does not – I want to begin by simply and blandly paraphrasing those elements of what he says which have proven themselves most susceptible to being accorded some meaning (or, at any rate, to being accorded the status of meaningfulness). We can leave aside, then, the odd assertion of 'the dialectic's' unflappability, as well as the insistence upon its revolutionary 'essence'.[2] The latter, in any event, is presumably meant to follow from the previous remarks. As for what remains, if we were to take Marx at the letter of these ostensibly ex-post metatheoretical indications, they would seem to suggest that the specificity of the 'dialectical method', at least in its 'rational' application, consists in the articulation of some moment of 'negation' which is supposed to be essential to the correct comprehension of any existing phenomenon.

Marx makes it quite clear that 'negation', though in its customary usage restricted to a *logical* application, is here to be given a *substantial* interpretation. Thus the 'negation' of what exists is paratactically expanded upon by Marx as 'its inevitable destruction'; and to grasp in a 'dialectical' manner some 'form' which has *come into existence* (*jede gewordne Form*) is said to involve grasping 'it according to its transient side [*nach ihrer vergänglichen Seite*] as well', hence grasping that and presumably also *how* it will *cease to exist* (*vergehen*). Marx's claim seems to be, then, that the comprehension of the conditions of emergence and the conditions of decease of some given thing is tantamount to the comprehension of what that thing at any given moment *is*, and, furthermore, that this way of grasping phenomena – grasping, namely, their 'being as becoming' – is precisely the achievement of the 'dialectical method'. To know something 'dialectically', on this view, would be to know it as the temporary result of a more comprehensive process wherein it will be dissolved in turn: hence Marx's allusion to grasping every form in 'fluid movement'.

2.2 'DIALECTICS' AND THE CONCEPT OF HISTORICAL CHANGE

Now, before going any further, we have at least to acknowledge a certain systematic ambiguity in the gloss on Marx's 'famous quotations' just proposed – especially since very much the same ambiguity gets continually exploited, however unwittingly, in the whole tradition of methodological commentaries on 'dialectics' which Engels was to initiate not long after the publication of Marx's 'Afterword'. If, on the one hand, we interpret the object whose knowledge is here in question as some *particular*, then the claim that it is only properly grasped in the process of its genesis and dissolution implies indeed the transience of *that particular*, but without thereby excluding the *permanence* of some *sort* which the particular instantiates. It might be interjected here that scientific inquiry is not in fact concerned with 'sorts' in any classificatory sense (or, alternately, that 'dialectical' science ought not to be so concerned), and that the relevant distinction is not, then, between particulars and general sorts to which they relate (or, perhaps better, are related) as instances, but rather between particulars and systems or 'wholes' to which they relate (or, perhaps better, in which they are interrelated) as elements. But just as the transience of the particular does not imply the transience of any sort under which it might be arrayed, so too its transience does not imply the transience of any system in which it figures as constituent. Since the identity of the system is determined by the character of the relations among its elements (and not by the positive character of any of those elements considered, as Hegel would say, simply 'in itself'), the degeneration of some particular which is functionally subordinated to it will not necessarily compromise the viability of the system as such: so long, namely, as it is in the nature of the system periodically to renew its own conditions.

Hence, if it is merely *particulars* which the 'dialectic' grasps in the process of their 'coming-to-be' and 'ceasing-to-be', then there is no reason to conclude that the 'fluid movement' which it is supposed to reveal should, so to speak, on the 'aggregate' level, follow anything other than a *cyclical* course – assuming indeed that this 'movement' at least exhibits *some* definite pattern. Barring this last assumption, matters would stand even *worse* for the promised 'dialectic': since it would then turn out to be nothing more than an empiricist ideology of the 'ceaseless flux' of the real. In which case, far from constituting a 'method' for the production of knowledge, it would seem to imply – as indeed so many of Engels's writings on 'dialectics' seem to imply – the very impossibility of knowledge.[3] But even under the assumption specified, supposing it does indeed make sense to speak of this 'dialectic' as a 'method', the alleged novelty of that 'method' would appear dubious: since hardly any theory, no matter what its 'methodological' orientation, could be accused of treating either nature or social life as if they were *absolutely* 'immobile' – as if, that is to say, they exhibited no phenomena of change at all.[4]

If, on the other hand, we interpret the intended object of Marx's comments as itself a *sort* of thing (as could be suggested by his use of the word 'form'), then its 'negation', its 'necessary destruction', implies not just change per se, but *historical* transformation. This is brought out quite clearly by considering the case of what philosophers would call a 'natural kind': say, for instance, a biological species. The 'ceasing-to-be' of some member of the species implies change, of course, but only in the sense in which, for example, the seasonal blooming and withering of vegetative life does as well. The 'ceasing-to-be' of *every* member of the species, however, the 'ceasing-to-be', namely, of the species *itself* (whether in the form of extinction or speciation), implies change in a more determinate sense. It implies indeed that the ecosystem as such has changed (whether the passing of the particular species is understood as cause or effect in this context). It is in invoking this latter sense of 'change' that we might say, for instance, that the becoming extinct of some species or its evolution into a new species represents an event in *biological history*, whereas the death of a member of the same species, regarded in isolation, is merely a biological event.

The point being made here is quite general. Indeed, it can be just as readily illustrated using an example of what we could call 'artificial' or 'non-natural' kinds. Since our special concern here is economics, let us consider, for instance, the case of an industrial machine. That some exemplar of the machine suffers wear and tear and hence requires eventually to be replaced implies merely the temporal existence of the economic system: it implies change, of course, but change merely as an *aspect* of the maintenance of those interdependencies which characterize some abiding state of the system. Such change occurs within the system, but the system per se does not undergo it. In this sense, the system is not affected by its own temporality. (It is to this peculiarity that I gather Althusser was alluding in calling the synchronicity of a system 'eternity in Spinoza's sense'.[5]) If, however, the sort of machine in question becomes *obsolete* – say, as the result of the development and diffusion of a new technology allowing for increased productivity in that sector (or those sectors) of production in which the now antiquated machine had previously been utilized – then this implies a whole series of correlative modifications in the attributes of the economic system itself.

In the interest of concreteness, let us pursue this example a bit further. Let us assume, just for the sake of familiarity, that the economic system is a *capitalist* one – though the point at issue in no way depends on this assumption. Let us assume too, for the sake of simplicity, that both the antiquated technology and the one which has replaced it have only one industrial application: that is, are or were used in the production of only one sort of good. Let us call the good in question 'good *x*'. Under the said assumptions, supposing that the fall in the unit-price of good *x* precipitated by the diffusion of the new technology is not fully offset by a proportionate rise in the demand for it at the new price, then either some portion of the capital invested in the *x*-producing sector will simply be destroyed or some portion of it will flow out of that sector or, as is indeed most likely, both processes will occur in some combination. Now, if capital flows *out* of this sector, then it will flow *in* to some others, thus increasing the overall supply of goods in the latter, intensifying competition and driving some 'excess' portion of capital from them in turn. This newly dislodged capital will then catalyse exactly the same reactions in still further sectors – and so on. The overall effect of the combined movements of the particular capital-fragments will be a redistribution of the total social capital among the various sectors of production and, as a function of this redistribution of the total *capital*, a redistribution of the total *labour* available to society.

The end-result of the obsolescence of the formerly prevailing technology in the *x*-producing sector will thus be either a decline in total employment (that is as measured in labour-*hours*, though not necessarily as measured in number of labourers employed) or a redistribution of the total social labour among the various sectors of production – *or* a redistribution of labour occurring in conjunction with a fall in total employment. This end-result would, furthermore, be the same under *any* economic system, though the mechanism bringing it about will, of course, differ (in a socialist system, for example – at least according to the classical model – depending upon macro-level planning decisions rather than micro-level investment decisions). It is because technological change thus entails a modification of the state of the economic system that we can say, in analogous fashion to the conclusion we drew from the biological example, that the obsolescence and replacement of some sort of machine represents an event in *economic history*, whereas the eventual scrapping of some exemplar of that machine is merely an economic event.

We could adduce still further examples. The case of specifically *linguistic* change, for instance, presents especially interesting modifications of the general rule, since the constituents of a semiotic system are arguably themselves sorts (viz. 'sign-types' rather than 'sign-tokens'). But rather than entering into subtleties which are not immediately germane to the task at hand, let us consider the consequences of what has been thus far established for the interpretation of Marx's comments on 'the dialectic'. What I have suggested by way of the above examples is, in effect, that change be considered *historical* change, as opposed to the regular pattern of transformation which the elements of a system might undergo (even indeed as an aspect of their functional subordination to it), if and only if it represents a transformation of the relations among those elements which taken as a whole determine either some state or, more comprehensively, even the very *nature* of the system as such. It follows – indeed it follows tautologically – that if in the cited passage from Marx we interpret the intended object of knowledge as precisely such a *system* (as might be implied by Marx's repeated use of the expression 'what exists', which could be interpreted to mean no less than the *totality* of that which exists), then the assertion that 'the dialectic', in contrast to other 'methods', grasps the object 'according to its transient side' equally implies not just change, but specifically *historical* change.

So long, then, as the object of knowledge is interpreted as something *other* than just some particular or (a bit more plausibly) some range of particulars, the alleged distinctiveness and, presumably, superiority of a 'dialectical method' will have to consist in its grasping the *historicity* of objects as essential to their nature: hence, to put this another way, in exposing the historicity of objects by *grasping* their nature. Now, whether or not some specific object or objective 'form' is in fact historically transient by virtue of *its nature* – and not, say, by virtue of circumstances extrinsic to its nature (as, for instance, the climactic change which is said to have spelled the doom of the dinosaurs or the volcanic eruption which destroyed Pompeii) – could be reasonably expected to depend on the object in question. Hence, to conceive the disclosure of this historicity as a matter of *method* is already somewhat odd. It is odd, at any rate, if we understand by 'knowledge' the comprehension of things as they are and not rather as we have predecided they ought to be. Nonetheless, such a conception of Marx's 'dialectical method' has, I would suggest, become in fact the habitual one – even if it is not always clearly distinguished from the view which emphasizes the centrality simply of change *tout court* and is often indeed treated as if it followed from the latter (which, as we have seen, it does not). In any event, this conception is surely that which, in more or less subtle forms, has traditionally dominated the philosophical discussions. It is only quite recently that a new current of academic opinion on the 'Marx–Hegel relation' has emerged, which takes much more seriously and literally the claims for 'dialectics' to represent a distinctive logical canon. But we will reserve judgement on this 'new' Hegelian Marxism until after having first disposed of the 'old' variety.

I propose to call the methodological conception just described a '*historicism*', or, more precisely, a '*dynamic* historicism', in order to distinguish it from other variants of historicism which are either fundamentally different or simply more modest in their claims. My contention will be that the 'dialectical method' thus construed is a strictly *imaginary* method: a method which Marx did not apply, because he could not apply it, because there simply is no such method to be applied.

2.3 THE THIRD FOUNDER – OR I.I. KAUFMAN'S 'MARXISM'

Before going on to characterize in greater detail the supposed properties of the 'dialectical method' conceived on the historicist pattern, I want to make a brief detour of a philological nature. For if we reconstruct the textual context of Marx's 'famous quotations', what becomes especially clear is the ambivalence of the sources upon which the historicist model has been based. Indeed, it turns out that one of the founding documents of the tradition of would-be 'dialectical' social science was not written by Marx at all, nor by Engels, but rather by one I.I. Kaufman: so identified by the editors of the *Marx–Engels Werke* as the author of a Russian-language review of *Capital* which provides the immediate occasion for the 'famous quotations'. Furthermore, this unheralded co-founder of 'dialectical' social science turns out to be a professed *opponent* of 'dialectical' modes of thought. Thus Marx observes that the cited review, which 'deals exclusively with the method of *Capital*', 'finds my method of inquiry [*Forschungsmethode*] severely realistic, but my method of presentation [*Darstellungsmethode*], unfortunately German-dialectical'. As illustration, Marx quotes a passage to the effect that 'at first sight, if judgment is made on the basis of the external form of the presentation, Marx is the most idealist of philosophers, and indeed in the German, i.e. the bad sense of the word' (*CI*, 100/25). 'I cannot answer the writer of this review in any better way', Marx continues, 'than through a few extracts from his own critique'.

There then follows in the 'Afterword' a very lengthy citation from the Russian review, which does not need to be reproduced in full here, though I would recommend that the reader sometime confer it. For if we compare these extracts with any of a remarkably wide range of would-be methodological resumes of *Capital* which have appeared since their (re)publication by Marx, it is difficult not to conclude that I.I. Kaufman has been a major influence upon the sort of 'Marxism' which such methodological discourses typically represent – perhaps even as much of an influence as Engels himself, and probably a greater one than Marx.

Consider just the following two passages from Kaufman's review; first, that with which Marx's extracts open:

> For Marx one thing alone is important [sic!]: to find the law of the phenomena with whose investigation he is concerned. And it is not only the law which governs these phenomena, in so far as they have a definite form and mutual connection within a given historical period, that is important to him. Of still greater importance to him is the law of their alteration, of their development, i.e. of their transition from one form into another, from one order of connections into another. Once he has discovered this law, he investigates in detail the effects with which it manifests itself in social life . . .; (*C*I, 100/25–6)

and that with which they conclude:

> With the varying degrees of development of productive force, relations and the laws governing them vary too. While Marx sets himself the aim of exploring and explaining the capitalist economic order from this point of view, he is only formulating, in a strictly scientific manner, the aim that every accurate investigation of economic life must have. . . . The scientific value of such an inquiry lies in the illumination of the special laws that govern the emergence, existence, development and death of a given social organism and its replacement by another, higher one. And in fact this is the value of Marx's book. (*C*I, 102/26–7)

Now, Kaufman, as noted, has already declared his hostility to idealist philosophy. After we have discussed the systematic sense of 'dialectic' in the Hegelian context, I hope it will be possible to appreciate the strangeness of the notion that a historicist approach such as the one outlined by him should represent some sort of 'materialist application' of a 'dialectical method' deriving from Hegel. I want to suggest that the self-evidence which is, nonetheless, often accorded to such a strange notion in Marxist debates stems not so much from serious consideration of the issues involved as from the gracious conceit with which Marx responds to the 'criticisms' of I.I. Kaufman (and indeed therewith introduces the 'famous quotations'). 'While the author describes what he calls my actual method in so striking and, as far as concerns my own application of it, so generous a way,' Marx writes, 'what else has he described but the dialectical method?' (*CI*, 102/27).

It is of some additional symptomatic interest to note that in Kaufman's original review, according to Marx's account, the passages extracted by Marx are themselves preceded by a citation – not, as one might expect, from *Capital* – but rather from yet another of *Marx's own* methodological resumés, and indeed one which has in the intervening years become at least equally renowned for its wealth of 'famous quotations': viz. the preface to the *Contribution to a Critique of Political Economy* of 1859. Indeed, Kaufman's allusion to 'relations' – he does not say what kind, but we can safely assume *relations of production* – changing along with changes in the level of development of 'productive force' is quite obviously just a gloss on the core proposition of Marx's 1859 text. By virtue of Marx's characteristic manner of expressing it and for ease of reference, we can call this proposition the 'fetters' (or '*Fesseln*') hypothesis. 'At a certain level of development,' Marx writes, in words which will no doubt be familiar to most:

> the material productive forces of society come into contradiction with the existing relations of production or – this merely expresses the same thing in legal terms – with the property relations within which they have moved hitherto. From forms of development of the productive forces these relations turn into their fetters. Then begins an era of social revolution. (*CPE*, 21/9)

Though the 1859 'Preface' provides the by now canonical statement of the 'fetters' hypothesis, it is important to be aware that this hypothesis first begins to appear in the Marx–Engels corpus more than ten years earlier: that is, *before* Marx had embarked upon the systematic economic investigations which would issue in the publication of *Capital*.[6]

Kaufman's allusion to the 'fetters' hypothesis is significant, I would suggest, because whereas Marx's endorsement of his presentation implies that the 'method' described is indeed the very organizing logic of *Capital*, if we take the risk of *testing* this description against its alleged object – namely, the analytical discourse whose *modus operandi* it purports to describe – we discover that the imputed 'method' is in fact nowhere to be found. This is not only because it happens not to have been 'Marx's method': but, more fundamentally, as I will try to demonstrate below, because it is quite simply *not* a method, and hence not susceptible of 'application' in any case or by anyone. Rather than a felicitous exposition of the actual 'method' put to work in *Capital*, what we are confronted with in Kaufman's remarks is, then, something more in the order of methodological commentary upon methodological commentary.

Sadly, such a discordant relation between methodological reflection and analytical discourse, between would-be *meta*-theory and 'first order' theoretical inquiry, has become an ingrained (and profoundly unhealthy) habit of the Marxist intellectual tradition. The celebrated 'dialectic' of relations of production and forces of production is in fact an especially conspicuous case in point. (And even just to call the decidedly unidirectional sort of causality involved here a 'dialectic' is itself symptomatic of the false Hegelianisms with which Marxist discourse tends to be rife.) For whatever Marx may have said in his 1859 'Preface', and however much both opponents and even some proclaimed allies (most notably, in recent years, G.A. Cohen[7]) may have taken him at his word, what he in fact succeeds in demonstrating in *Capital* is not how some putatively autonomous (as Cohen says, 'extra-social') evolution of the productive forces precipitates a transformation in social relations of production, but rather *the reverse*. What he in fact demonstrates is how a transformation of relations of production – namely, the replacement of feudal relations by specifically capitalist ones (or the so-called 'formal subsumption' of labour to capital) – precipitates a massive acceleration in the pace of development of the productive forces (or, in other words, in the pace of productivity-increasing technical change).

3 'Dialectics', Historicity and the Logic of *Capital*

3.1 THE HISTORICIST DISCOURSE

Invested with canonical authority by Marx's imprimatur, the historicist model contained in the Kaufman extracts has exerted great power over the Marxist tradition. This power can best be gauged by reviewing some citations from other authors. I do not want here to consider in detail any of the cited passages. I want simply to show by way of exemplification how the historicist model has in fact come to provide the norms of what we could call an entire methodological discourse: the norms, that is to say, of a sort of discourse *about method*, though not, I am suggesting, of any analytical discourse which actually *employs* the 'method' in question.

This is in no way to deny that the basic model has in practice been subject to very significant variations: so significant in fact as to preclude passing any blanket judgement upon the results achieved by authors drawing on its conventions. A 'discourse' (or 'discursive formation', to use Foucault's coinage) is, after all, an abstraction which can only be reconstructed *ex post* from the evidence of actual sequences of writing and speech: which is to say, that any given 'discourse' only ever acquires practical existence by intersecting with, modifying and being modified by other sorts of discursive practice. What is, however, precisely so conspicuous and so indicative of the power which the historicist model of Marx's 'dialectics' has had, is the degree to which its norms have been respected and reproduced by authors of otherwise such widely divergent political commitments and theoretical conceptions; authors also, it should be added, producing under the most varied of general societal and specific institutional conditions. All of which, incidentally, lends unmistakable support to the thesis of what we could call the 'relative autonomy' of discourse.

It should be obvious that I am not in what follows making any pretence of comprehensiveness. If what I have proposed concerning methodological historicism as a 'discourse' is true, then, in the first place, it would not be possible to be comprehensive, and, in the second place, it would be tedious to try. Nor have I selected examples for their special historical importance. I have selected them only for their typicality. Indeed, as judged by the criterion of historical significance the cited authors are likewise extremely diverse: ranging from a (perhaps *the*) canonical figure in the tradition of so-called 'Western Marxism' to a contemporary whose writings on Marx will, I should think, prove to have been little more than an eddy produced by changes in the currents of intellectual fashion.

Case 1

Consider, then, to start with, the following observation from a contribution to the post-war Eastern European discussions of 'dialectical materialism':

> The 'concept' is, according to Marx, the intellectual reproduction of the internal articulation, the internal structure of an object, and indeed of this internal structure in its development, in its emergence, in existence and decline [*Untergang*].[1]

The same author writes:

> As soon as capital moves upon its own foundation, the history of the emergent object [*des gewordenen Gegenstandes*] begins. This possesses different phases: from the beginning phases through the phases of classical maturity to the phases of disintegration, of the transition into another object.[2]

All of this is quite clearly direct paraphrase of Kaufman's remarks (and sometimes barely even paraphrase), though with traces, as in Marx's 'famous quotations', of a more self-consciously Hegelian idiom: '*der gewordene Gegenstand*' echoing Marx's '*jede gewordne Form*', and in both cases the *werden* (or 'becoming') of the object or form being conjoined with its *untergehen* ('destruction') or *übergehen* ('transition') into another object or form. A little further on in the same text, the author declares it a 'generally valid principle of Marxian dialectical-materialist analysis' that the 'internal' properties of an object should be 'investigated in a . . . unity with the history of the object'.[3]

Case 2

As is well known, Lukács makes the 'relation to the totality' the touchstone of his conception of 'dialectical method'. His elaboration of just what sort of 'totality' is supposed to be implied by this, however, exhibits all the symptoms of indeed an especially virulent attachment to the conventions of the historicist model. Thus he writes, for example, in a famous phrase: 'Whatever the subject of debate, the dialectical method is concerned always with the same problem: knowledge of the historical process in its entirety'.[4] And again, in a paradigmatic statement of methodological historicism: 'The knowledge of the real, objective nature of a phenomenon, the knowledge of its historical character and the knowledge of its actual function in the totality of society form . . . a single, undivided act of cognition'.[5] And once more, in his exposé of the 'antinomies of bourgeois thought': 'the concrete totality of the historical world, the concrete and total historical process is the only point of view from which understanding becomes possible'.[6]

That Lukács's version of historicism is 'dynamic', in the sense to be outlined below, can be seen from his characteristic tendency to infer from some objective form's having *come into existence* that 'theory' – that is, if it is 'dialectical' – ought then to be able to demonstrate just how it will *pass out of existence*. This reflects once more the historicist appropriation of Hegel's *werden–vergehen* couplet, as already noted in Marx's 'famous quotations', whereby *historicity* gets equated with *transience*. Such an equation is in fact everywhere at work in Lukács's writings. Thus, for example, in criticizing Max Adler, Lukács concludes that, as a consequence of the latter's disavowal of 'dialectics', 'neither the emergence of internal problems, nor the collapse of capitalist society, can be seen to be necessary'[7] – this from a professed *critic* of economic fatalism!

Case 3

For readers conversant in this literature, it will not be surprising to discover evidence of methodological historicism in the writings of authors whose theoretical efforts are bound up with the twentieth-century history of Communism, both as political movement and existing socio-economic system. It is perhaps more novel, however, to find such evidence in the writings of an author reputed to be an 'expert' on Marx in 'deconstructionist' circles. Yet a recent interpretation of Marx's value-theory which exhibits a more obviously Lacanian than Leninist inspiration is, nonetheless, replete with historicist *obbligatos*. Consider, for instance, the following remark:

> It is in basing oneself principally upon the genesis of the money-form and of capital, a historical and dialectical genesis, that the materialist mode of re-elaboration of Hegelian logic can be discovered;[8]

or this one:

> The genesis of the forms of (economic) exchange constitutes a dialectical logic of the process of historico-social substitution.[9]

That such traces of an historicist standpoint, however eviscerated, appear in a text dedicated to drawing analogies between money as the general equivalent form of value and a whole series of other alleged 'general equivalents' – 'the father, the phallus, the monarch, language [sic.]' – is compelling testimony to what I have called the 'relatively autonomous' effectiveness of the historicist discourse.[10]

Case 4

I have already suggested that the historicist model, despite the manner in which it has come to shape the philosophical discussions of the 'Marx–Hegel relation', is in fact quite unrelated to the Hegelian conception of 'dialectic'. It is thus not unusual that aspects of a historicist discourse should also be discernible in pronouncements on Marx coming from writers for whom Hegel and 'dialectics' are matters of indifference. Indeed, as we shall see directly, they are even discernible in the work of an author who explicitly *denies* the relevance of Hegelian 'dialectic' to Marx's economic analyses. Nonetheless, even in such cases the effects of the historicist model are still to be detected in the insistence that Marx did indeed provide in *Capital* proofs of the necessity of both the emergence and the transcendence of a capitalist mode of production. Since the textual evidence, despite the occasional rhetorical embellishment tending in this direction, offers no substantive support for such a contention,[11] the conviction with which it is accompanied must derive from other sources.

The above-mentioned 'fetters' hypothesis is normally invoked in such discussions as the general grounds upon which Marx is supposed to have based his analyses (even if the connection between the general 'law' and its specific applications is more often than not left to wishful thinking). This is obviously the case in the crude variant of technological determinism resurrected by G.A. Cohen as 'Marx's Theory of History'. Though, apart from Cohen and his followers, it is in fact rare to discover the attribution to Marx of a crude technological determinism in anything but overtly *anti*-Marxist diatribes. It is also the case, however, in the more nuanced work of Maurice Godelier – who, it should be noted in this context, is unequivocal in concluding that Hegelian 'dialectic' is 'useless for scientific work'.[12] Thus, Godelier writes, for instance:

> Ultimately, the scientific explanation of the comparative rationality of a particular mode of production, of its relative superiority in comparison with another, is based on the hypothesis of a law of necessary correspondence between the structure of the production-relations and the structure of the productive forces. This hypothesis enables Marx to analyze both the historical necessity of the appearance of capitalism and the necessity of its disappearance. . . .[13]

Godelier's allusion in this passage to the '*structure* of the productive forces' is reflective of the subtlety of his account. Thus, for example, what is supposed, according to Godelier, to necessitate the transformation of capitalist relations of production, is not something 'extra-social', but rather precisely the increasing centralization of *juridical control* over the productive forces (or, in other words, an increasing consolidation of the titles to ownership of the means of production in relatively ever fewer hands). This suggestion is, incidentally, drawn directly from Marx's own scattered remarks in *Capital* on the conditions for the transition to socialism. Its very subtlety, however, makes it all the more obvious that there is nothing in the development invoked which entails the *necessity* of the transition to a 'superior', viz. a socialist, mode of production. The increasing 'centralization' of capital implies perhaps the 'rationality' of such a transition (though, despite all of Godelier's pleadings to the contrary, there is clearly a normative judgement involved in drawing such a conclusion) or maybe just its greater *feasibility* (and this is the actual implication of Marx's analysis), but certainly not its necessity. Though we cannot enter into the details here, if taken to its logical extreme, the process of centralization would have indeed ultimately to result in the suspension of all the most characteristic 'laws of motion' which govern capitalist development under competitive conditions. But it would not in and of itself alter the structure of those property relations which are constitutive of *capitalism* as such, much less transform the latter into socialism. For such a transformation to occur, a political *act* of expropriation is clearly required.[14]

The only thing that sustains Godelier in, nonetheless, continuing to attribute necessity to the transition in question is, I would suggest, the acquired habits of Marxist historicism. This can be appreciated from the following strangely tentative formulation – and note the symptomatic regression here to posing the issue as a matter of 'dialectic':

> . . . dialectical analysis of the capitalist system, of its origin, its growth, etc., brings out the relative nature of this system. On this relativity is based the rational prediction of the necessity for the capitalist system to disappear, but this prediction is of an overall character and supplies no particular date.[15]

3.2 THE VARIETIES OF HISTORICISM

The tenor of the discourse which the cited passages exemplify will no doubt already have been familiar to many. Indeed, given its prevalence, it would even be possible to believe that such a discourse is nothing other than 'Marxism' itself. I want now to try to reassemble the distinctive features of the historicist model whose norms that discourse obeys. In order to facilitate this task, it is essential that we start by clearly distinguishing two general variants of traditional historicism which, though – unfortunately for us – they have often been uneasily combined or simply conflated in both Marxist and Marxological discussions, have otherwise normally operated in independence of one another. The one variant of traditional historicism I propose to call *synchronic* or *epochal* historicism; the other, *genetic* historicism.

Synchronic historicism is characterized by the claim to have demonstrated the *relativity* of some phenomenon by referring it to the totality of empirical conditions/relations obtaining at some particular moment or abiding over some particular span of time. If the reference is to a *span* of time, then that span is normally delimited and individualized by appeal to some governing principle which is supposed to unify the totality of relations in question, thus converting them into the elements of a determinate *epoch*. This is at least so when its invocation is in fact meant to bear any explanatory value, rather than simply serving as an alibi, in which case arbitrary chronological limits are perfectly serviceable.

The purely chronological form of historicism – easily the most impoverished form of them all – is not, however, much relevant to discussions of Marxism, except insofar as it has become a stock-in-trade of precisely *anti*-Marxist styles of discourse. The latter, when all else fails, remind us that 'Marxism' is a 'nineteenth-century theory'. (It is not even clear, however, what exactly that is supposed to mean. Are 'Platonism' and 'Aristotelianism', for example, 'fourth-century BC theories'? In that case, virtually the entire history of medieval philosophy must be dismissed as an anachronism. And why, in any case, should precisely a *century* be the relevant temporal measure?) From this fact it is apparently supposed to follow that 'Marxism' must by now have (somehow) lost whatever legitimacy it may once have possessed. Of course, were this pattern of argumentation in general a valid one, it would bode ill for the fate of our own theoretical efforts in this *fin de siècle*.

Epochal historicism is clearly manifest in Hegel's philosophy of history: namely, in the sequence of 'world-historical realms' it portrays. Each alleged 'world-historical realm' is, according to Hegel's conception, associated with some 'people' or '*Volk*' by which it is supposed to be dominated. Hence, we have the 'Oriental', 'Greek', 'Roman' and – needless to say, at the 'highest' stage of development – the 'Germanic' realms. The totality of relations pertaining to the realm in question is supposed to be unified by the 'principle' or (more vaguely, though also more significantly in the Hegelian context) the 'spirit' of the 'people' which dominates it. This 'principle' or 'spirit' suffuses the entire range of phenomena characteristic of the epoch it unifies: or rather, to employ a Hegelian idiom with which we will have to become familiar, only those phenomena have 'actuality' in a given epoch which prove themselves to be determined by its dominant principle. The unifying function of such a 'national spirit' or 'spirit of a people' (*Volksgeist*) with respect to the historical totality it is supposed to dominate is abundantly in evidence in a passage such as the following:

> Here we only have to take up this point: that each stage as distinct from the other has its own determinate principle. Such a principle is in history the determinateness of the spirit of a people. In this determinate form it concretely expresses all aspects of its will and consciousness, its entire actuality. This determinateness is the common stamp of its religion, its political constitution, its ethical life, its legal system, its customs, also of its science, art, and technical skill, and of the orientation of its industrial activity.[16]

Though there is a great deal to discuss in this regard, I do not want to comment upon the connection between what Hegel says here and the *völkisch* ideology whose dominion over German public discourse in the nineteenth and twentieth centuries is well enough documented and whose disastrous results well enough known.[17] For our purposes, it is above all important that we notice in such passages the peculiar sort of determinacy which the alleged dominant principle gives to the diverse phenomena which it is supposed to unite. Althusser introduced the notion of an 'expressive causality' to describe this sort of relation.[18] Although I am not sure that 'causality' is exactly the word which we want to use in such cases, nonetheless the description of the relation between dominant principle and subordinate phenomena as one of 'expression' is especially apt: and even more obviously so where the principle appears under the guise of an animating 'spirit'. The Hegelian conception of 'world-historical realms' makes the expressive character of this relation especially plain. But an expressive model of determinacy is, I would suggest, at least implicit in every sort of epochal historicism.

In the Hegelian scenario, the particular *völkisch* 'principles' are supposed in fact to represent but assignations *to* specific 'peoples' of principles requisite for the realization of the absolute aim of the 'world-spirit': viz. to develop itself into an objective world and thus become conscious of itself as such. Since the '*national* spirits' which in any given epoch gain dominance are thus reduced to but 'moments' in the process of the coming to consciousness of the '*world*-spirit' or '*absolute* spirit', the Hegelian scenario implies the necessity – albeit a 'necessity' which is manifestly external to the 'epochs' themselves under consideration – of the transitions from one epoch to the next (and it is precisely this external criterion, and not any simple chronological sequence, which allows Hegel to treat certain epochs as representative of a 'higher' stage of development than others). This is, however, a peculiarity of *Hegel*, *not* of epochal historicism per se.

Thus, to take an influential recent example, it could be argued that many of Michel Foucault's early 'archaeological' studies – however disruptive they may be of the other conventions of traditional intellectual history – nonetheless remain firmly within the tradition of epochal historicism. This is especially clear in *The Order of Things*, which arrays its material into bulky historical totalities ('the Renaissance', 'the Classical Age', 'Modernity'), each of which is supposed to be unified by its characteristic '*episteme*'. Consider just a brief remark such as the following: 'What changed at the turn of the century [that is, 'around' 1800, with the alleged shift from the 'classical' to the 'modern' *episteme*], and underwent an irremediable modification, was knowledge itself as an anterior and indivisible mode of being between the knowing subject and the object of knowledge'.[19] A change in 'knowledge itself', as defined at the 'level' of the '*episteme*' (though just where this 'level' ought to be located is not at all clear), is supposed then to account for changes undergone in a whole range of specific sorts or 'regions' of knowledge. Foucault does *not*, however, venture to *explain* the transition which is alleged to have taken place, nor does he in any way attempt to place the individuated '*epistemes*' in any more comprehensive order of development which would allow them to be judged as more or less 'advanced' or, for that matter, 'higher' or 'lower'.

Now, epochal historicism is certainly not alien to Marxist styles of discourse. The familiar Marxist variant discovers the unifying principle of an epoch at the 'level' of the economic 'base', and then reduces phenomena proper to the other 'levels' of the social totality (namely, the political-juridical and ideological 'superstructures') to but so many forms of expression of this principle to which they are all supposed to be subordinated. I have even heard this Marxist variant of epochal historicism summarized in paradigmatically crude fashion in the proposition that 'Everything in capitalism is capitalist'. This may well be true – though if it is to be anything other than tautologically so, we would need, to begin with, at least some criterion for distinguishing that which is 'in' capitalism from that which remains 'outside' it. (This same tautological quality, incidentally, accounts for the explanatory deficits of the culturalist brand of 'Marxism' associated especially with Adorno – even if in his case, one ought perhaps to substitute, say, 'bourgeois civilization' and 'bourgeois' for 'capitalism' and 'capitalist' in the subject and predicate terms of the proposition respectively.)

What makes a claim such as this *historicist* is the implication that everything which just so happens to exist *simultaneously* with the dominance of a capitalist mode of production is thereby itself stamped as essentially 'capitalist'. Presumably, the phenomena in question would have to be in some demonstrable way really subject to this dominance (hence, for instance, the Soviet political system under Brezhnev would not be 'capitalist', despite the fact of the simultaneous dominance of a capitalist mode of production in Western Europe). The scope of the claim is also, of course, presumably limited to just specifically social phenomena. But, in any case, the sorts of discourse which give rise to such claims rarely achieve the degree of analytical precision which would even make it meaningful to pose them such questions.

Althusser's critique of historicist currents in Marxism is principally directed at more or less nuanced forms of what I have here described as *epochal* historicism. It is a real achievement of that critique to have demonstrated how *even* elements which may figure among the strictly economic conditions of some existing capitalist social formation need not themselves have a specifically capitalist character. Or rather: attention to (and empirical study of) the reality of existing capitalism shows that this is the case, and Althusser has formulated a set of conceptual distinctions of sufficient precision for us to be able consistently to *say* that it is the case.[20] The dominance of a capitalist mode of production, which is what gives to an existing social formation taken as a whole its specifically capitalist character, does not preclude and may indeed even *require* the coexistence within that formation also of other forms of production which are not themselves specifically capitalist. Much of what gets called the 'informal sector' in the current economic literature provides unmistakable testimony to this fact. Consider too the entire domain of activities comprised by so-called 'domestic labour': viz. such activities as directly contribute to the reproduction of labour-power. For essential reasons, these are not susceptible to a specifically capitalist principle of organization; and yet it does not require much reflection to conclude that they are indispensable to the existence of a capitalist economy.

If this is so even for forms pertaining to the economic 'base', then *a fortiori* it is certainly not necessary (in fact it is not even conceivable) that all the 'superstructural' elements of a capitalist social formation should themselves have a specifically capitalist character. Capitalism as a system does not create its real conditions of existence *ex nihilo*. What determines the appurtenance of a political form (say, for example, parliamentary democracy) or an ideological configuration (say, for instance, nationalism or racism) to some existing capitalist social formation is their functional subordination under specific circumstances to a capitalist logic of material reproduction – their 'functionalization', if you will – *not*, however, anything which marks such forms considered simply *in themselves* as essentially 'capitalist'. Certain political or ideological forms may well share a *common* history with the capitalist mode of production. However, as Althusser rightly stressed, their own histories are never *reducible* to the history of the latter: they do not, that is to say, have the *same* history. This is indeed the very crux of Althusser's critique of historicism.[21] A form, then, which may have come to *function* as a reproductive condition of a capitalist society as it exists may well antedate the emergence of specifically capitalist relations of production and may well survive their disappearance; by the same token, the said form may well become obsolete without threatening the viability of capitalist reproduction as such. This can be confirmed by considering any of the examples mentioned parenthetically above: the character of the relation between each of them and a specifically capitalist logic of material reproduction has to be established by empirical research and for specific cases. It cannot simply be decided upon by methodological fiat or deduced, say, from 'the concept' of capital.

Althusser's exposé of the failings of epochal historicism – above all, his insistence that the constituent elements of a society not be attributed the kind of spiritual unity which characterizes what he calls the 'Hegelian totality' – is, then, of great value in correcting what are definite and harmful tendencies in the Marxist tradition (and not only in the Marxist tradition). Indeed, it is a shame that, for the most part, the content of such subtle analyses as these has simply been forgotten, while Althusser's name gets invoked instead in connection with pseudo-epistemological banalities. Nonetheless, Althusser's critique is not of direct relevance for us here. The reason for this can be appreciated simply by reviewing the passages cited above as artefacts of the historicist discourse. The conventions of epochal historicism are normally drawn upon in Marxist discussions when it is a matter of relating the content of Marx's economic analyses to phenomena pertaining rather to the 'spheres' of, say, culture or politics, *not*, however, in connection with the protocols governing those economic analyses themselves. In this latter connection, as the cited passages bear out, it is more common to find evidence of what I have proposed to call *genetic* historicism.[22]

We can define *genetic* historicism as a style of discourse professing to *explain* something by reference to the specific conditions of its historical genesis: to clarify what (and indeed how) it *is* by reconstructing how it *came into being*.[23] Now, to a greater or lesser degree, all the 'methodological' texts cited above bear traces of such genetic historicism. It is evident from their inspection, however, that the methodological historicism which has dominated the discussion of Marx's 'dialectics' is not *merely* genetic in character. Recall Marx's own contention regarding his demystified 'dialectic': 'it grasps every form which has come into existence in fluid movement, and therefore grasps it according to its transient side as well'. It is this emphasis on the '*transient* side' of the object under investigation which constitutes the distinctiveness of the Marxist variant of methodological historicism as against the traditional genetic sort.

For a traditional genetic account, in order to grasp the nature of some phenomenon it ought to be sufficient to demonstrate the conditions which give rise to it historically. (Clearly, genetic historicism cannot tolerate any 'multiplicity of origins': there must be one *unique* set of historical conditions which determine the emergence of every phenomenon – otherwise the characteristic claim of genetic historicism becomes ambiguous.) But according to an historicist construal of 'the dialectic', nothing is properly grasped except as, so to speak, articulated *between* the conditions of its emergence and the conditions of its decease: the form of existence of the object of investigation is thus not only conceived of as a *result* (per the requirements of genetic historicism), but also as a *phase*. This is manifest in nearly all of the citations reviewed.

The defining claim of a 'dialectical' method construed in this way – what makes it precisely 'dialectical' and not merely genetic – is that an adequate understanding of some (presumably, *any*) object of inquiry is obtained via the demonstration of its historicity, not *only* in the sense of its being something historically *originated* (or 'evolved'), but also in the sense of its being *qua* something historically originated thereby, so to speak, progressively delimited as well: something, that is to say, which is destined (if it has not already done so) *to perish*. As will be seen in a moment, this sort of formulation does indeed have a Hegelian source: not, however, in anything which Hegel has to say concerning specifically *historical* transitoriness, but rather in his treatment of transitoriness as an essential characteristic of finite existence as such.

Writing of finite things in general, Hegel observes, 'the hour of their birth is the hour of their death'. We will be examining in detail the significance which this ominous pronouncement takes on in the context of Hegel's idealism. But it is clear that an analogous precept underlies the historicist conception even of Marx's allegedly materialist 'dialect'. Every general form of existence is supposed to be grasped as the product of the conditions which have brought it about, but these conditions are in turn supposed to resolve themselves into a set of conditions which determine *the necessity of its demise*: the very conditions of existence of the form under investigation are thus revealed to be nothing but the transition between these two stages which encompass its emergence and decline. The form is grasped 'in fluid movement': namely, as a temporary constellation in a more comprehensive process. It is this sort of historicism which I propose to baptize '*dynamic* historicism'.

3.3 THE 'METHOD OF *CAPITAL*' AS DYNAMIC HISTORICISM

The most symptomatic form of expression of dynamic historicism in the methodological discourse we are examining here is the contention, articulated with paradigmatic clarity in the Kaufman extracts, that Marx, as required by the protocols of his alleged 'method', presents in *Capital* a continuous set of laws governing the 'emergence, existence, development and death' of his chosen object of investigation: namely, of a capitalist economic order. Special emphasis needs to be placed here upon the alleged *continuity* of the 'laws' in question. It would not involve any sort of historicism at all, for instance, to suggest that Marx: (1) established the 'laws' of 'existence and development' of a capitalist economic order (or, more precisely, that he established (a) the constitutive conditions of such an order and (b) definite patterns of development they entail – in other words, what have come to be known as the 'laws of motion' of capitalism); (2) offered some interesting observations on the historical processes resulting in its formation (in other words, on historical processes resulting in the emergence of a society in which those constitutive conditions are *really satisfied*); and (3) adduced some considerations intrinsic to the nature of such an order militating against the long-run viability of its reproduction and even, say, favouring its transformation into some specifiable other sort of economic order.

Indeed, the last claim could be formulated in yet stronger fashion. Let us suppose for the sake of argument that Marx attempted in *Capital* to demonstrate the *necessity* of the dissolution of a capitalist order and, furthermore, to demonstrate this on the basis *solely* of features inherent to it: that he proposed, in short, a *law of dissolution* of a capitalist economy. (We leave aside, just momentarily, one last possible variant: viz. that according to which the emergence of a socialist order out of the dissolution of the capitalist one is likewise ascribed necessity.) Even if this were so, *still* there would be nothing specifically historicist about the theoretical project described. The peculiarity of the dynamic historicist construal lies in the claim that the three components of this project – let us call them, for sake of convenience, analytical sequences 1, 2 and 3 – represent an indissoluble unity: that they are *logically interdependent*, such that the one analysis can only be completed *on the condition* that the others are as well.

Now, if we examine the *précis* of these components just given, it becomes clear that analysis 3, supposing it were carried out, would have indeed to *derive* from 1: whatever interpretation we choose to give to 3, if the claim for the *immanence* of the grounds adduced is to be maintained, then it would have, in effect, to represent merely a logical extension of 1, though, equally clearly, this has nothing to do with 'method', but has to do rather with the character of the claim which analysis 3 is supposed to support. We will return to this point below. What a dynamic historicist interpretation of Marx does, however, is to insist that components 2 and 1 are *also* interdependent – which is not only not obvious from their descriptions, but indeed, as will be seen momentarily, *impossible*. By the same token, a dynamic historicist reading requires that we interpret 3 in the manner of the stronger variant suggested above: the immanent law of development of a capitalist order, if allowed to remain in operation for a sufficient length of time, must reveal itself to be the very 'law' of its ultimate demise. This is important, since though the presence in *Capital* of some argument attempting to demonstrate the existence of such a 'law' would not per se count as evidence in favour of the historicist interpretation, the *absence* of such a demonstration is alone sufficient to disqualify the latter.

Since, moreover, what remains in the aftermath of the dissolution of the capitalist order is presumably something other than just economic disintegration *tout court*, historicist interpreters of Marx have tended to go still further and to suggest that the alleged 'law of dissolution' is at once a *law of transition* by which a capitalist order is necessarily transformed into a socialist one – exactly as the 'law of emergence' of a capitalist order, supposing there was such a law, must in fact have been a 'law of transition' between a pre-capitalist, viz. a feudal, order and a capitalist one. Indeed, a consistent and comprehensive dynamic historicism would have to depict each of these 'laws' as, in effect, *three* laws: the 'law of emergence' of capitalism as also a 'law of dissolution' of feudalism and a 'law of transition' between the two; and the 'law of dissolution' of capitalism as also the 'law of emergence' of some other economic order (a socialist one being, of course, the preferred choice) and a 'law of transition' between them.

It should be added that *if*, for instance, we maintained that the economic transformation in question is necessarily accompanied by parallel transformations in, say, political institutions and 'modes of thought' – if, that is to say, we conceived of society according to the conventions of *epochal* historicism and identified the organizing principle of material reproduction as the basic principle which gets expressed at every 'level' of the social whole – then we would have what could be called an 'inclusive' historicism. Lukács is especially inclined to combine the conventions of epochal and dynamic historicism in this way, and presumably indeed the dream of such an inclusive historicism has occupied the methodological imagination of many a would-be 'orthodox' Marxist. Nonetheless, it will not be our theme here, since, as already indicated, discussions concerning the relation between 'base' and 'superstructures' typically only serve to divert attention from the specific content of Marx's economic analyses.[24]

Now, as compared to either a synchronic historicism or a simple genetic one, what is especially conspicuous about a dynamic historicism is the exorbitance of its claims. The former claim only to grasp the nature of some object each according to distinctive explanatory procedures – in the one case, by referring it either to an epoch or a 'moment' to which it is supposed to belong, in the other, by reconstructing the conditions of its genesis. In contrast, *dynamic* historicism is distinguished by the claim not only to grasp the nature of some object as it exists, but also, precisely *by virtue of* grasping its nature, to demonstrate the inevitability of the *transformation* of this object into an object of some different sort.

Recall the passage from Godelier in which he contends that Marx was able 'to analyze both the historical necessity of the appearance of capitalism and the necessity of its disappearance'. Well, assuming that capitalism exists, to analyse the 'historical necessity' of its appearance is nothing different than simply analysing how it in fact came into being: whatever the peculiar conditions of this process happen to have been, that it was 'necessary' – metaphysically considered, at any rate – is shown by the simple fact that it occurred. On the other hand, to analyse the 'historical necessity' of its *dis*appearance – supposing, namely, that it *still* exists – is evidently a matter of greater distinction. To perform such an analysis presupposes that we have the capacity not only to *reconstruct* the governing principle of *anterior* historical development, but also to *extrapolate* the character of *future* historical development. It is, incidentally, precisely this last aspect of the method which Marx is alleged to have followed in *Capital*, i.e. the implication of there being incontrovertible and universal 'laws of historical development', that inspired the special ire of Karl Popper and it represents the core of the doctrine which Popper identified as 'historicism'.[25]

3.4 THE POVERTY OF THE HISTORICIST INTERPRETATION

What, then, exactly is wrong with dynamic historicism? In summarizing the conclusions of his *The Poverty of Historicism*, Popper wrote:

'I tried to show . . . that historicism is a poor method – a method that does not bear any fruit'.[26] I think Popper would in fact be quite right about this – *if*, that is, historicism of the dynamic variety was a method at all. I want to show here that it is not, that the dominant form of historicism in the Marxist tradition is even more impoverished than Popper thought. My proposal is that dynamic historicism is not a 'method', but merely a methodological fantasy. The historicist model which we have examined lays down the norms for a discourse *about* method. It does not, however, lay down norms which have guided or could guide the theoretical investigation of any definite subject-matter. Does this proposal, if justified, represent a devastating critique of Marx, as Popper supposed his treatment of historicism did? Still more: does it represent sufficient grounds for laying at Marx's doorstep the souls of 'the countless men and women of all creeds or nations or races who fell victims to the fascist and communist belief in inexorable Laws of Historical Destiny'?[27]

The answer to both questions is: quite obviously not. (And Popper's assimilation of communist to fascist 'belief' in this regard is tendentious in the extreme, since fascist ideology is not in fact characterized by any insistence upon scientifically ascertainable 'laws' of history, but – on the contrary – typically employs the motif of an historically unique 'crisis' of 'civilization', which is only to be overcome by an heroic initiative breaking with the entire previous trend of development.) Exposing the illusory character of dynamic historicism proves merely that Marx was capable on occasion of making overblown and ill-conceived pronouncements (though he almost always corrected them in calmer moments) and, above all, that Marxists and anti-Marxists alike have felt more comfortable reading the prefaces and afterwords where such pronouncements mainly occur than the texts they accompany.

Regardless of what Marx himself may have seen fit to remark with respect to the 'dialectical' nature of his economic analyses, there is no evidence that he ever in fact 'applied' in *Capital* a 'dialectical method' of the sort suggested by the historicist model. One, albeit rather laborious, way of showing this would be simply, as suggested above, to *test* the model against its supposed object: viz. the actual order of theoretical demonstration which *Capital* displays. We have seen that if the historicist conception is correct, then the discourse of *Capital* must include the formulation of determinate, so to speak, 'laws of transience' of a capitalist mode of production: a law governing its emergence and a law governing its decline. Indeed, as we have also seen, a consistent historicism would have in fact to regard the 'laws of transience' proper to a capitalist order as both of a piece with its own distinctive 'laws of motion' and at once 'laws of transition' between it and other sorts of socio-economic order. Presumably, if it is really here a 'method' which is at issue, the entire expository structure of *Capital* ought to be dictated by requirements associated with the demonstration and presentation of such laws. The proof that this is not the case is quite simply *Capital* itself. But we need not lend the systematic pretensions of historicism quite so much credence. The mere fact that the 'laws of transience' should turn out to be 'missing' from the discourse of *Capital* would provide sufficient grounds for concluding that Marx did not, in any case, employ a dynamic historicist 'method' in composing it.

Of course, even with regard to this more limited 'test', the burden of proof must in the first instance fall on those who defend the affirmative position. It is up to the adherents of the historicist model to propose particular analytical sequences in *Capital* as those fulfilling the promise of their 'dialectical laws', and some have indeed done so. Thus, though the historicist model is the product of a methodological discourse which has gained a kind of spurious autonomy from first-order theoretical inquiry, nonetheless it has inspired a certain 'reading' of *Capital*. In order to discredit the historicist conception by, so to speak, 'a posteriori' means, it would be enough, then, to demonstrate that the various candidates put forward do not in fact discharge the function which has been ascribed to them. Indeed, this would show that the historicist conception of 'Marx's method' is not merely *false*, but *systematically misleading*: in the sense that once accepted *en gros*, it predisposes the reader to misconstrue the details of Marx's analysis – or at least all such of those as are not simply ignored altogether.

The confusion which has been created by an historicist reading of *Capital* is especially great as regards Marx's presentation of the famous 'law of the tendency of the rate of profit to fall'. This supposed law derives much of its fame – as well as its infamy – precisely from its being construed as just that 'law of motion' of a capitalist economy which, given a long enough time, is supposed to reveal itself as also the 'law' of its ultimate demise. In fact, if we take seriously the 'methodological' requirement that a 'dialectical law' be not only a 'law of transience' but also one of *transition*, then the law of the falling rate of profit is obviously unsuited for the role. Even if it could be demonstrated that the 'law' entails the demise of the capitalist system, there is certainly nothing about this anticipated demise which would suggest an '*Aufhebung*': that is, the transformation of the capitalist system into some other and indeed 'superior' socio-economic system. Judged according to the stated criterion, the law of the 'concentration and centralization of capital', Marx's own choice for the 'law of transition'[28] is indeed the far more alluring candidate – even if it too, as we have seen, is not finally equal to the task.

But never mind: there is a remarkably stable consensus, encompassing both 'orthodox' Marxists and anti-Marxists, that with his analysis of the tendency of the profit rate Marx attempted to demonstrate that capital accumulation is subject to a law entailing its own ultimate cessation and hence the 'breakdown' of the capitalist system. This consensus has not been disturbed in the least by the fact that in his most mature presentation of the 'falling rate', viz. in the third volume of *Capital,* Marx explicitly and correctly acknowledges that as formulated by him the law does *not* in fact entail any such consequences. Indeed, throughout his discussion, Marx even treats a growing mass of profits as an aspect of the very same law which is supposed to govern the profit rate's decline. Thus, for example, he asks: 'How, then, should we present this double-edged law of a decline in the profit *rate* coupled with a simultaneous increase in the absolute *mass* of profits, arising from the same reasons?' (*C*III, 326/230). This way of posing the problem in fact represents a significant departure in Marx's own thinking on the subject, for which historicist interpreters of *Capital* would be hard pressed to give an account.[29]

It is not necessary, however, to enter here into all the Marxological details that an a posteriori refutation of the historicist model would require us to review. For there is also available to us a more concise, so to speak, 'a priori' route to the same end. I have, after all, claimed not only that Marx *did not* employ the 'dialectical method' ascribed to him on the historicist interpretation, but that he *could not* have employed it, since there is no such 'method'. The 'method' described by the historicist model is simply not a method of scientific analysis at all. Two distinct considerations will make this clear.

In the first place, and as we have seen, *if* the 'method' of Marx's investigations was historicist in character, then we ought not only to find in them the presentation of some 'law of emergence' of a capitalist economy, but, furthermore, this 'law', which is supposed to govern the consolidation of the specific conditions of such an economy, will have to be continuous with the very economic 'laws of motion' which are determined *by* those specific conditions. The former and the latter will have, in effect, all to share a common principle. Now, many interpreters of Marx have insisted that the expository structure of *Capital* reflects exactly such an approach, and some have even undertaken quite remarkable contortions in order allegedly to prove it. However, by even just inspecting the claim which this sort of interpretation suggests that Marx's analysis is designed to support, we can see that it is false. It is, namely, *logically false*: it is not only *not* the case, it *cannot be* the case.

If the laws of motion of a capitalist economy *are* precisely laws of motion of a *capitalist* economy and not simply economic 'laws of motion' as such, then they will, as indicated, have to be determined by whatever conditions are specifically constitutive of a capitalist economy. Hence, they will have precisely to be *dis*continuous from any principle that may have governed the process through which those conditions come to be satisfied in fact – this quite apart from the question of whether the latter process ought properly to be regarded as lawlike or not. (In his own discussion, Marx briefly invokes the 'fetters' hypothesis in order to suggest that it indeed ought to be.[30] But his actual account of the various 'levers' of the 'so-called primitive accumulation of capital' – spoilation of church property, theft of common lands, 'clearing' of feudal estates, and so on – suggests anything but a lawlike process.) Here, then, is a first reason for considering dynamic historicism to be not an actual 'method', but an imaginary one: since any 'method' of analysis which requires the demonstration of impossible claims will not find many occasions to be 'applied'.

In the second place, and as we have also seen, *if* the 'method' of *Capital* was 'dialectical' in the sense implied by the historicist model, then we would have to find in it the presentation of some 'law of dissolution' of a capitalist economy (which would have, according to the most ambitious and indeed consistent variant, to be at the same time a 'law of transition' to a socialist one). Now, as just discussed, even if he too was prepared to say that some such law must obtain, Marx did not in fact derive any such law in *Capital*. There is, however, nothing a priori problematic about the suggestion that he did. What is problematic is the unusual (and unflattering) suggestion that he was *required* to do so by the protocols of *his method*. If Marx's analysis so happened to demonstrate that the constitutive conditions of a capitalist economy entail the inevitability of the dissolution of any actually-existing capitalist order, then the validity of this conclusion would consist in its having been shown to follow *from the nature of capitalism*. To suggest that it follows from the 'dialectical' nature of *Marx's method* is, in effect, to suggest that Marx has not *proven* it at all – and this is indeed precisely what *anti*-Marxists mean to suggest when they accuse Marx of 'Hegelianism' in this context.

Here is, then, a second reason for concluding that dynamic historicism is not a method, but merely a highly misleading way of talking *about* 'method': since – and we have already noted that a historicist discourse of an epochal variety involves exactly the same fallacy – it presents as a matter of *methodological choice* what ought rather, if it were really a 'method' that was here in question, to be a matter *of proof*. Either it lies in the nature of a capitalist economy to be subject to some law which would, given a sufficient length of time, result in its dissolution or it does not lie in the nature of a capitalist economy to be subject to such a law. It does not belong to any 'method' to decide this.

3.5 THE HISTORICIST MODEL AND HEGEL

It might be presumed at this stage that having put paid to the historicist model, we have conclusively shown that – occasional philosophical flourishes aside – the actual scientific discourse of *Capital* must be quite free of any distinctively Hegelian aspect. That, however, will depend on the accuracy of what the historicist model implies concerning the character of 'dialectic' in its archetypal Hegelian setting. In fact, if it is the case, as I have suggested, that Hegelian Marxism of the traditional historicist variety predisposes a misleading and impoverished interpretation of Marx's *Capital*, it is no less the case that it presupposes what I would call a *banalized* interpretation of Hegel's *Logic*. Recall Marx's 'famous quotation' on 'the dialectic': 'In its rational form it is a scandal and abomination to the bourgeoisie, because it includes in its positive understanding of what exists a simultaneous understanding of its negation, its inevitable destruction'. Now, following Marx's example, let us indulge ourselves just for the moment in a Hegelian metaphoric, before going on in the sequel to ascertain what theoretical content such metaphors can be made to bear. To reveal the 'negative' ensconced at the heart of the 'positive' is, then, indeed precisely the task which Hegel assigns to dialectical thinking. But, as already indicated above, the problem is how exactly we are to interpret the 'negativity' in question. Marx's formulation suggests that what is 'negated' thereby ceases to exist – hence the *temporal* connotation attaching to his use of 'negation' here. To demonstrate the 'negativity' inherent in the object of investigation is to demonstrate the necessity of its dissolution: namely its 'transience'. We have noted the repercussions that Marx's usage in this passage has had for the subsequent

Marxist tradition, which has for the most part been content to glean its 'dialectics' from such sources (if not much worse ones).

In Hegel's own usage, however, the inherence of the 'negative' in some phenomenon abstractly conceived of as self-subsistent, and hence 'positive', implies in the first instance not the necessity of the latter's *dissolution*, but rather the essentiality of its *limitation*. According to Hegel, for any given thing, what it is *not* is precisely a condition of what it is, a condition of its determinacy as such: hence Hegel's fondness for the Spinozistic dictum '*Omnis determinatio est negatio*' – or, as Hegel himself renders Spinoza, 'The foundation of all determinateness is negation' (*En.L*, §91, add.).[31] In Hegelian parlance, what is determinate 'passes into' its opposite, the one 'passes into' its other – it does not simply pass *away*.

If the significance of such characteristically Hegelian formulations is not immediately evident, that need not concern us too much at this stage. We will have occasion enough to familiarize ourselves with them in Part III below, where we will treat Hegelian 'logic' in its own right. For present purposes, it is only crucial to appreciate that in its archetypal 'dialectical' application the category of negation does not, as in its historicist appropriation, pertain to the transient quality of existing phenomena, but rather to what we can, for the moment, call the constitutive alterity (or 'Being-for-another') that provides the condition by virtue of which anything can even be ascribed determinate being at all.

I have to confess, however, that in order to make Hegel seem a bit more coherent and plausible in this initial approach, I have smuggled into his doctrine an element which is in fact foreign to it: viz. by referring in this last sentence to an '*ascription*' of determinacy. As we shall see in some detail later on, Hegel is not himself so concerned to specify the condition in question as a *logical* one – or rather he is not concerned to specify it as *merely* a logical one. This has immediate implications for the problem at hand. Though I have stressed that the category of negation in Hegel's 'dialectical' usage does not *in the first instance* imply the dissolution of 'the positive' (but rather the determinate limitation of the latter), this is not in fact the whole story. For the negativity which constitutes the determinateness of the determinate 'something' (or '*Etwas*') is interpreted by Hegel as the ground of its *finitude*, and the very principle of Hegel's idealism is that the finite (precisely as the positive form of appearance of the infinite) lacks 'absolute being' and hence is condemned precisely to *cease* to be. 'The being of such finite things', Hegel writes in the ominous passage to which allusion has already been made, 'is to have the germ of decease as their being-within-self: the hour of their birth is the hour of their death' (*SL*, 129/I, 140).

The speciousness of Hegel's annexing the connotation of a real *passing away*, and even the figure of a *biological* mortality, to his interpretation of determinate negativity can be gauged by considering his own examples. Thus, in the *Science of Logic*, Hegel (amazingly) arrives at his conclusions concerning the 'mortality' of the finite by way of – or, at any rate, *after*! – a consideration of *pure spatial objects*: viz. points, lines and planes. If we grant for the sake of argument that such pure spatial objects are 'determinate beings' (or '*Daseiende*') by virtue of the limitation which constitutes their specificity, just as empirical objects are in their specificity so determined, then it is clearly impossible to regard the determinacy of the determinate per se as the pronouncement of its 'death sentence': for, as the examples unwittingly bring to mind, not *everything* determinate is subject to such a fate. It may be that logically considered the point is, as Hegel puts it, '[the] dialectic of its own self to become a line, the line the dialectic to become a plane, and the plane the dialectic to become total space' (*SL*, 128/I, 138). But having thus 'become' other than themselves, point, line and plane have certainly not '*ceased to be*': the negativity intrinsic to their identity has not, after all, proved the 'germ of their decease'. The earnestness with which Hegel insists upon the contrary cannot but remain utterly mysterious for those unwilling to take serious account of the theistic commitments informing his idealism. By persistently conflating logical transition and empirical transformation (in instances such as the one reviewed here quite simply by exploiting an ambiguity in the word 'become'), Hegel thus provides himself the means to conclude that the subjects of the latter are in fact themselves 'ideal' and precisely *not* 'real' – or, in other words, that they lack 'intrinsic' being.

Even prior to the advent of 'Hegelian Marxism', then, Hegel is himself prone to give his insight concerning the inherence of the negative in the positive a substantializing and hence *temporalizing* turn. At especially crucial junctures he thus slides in his argument from *alterity* (*Anderssein*), which is clearly a *logical* category applying to objects only insofar as they have been distinguished (whether into sorts or simply numerically) and *compared* (or, in other words, which applies to objects from the perspective of what Hegel would call 'external reflection'), to *alterability* or 'mutability' (*Veränderlichkeit*), which describes a condition that ought to pertain to objects considered simply *in themselves*. In a typical passage from the *Encyclopedia*, paralleling the one from the 'greater' *Logic* discussed above, Hegel follows the observation that something 'is what it is, only in and through its limit' by remarking:

> For the imagination existence appears in the character of something solely positive, and quietly abiding within its own limits; though we also know indeed that everything finite (and existence is such) is subject to change [*Veränderung*]. . . . The fact is that it lies in the concept of determinate being to change, and change is only the manifestation of what determinate being implicitly is. The living thing dies, and indeed simply because as living it bears within itself the germ of death. (*En.L*, §92, add.)

The invocation of *change* in this connection is, however, a non-sequitur: what Hegel has shown in the preceding development is that *alterity* lies in the notion of determinateness, *not* that alterability does.[32]

As we will have ample opportunity to confirm, such non-sequiturs are not merely on occasion characteristic of Hegel's argumentation. The slippage from logical alterity to empirical mutability – and let there be no mistake, what occurs here is a *slippage* and no 'transition' – is part and parcel of Hegelian metaphysics as such. This is no doubt what has given courage to so many of its would-be Marxist 'friends'[33] in construing 'the Hegelian dialectic' simply as a principle (in fact, an ontology) of all-encompassing change. It should be stressed, however, that in so doing they have in fact taken a step back *behind* Hegel: in effect *ignoring* the logical insight altogether, while adopting the banalities which are the result of the illicit empirical employment of the latter as the very essence of 'dialectics'. Contrary to stated intentions, the traditional procedure of 'Hegelian Marxism' has more often than not been to discard whatever 'rational kernel' is to be found here.

If, then, as Marx himself insists we should, we take Hegel as our standard of what counts as 'dialectic', a 'dialectical method' of the sort described by the historicist model would not even be 'dialectical' – except to the degree that the sense this modifier has in Hegel's usage is pared down to the bare figurative connotation of movement (as opposed to 'fixity'), irrespective of the nature of the objects (categories of thought, pure spatial objects, natural phenomena or forms of social life) to which such 'movement' is attributed. The figure of 'movement' in such 'dialectical' styles of discourse is, incidentally, a figure both in the sense of invoking an *image* and in the sense of being a *rhetorical* figure. More precisely, it is a *synecdoche*, with one sort of change, viz. *change of place* or 'movement', serving to represent all sorts of change – or even, perhaps more typically, change of place serving to represent *change of condition*.[34]

3.6 THE HISTORICITY OF CAPITALIST PRODUCTION AND THE CRITIQUE OF POLITICAL ECONOMY

In order to evaluate whether the logical peculiarities in the discourse of *Capital* are indeed a function of the Hegelianism of its 'method', and to assess what the substantive implications of this might be supposing it were true, we have no choice but to return to the alleged source. As noted, there has of late emerged a 'new' Hegelian Marxism which is much more conscientious than its traditional predecessor in trying to extract from Hegel principles of reasoning for which a serious claim could be made of their having somewhere been applied. Representatives of this current have, however, typically been content to provide brief summaries of these supposed principles of 'dialectical logic', before moving on straightaway to an examination of alleged instances of their application by Marx. We cannot be content to do the same here. The only standard for judging what Hegel's distinctive 'method of analysis' might be is, of course, the 'method' which Hegel's own exposition obeys – and not what Hegelians, nor, for that matter, Hegel may have said on the issue. It could turn out that Hegel did not even himself follow the precepts which he laid down for 'dialectical' thought. In which case, what sense would it make to insist that Marx did?

Before setting off on the tortuous detour through Hegel's *Logic*, however, one further confusion created by the historicist model should be cleared up, for, ironically, that model has had the consequence of obscuring even the very sense in which the historicity of Marx's object of investigation in *Capital* is indeed *at stake* in the analysis he makes of it. Despite all our criticisms of histori*cism*, viz. as a methodological postulate, the demonstration of the historical character of capitalist production is not only a pivotal accomplishment of *Capital*, but indeed among those accomplishments which earn it the title of a *critique* of political economy. This accomplishment, however, does not depend upon any special attributes of Marx's 'method'; nor does it involve reconstructing the actual historical genesis of a capitalist mode of production, nor proving the inevitability of its decline. It depends upon the fact that capitalist production is indeed *capitalist*: it is, namely, only one specific *social form of production* and not simply production *as such*. In this sense, Marx's object of investigation is in itself *objectively* *historical* – quite apart from anyone's 'methodological' preferences. The demonstration of the historicity of capitalist production is, then, nothing other than the demonstration of its constitutive conditions: *not* the demonstration of how they *came into being*, but the demonstration of *what they are*.

Perhaps the most common manner of interpreting Marx's departure from classical political economy in this regard is as a repudiation of the assumption of the *homo oeconomicus*. Now, it would hardly make sense to accuse the political economists of having altogether ignored the historical novelty of the socio-economic order whose basic norms they attempted to grasp. They were, after all, in a way publicists for that order and indeed advocated specific policies for consolidating it. The more exact charge against them is rather that they illicitly sought to derive the characteristics of a market system from postulates concerning the behavioural propensities of individual economic agents, thus ultimately basing their entire analysis upon an unsubstantiated conception of 'human nature'.[35] In this sense, classical political economy provided a kind of 'ideal derivation' of such a system, from which it followed that the existence of other sorts of economic systems, however undeniable, was, so to speak, '*merely*' historical and '*un*natural', since contrary to the fundamental motive forces of human behaviour as such.[36]

Marx is supposed to have broken with this whole construction: viz. by anchoring his theory in an analysis of the structure of those social relations which lend to capitalist production its specifically capitalist character, and treating various patterns of individual economic behaviour merely as so many effects of that structure. It was not the 'natural' propensities of concrete individuals which determined the socially-prevalent patterns of behaviour (much less which determined the movement of the system as a whole), but rather the constraints placed upon such individuals by the structural 'sites' of economic activity they occupied. In this way, Marx succeeded in undercutting the anthropological postulates through which political economy fulfilled its ideological vocation of 'naturalizing' capitalist production. The details of this account of Marx's innovation will be familiar to readers of Althusser.[37] Although it should not be thought, of course, that the critique of the *homo oeconomicus* is as such a monopoly of his.[38]

The basic position outlined above has many merits: it provides what is surely the crucial element of any critique of modern 'bourgeois' social science more generally and it helps indeed to establish the specificity of Marx's procedure in opposition to the latter.[39] It is, however, equally clear that classical political economy in particular is not systematically quite so dependent upon the supposition of the 'rational economic man' as has been suggested. The political economists, so to speak, 'promoted' such a supposition. But neither the theories of value nor the analyses of distribution which they developed in any obvious way require it. By contrast, the thoroughgoing logical dependence of neoclassical economics upon the postulate of the *homo oeconomicus* is conspicuous, and that this postulate acquires such an enhanced role there is indeed precisely a consequence of the neoclassicals' *rejection* of the classical theory of value and their replacement of the latter by a 'subjective' theory.[40] Marx himself, incidentally, already commented upon this special dependence of a 'subjective' theory of value upon an assumed anthropology in criticizing the 'vulgar economic' ancestors of the 'marginalist revolution'.[41] It is not surprising, then, that in his most developed criticism of the classicals he did not in fact place any great emphasis on this point. The obfuscation of capitalist production in classical political economy is precisely of a more subtle and sophisticated sort.

In order to understand the basis of this obfuscation and of Marx's critique of it, it is especially important that we take account of the distinction he draws between, on the one hand, the material 'content' of economic processes – namely, the material elements of the production process and the goods which are its result – and, on the other, the 'form-determination' (*Formbestimmung*) which under conditions of commodity-exchange gives to these material items a second 'social objectivity' in addition to and superimposed upon their simple physical objectivity. This social objectivity of things is, namely, the objectivity which they possess as *values*. Now, Marx would repeatedly chastise the political economists for having confused the material 'content' of capital, understood in this context simply as produced means of production, with the 'form-determination' which first converts this material 'content' *into* capital, viz. the application of such means of production within those determinate relations of production which allow them to function simultaneously as *means of valorization*. Thus he writes, for example, in the *Grundrisse*:

> If, then, the specific form of capital is abstracted from and only the content is emphasized, *as which it is a necessary moment of all labour, then of course nothing is easier than to demonstrate that capital is a necessary condition for all human production*. The proof of this proceeds precisely by abstraction from the specific aspects

> which make it the moment of a specifically developed *historic* stage of human production. The joke is that if all capital is objectified labour which serves as means for new production, it is not the case that all objectified labour which serves as means for new production is capital. (*Gr.*, 258/182–3; cf. also *Gr.*, 86/21)

It is, I will argue, by virtue of their subsumption under the value-form, that is to say, by virtue of their legal status as private property and the continuity and systematicity of their exchange as such, that products of labour acquire their 'social objectivity' and certain, so to say, *socially objective* properties associated with the latter. I commented at the outset on the practice customary among economists of interpreting Marx's value theory simply as a special theory of price-formation: a 'labour theory of value', distinguishable from that of Ricardo at best only by its greater refinement. Marx himself, however, was unequivocal in specifying the failure to analyse the value-form as 'one of the basic defects of classical political economy' (*CI*, 174/95), and he was unequivocal in concluding that this defect resulted in nothing less than the incapacity of classical political economy to grasp the specific character of the relations of production proper to a capitalist society. It is this aspect of Marx's critique of political economy – an aspect which is alluded to in the historicist discourse, but in a mystified form – to which we will now turn.

Part II

Reification and Exchange

4 Concepts and Objects

4.1 THE CATEGORIES OF POLITICAL ECONOMY

As early as *The Poverty of Philosophy* of 1847, Marx comments upon what he takes to be the ahistorical quality of the treatment of economic categories in classical political economy. These critical remarks – which are indeed just remarks made in passing in the midst of a critique of Proudhon's Hegeloid appropriation of the political economists ('The material of the economists is active and effective human life; the material of M. Proudhon are the dogmas of the economists'[1]) – have served as a rallying point for historicist interpreters of Marx. Lukács cites them with evident enthusiasm.[2] Althusser cites them as well, though to opposite ends. For heuristic purposes, it will be useful to cite them here yet again: since precisely by virtue of their ambiguity, the remarks in question can be interpreted such as to yield *both* an anticipation of Marx's mature critique of political economy – a promising 'insight', if you like, but not yet a coherent analysis – *and* a symptomatic expression of the methodological historicism which I am suggesting is the mystified reflection of the former. Thus Marx writes:

> The economists express the relations of bourgeois production, the division of labour, credit, money, etc., as fixed immutable, eternal categories.... The economists explain how production takes place in these given relations, but what they do not explain is how these relations themselves are produced, that is, the historical movement which gives them birth.[3]

Althusser annexes to this passage a remark from another passage which occurs in fact in the following section of Marx's original text: 'these categories are as little eternal as the relations they express. They are historical and transitory products'.[4] This might seem like mere amplification upon the previous remarks. As we shall see, it is not. A notable slippage takes place in Marx's text in the space between the two passages and one which pushes the sense of the former in an unmistakably historicist direction: in the direction indeed of what I have above described as an 'inclusive' variant of historicism. Thus, whereas Althusser with some justification describes the criticism of classical political economy which Marx makes in this context as 'superficial and ambiguous', he has by his manner of quoting Marx in fact impeded our ability to reconstruct, so to speak, the system of this ambiguity.

In any event, superficial and ambiguous as it may be in a relatively early text like *The Poverty of Philosophy*, the charge that the political economists had an ahistorical conception of economic categories will remain an essential part of Marx's evaluation of the failings of his classical predecessors. Althusser is, of course, right to reject the view which locates the whole of Marx's theoretical innovation in his supposed 'historicization' of these categories: since such a view would suggest that there is nothing distinctive about the conceptual order of Marx's economic analysis per se, but merely a distinctiveness deriving from the application of his 'dialectical method', which – somehow – is supposed to have revealed the historical relativity of what the political economists presented as absolute. But, as against Althusser's interpretation, it is important to note that in the cited passages (unlike, say, in the 'famous quotations' from the 1873 'Afterword') Marx is simply not making any positive methodological recommendation – and he is certainly not giving his endorsement to a specifically *'dialectical'* method. *The Poverty of Philosophy* is, after all, an explicitly *anti*-Hegelian text, which is dedicated precisely to the task of exposing the mystifications wrought by a would-be 'dialectic method'.[5] Marx is not, then, as Althusser suggests, claiming that the categories of classical political economy 'must be historicized' in order to be understood,[6] but only that *in fact* their validity is historically limited in a way that the classical political economists managed to obscure.

This criticism is indeed still 'superficial', since by way of it Marx tells us neither what exactly *determines* the historical limits of applicability of these concepts, nor just *how* the political economists obscured such limits. But, on the other hand, rather than being simply abandoned, it will in Marx's mature critique be developed and specified in a manner that the 'young Marx' was not yet able to accomplish. The historicity of economic categories which Marx will continue to insist upon in critically evaluating the procedures of political economy has nothing to do with the actual sequence of events through which a specific set of social relations arise ('the historical movement which gave them birth'), nor much less with any general 'dialectical' precept to the effect that 'everything is transitory' (and hence so too must the relations expressed in political economic categories be transitory). Rather, this historicity has to do with the simple fact that the categories peculiar to political economy as a science *are* indeed 'expressions' of social relations, viz. social relations of production. In *The Poverty of Philosophy*, Marx already *says* this: 'Economic categories are nothing but the theoretical expressions, the abstractions of social relations of production'.[7] But he does not yet add, as he will later, that being 'expressions' of social relations, economic categories are not, then, to be confused with general empirical concepts applying to independently existing *things*.

Indeed, in a manner symptomatic of the continuing influence upon his thought of Feuerbach's materialism, Marx actually *encourages* such a confusion. By persistently and rather carelessly making appeal to an empiricist conception of abstraction, Marx seems to imply that the categories of political economy relate to their objects in much the same manner as, say, the categories of zoology relate to theirs. If such a model were actually relevant in this context, then the category *money*, for example, ought merely to be the product of a mental act of 'abstracting' from the intuited particularities of many empirically-existing specimens of money, just as the category *horse* should be the product of 'abstraction' from the particularities of many empirically-existing horses. Later, however, Marx will come to recognize that precisely *the reverse* is the case: viz. that the very existence of the particular specimen of money *qua* money is a function of its subsumption under the general form of value which it instantiates.

4.2 THE DIVISION OF LABOUR AND THE CONCEPT OF SOCIETY

By virtue of developing the insight that categories of social relation have a distinct logical status from general empirical concepts, Marx is able to go beyond merely chiding the economists for not explaining the historical provenance of the specific relations their categories 'express'. Why, after all, should economists do the work of historians? In his mature critique he is able to expose rather the (para-)logical mechanism whereby the analyses of the economists serve in fact *actively* to 'eternalize' such categories: which is to say, to obscure the historical limits of their applicability. This insight alone, however, is not sufficient to carry through Marx's critique, and this for two reasons in particular. In the first place, *all categories of relation*, not only those of specifically *social* relations, have a distinct logical status from general empirical concepts. For categories of relation as such, however, this by no means implies the historicity of their objects.

The category *circle*, for example, is just as much a category of relation as, say, the category *division of labour*. From this it follows that it is not arrived at by 'abstracting' the common features from a range of particulars. Rather, the object of the category is just the pure spatial possibility of a two-dimensional figure, all of whose points are equidistant from a common centre. In this sense, *there is no* range of particulars to which the category *circle* applies; there is just *one* circle, which can be variously represented. Such 'mathematical species', to use Leibniz's expression,[8] are not abstracted from a range of particulars, because the members which comprise them (in each case being unique) already *exist abstractly*.[9] Thus, insofar as 'mathematical species' are completely independent of any *particular* instantiation, the categories applying to them, far from being historically limited in scope, *are* precisely 'eternally valid' – which is to say, *a*historical.

Although for different reasons, the same holds true for the most general sorts of relation which obtain among objects conceived of simply as physical things. Thus the 'categories of relation' in the Kantian sense (substantiality, causality and interaction) are supposed to lay down the relations which physical objects as such not only *may* bear to one another, but *must*, at any event, *be thought of* as bearing to one another in order to be objects of experience at all. Since the application of these categories to the raw data of intuition ('appearances' in Kant's sense) is thus a *transcendental* 'condition of the possibility of experience in general', they are not only – unlike the concepts, say, of pure spatial (or, in other words, geometrical) objects – susceptible to particular instantiation, *every* particular experience is necessarily a particular instantiation of them (that is, in respect to its form). But this clearly leads us to the same conclusion as that which we reached with regard to the pure 'mathematical species', viz. that the Kantian 'categories of relation' – precisely *in* their application to experience – are likewise 'eternally valid'. Either that or they are 'eternally *invalid*', the latter possibility representing the sceptical option that Kant attempts to combat. But in either case – which is what is of relevance for our purposes – the most general categories of relation among physical objects certainly *cannot* be attributed a merely *historically-limited* validity.

One might suppose, then, that if the relational character of political economic categories does not of itself entail the historicity of their objects, then it must be the fact that the relations here in question are not just any relations, but rather specifically *social* relations that does so. But – and this is the second of the two reasons alluded to above – neither is *every* category of specifically social relation historically restricted in scope (except, of course, in the tautological sense that its application is restricted to societies). Consider the examples which Marx mentions in *The Poverty of Philosophy*: the division of labour, credit and money. These are supposed to be 'relations of bourgeois production' which the economists 'express as fixed, immutable, eternal categories'. Leaving aside credit and money for the moment (though these are clearly categories applicable to other modes of production besides just the specifically 'bourgeois'), in what sense is the division of labour *not* in fact 'eternal' – or at least as 'eternal' as the political economists can reasonably be accused of having 'expressed' it?

As I have already suggested, by the charge of 'eternalization', Marx understands more precisely that classical political economy succeeds in *de*historicizing economic categories, which is to say, in obscuring the specificity of the historical conditions under which they are applicable. Thus, for example, to label every piece of gold as 'money', just by virtue of its physical features, would be to obscure the fact that *the physical thing* gold takes on *the social function* of money only to the degree that it serves to mediate the relations entered into by economic agents through commodity exchange. Indeed, more exactly and as we shall see at length below, under such conditions as this thing becomes money, it does so by virtue of its being enlisted to represent the very social relatedness of individuals in objective form. Hence, though gold is always gold, it is not always – 'eternally' – money.[10]

But what about the division of labour? *Division of labour* is not a category of a thing insofar as it mediates a social relation, or, for that matter, of a social relation which gets represented 'in the form of' a thing. Rather, *division of labour* is explicitly and unmistakably a category of a social relation as such. It refers to *the relation* itself and not to the relation alloyed with some objective form in which it might under particular circumstances be represented. In this case, then, there is no opportunity to 'eternalize' any social relationship by mistakenly identifying it with a thing. If the political economists, nonetheless, portray the division of labour as an 'eternal' condition of production, then either they overlook the fact that there have existed societies without any division of labour (and, in which case, they are guilty not of a mystifying paralogism, but merely a simple mistake) or they are within their rights, because the division of labour *is* in fact such a condition.

In *The German Ideology*, Marx himself suggests precisely the latter: arguing that *some degree* of division of labour, if only a gender-based division between 'reproductive' (that is, biologically reproductive) and productive labour within the family, is indeed characteristic of all modes of production, including the most 'primitive'.[11] Moreover, quite apart from any empirical grounds for maintaining the universality of the division of labour, there are conceptual reasons for doing so. For what, after all, *is* society without a division of labour? What transforms a mere collection of biological individuals into the members of a common society, if not a functional differentiation which makes the activity and reproduction of each dependent upon at least some aspect of the activity of the others?

This differentiation need not, of course, be unhierarchical, and, in the event it is not, nor must it include only *labour*-functions strictly speaking. Thus, any given social formation may include, in addition to the labouring population, a functional strata of non-workers, whose participation in the consumption of the social product is determined by something other than their contribution to its production (for example, ownership of the means of production or seigneurial right).[12] Nonetheless, some aspect of the activity of the members of such a strata taken as a whole – to the degree, that is, that it actually forms part of the social formation in question, and is not merely a remnant of a previous one – must at the very least contribute to the reproduction of the *social form* of production: which is to say, among other things, to the reproduction of the conditions of its own claim upon the surplus-product.

The division of labour *is*, then, a universal feature of production as such, or at least of all production in society, which is all that is relevant for our purposes.[13] If the object of inquiry is 'society' or rather specific social formations, which we take as being unified at the level of their (dominant) modes of production, then the division of labour belongs to those 'general conditions of production' which define social production as such. Even at the extreme where production is *exclusively* for immediate subsistence requirements, and no redistribution of the product takes place, the collective existence of the members of the family or clan implies some sort of parcelling out of tasks and hence, however rudimentary, a division of labour. In this sense, the treatment of *the division of labour* and related categories as transhistorical is perfectly legitimate. They are not *a*historical, as we saw was the case with pure spatial or transcendental categories of relation. They are valid rather for every phase in the historical development of the specific object of inquiry, since taken together they determine the very concept of that object – in this case, the concept of 'the social' – and hence the bounds of any possible history which it can undergo.

4.3 THE DUAL OBJECTIVITY OF MONEY AND COMMODITIES

If not categories of social relation as such, just what sort of categories of social relation are then susceptible to the dehistoricization for which Marx criticizes classical political economy? Our earlier counter-example of *money* is instructive in this regard. Money is, Marx will suggest, a material thing in which a social relation is represented. More exactly, money is a material thing which, by virtue of the function assigned to it within a peculiar mechanism of social integration, comes to represent social relationship as such. It is, to adopt an expression with some cachet in the Marxist tradition, a 'reified' index of the social relatedness of its possessors. Let us attempt at this juncture merely to sketch out in a preliminary way the meaning of this proposal. We will return to it to fill in the details later on.

In a society of generalized commodity production, the real material dependencies among individuals are mediated by the exchange of the products they possess in their capacity as formally independent commodity owners. The definite ratios in which these commodities exchange among their owners are regulated by the values they respectively represent as objectifications of some portion of the total labour employed by society (or the 'social working day'). This is of course a claim which has been subject to more than a little and indeed one could even say 'epoch-making' controversy. It will have at this juncture to stand as simply asserted. Nonetheless, the basic 'intuition' underlying the claim – whether in the simple form of Adam Smith's deer and beaver economy or the much more intricate variant developed by Marx – should already be clear: viz. that commodity exchange is the mode of integration of a spontaneously evolved (that is, unplanned) division of *labour*. What can be had *without exertion* – this is the essential point and not considerations of scarcity or abundance – provides no one the occasion to enter into exchange relations.

Merely incidental exchange of goods can take the form of barter. But insofar as commodity exchange has become *the universal social bond* articulating the diverse productive activities of individuals into a functionally interdependent whole, the very nature of this complex 'social metabolism' (*CI*, 119/198) necessitates that the value of commodities obtain an independent form of existence which is universally alienable: which is to say, alienable in some proportion against all goods and at all times. Now, supposing for the moment that only that can be alienable which is itself a commodity, the practical requirements associated with such *universal* alienability will have the consequence that just some goods as opposed to others are, by virtue of their physical properties, especially well-adapted to fulfil the money-function.[14] But to confuse these physical properties with the social power which thus becomes associated with them, as if the latter were just *one more* intrinsic property of the species of thing exhibiting the former, would result precisely in a sort of 'naturalization', hence a '*de*historicization', of the concept of money. *Gold*, for example, is not simply as such universally alienable. Rather commodity exchange as a mechanism of social integration creates the functional requirement for an independent form of value which is universally alienable. As a function of this specific mode of sociality, *money* is universally alienable, and gold, among other things and in specific historical contexts, discharges the money-function.

The example of money thus provides us with all the elements for the solution of our problem. As what I will call a 'practical concept' of commodity-producing societies, *money* refers simultaneously to a functional aspect of the specific sort of 'social metabolism' which defines such societies as 'commodity-producing' *and* to the particular physical items upon which in a given social formation that function happens to devolve. This is not a matter of an ambivalence of reference affecting the *word* 'money'. The duality in question belongs not to the linguistic sign but rather to the object it designates, to that which money *is*. As Marx puts it, money has both a 'functional existence' and a material one.[15] Now, it is precisely this dual functional/material nature of its referent that allows the category to serve as the vehicle for the sort of dehistoricizing conceptual slippage described above: insofar as money in its material existence is attributed qualities which it only acquires in its functional existence. To the degree that it identifies precious metals simply *as such* with the absolute form of wealth, thereby ignoring the specificity of the mode of social integration which impresses this formal determination upon them, mercantilism was, for instance, guilty of just such a dehistoricizing move.

The acquisition by some particular species of alienable thing of the property of universal alienability – of, so to speak, the mantle of absolute wealth – is itself a consequence of the acquisition by the product of labour in general of the property of exchangeability in regular proportions, or what we could call a *specific alienability*. The money-form comes to be impressed upon some particular sort of commodity to the degree that the commodity-form comes to be impressed upon the product of labour in general. The real ground of both formal determinations is the same: viz. an economic system distinguished by the fact that the range of productive activities it comprises are only articulated into an interconnected whole a posteriori through exchange. Where this articulation through exchange has become the organizing principle of social production, private individuals are only able to satisfy their own needs to the extent that the status of their labour – or the labour they directly control – as a necessary component of the aggregate labour of society is confirmed through the purchase of its products.

Under such conditions, the product of labour in general acquires a dual existence, of which the dual existence of the specific money-commodity – continuing to suppose that money must be a commodity – is just a special case. On the one hand, the product of labour remains, as it is in all social formations, a use-value: a physical thing, capable by virtue of its material properties of fulfilling specific needs or wants. On the other hand, it now acquires, in addition to its material existence as a use-value, also a formal existence as a value. Under this latter aspect, the product counts merely as an objectification of some definite portion of the total labour employed by society. As such, it confers upon its owner command over a commensurate portion of the total social product: in other words, command over some potential set of produced goods, however heterogeneous in physical respects, commensurate in respect to its labour requirements with the particular product s/he has to alienate. For the immediate producer (or rather, for the legal owner of the product of the immediate production process, whether or not s/he is the immediate producer), the product of labour has become a mere representation of the socially necessary labour-time required for its production.

The qualifier 'socially-necessary' is, of course, essential here, since the commensuration that occurs between some product and the products against which (via the mediation of money) it exchanges is not made in respect to the actual labour expended on its production (or, in other words, the labour it 'embodies'), but rather the average amount of labour required for its production under the reigning technical conditions. Furthermore, even with respect to labour which is 'socially-necessary' in this limited sense of conforming to the societal norm of productivity, the commensuration is in most cases not exact. Indeed, it is even a functional requirement of generalized commodity-production that as a rule this commensuration *not* be exact, since the criterion of the 'social necessity' of labour applies to the *total labour expended in a branch of industry* and only to that expended in the individual production process inasmuch as a component of the latter. If, for example, the market for a given sort of commodity is oversupplied, then it not only might happen, it *must* happen that even those producers of the commodity operating with average technical conditions will exchange their product against a sum of money representing a labour-time less than that in fact required for its production – or, in other words, the 'market price' of the good will fall below its value. The converse is, of course, also possible, and indeed necessary if we view social production as a whole.[16] But as the nuances affecting the quantitative determination of value are not immediately germane to the formal question at issue here, we can leave them to one side.

Under conditions of generalized commodity production, the product of labour is for its seller merely a (particular) value-equivalent (immediately for money, and mediately) for some portion of the remainder of the total social product which s/he may subsequently purchase: it is an exchange-value, but not a use-value. On the other hand, in order for it to fulfil this function of value-equivalent for its seller, the product must prove itself (that is, precisely in exchange) to be endowed with the material properties which make it a use-value after all – namely, *for someone else*.[17] Once the product of labour has acquired this second 'social objectivity' of being a value, it is then the physical objects themselves which, so to speak, bear this social form that thereby acquire the attribute of exchangeability in regular proportions. They acquire, that is to say, a 'specific alienability' against other products – or, more simply and much more concretely, *a price*. It is this coincidence of social form and physical thing which is the basis for what Marx famously describes as the 'fetishism of commodities'. Thus he writes,

> The mysterious character of the commodity form consists . . . simply in the fact that it reflects the social characteristics of people's own labour as objective characteristics of the products of labour themselves, as the social natural-properties [*gesellschaftliche Natureigenschaften*] of these things. Hence, it also reflects the social relation of the producers to the sum total of labour as a social relation of objects, which exists outside and apart from them. Through this quidproquo, the products of labour become commodities, sensate suprasensate [*sinnlich übersinnliche*] or social things. (*CI*, 164–5/86)

4.4 THE 'PRACTICAL CONCEPTS' OF EXCHANGE

I have argued here that what would according to the conventions of the historicist interpretation of *Capital* be understood as Marx's 'historicization' of economic categories is in fact more properly understood as a restitution rather than any methodological accomplishment. What Marx does, in effect, is to excavate the historical conditions of validity of concepts which in the usage of the political economists had, by way of a very precise sort of conceptual slippage, been deprived of their social significance and to that degree 'naturalized'. Now we find, in addition, that the sort of 'naturalization' or 'dehistoricization' for which Marx accuses classical political economy is *itself* tied to specific historical conditions. It is a dehistoricization which could only occur in the theoretical treatment of economic relations founded upon specifically *commodity* production.[18] For only that peculiar subset of categories of social relation is susceptible to dehistoricization which, so to speak, refer *obliquely* to social relations, namely by referring *directly* to physical objects which acquire 'social properties' by virtue of the mediating function they discharge with respect to those relations. Such categories, as we have just found out, are in fact the symptomatic expressions of one specific sort of social organism. They are, as I would propose to call them, the 'practical concepts' of commodity exchange.

I call these categories '*practical* concepts' in order to highlight the fact that they are not the result of theoretical reflection upon commodity exchange. They are immanent rather to the very practice of exchange, even indeed in the manner of transcendental conditions of the possibility of the latter. It is economic agents who in exchanging them disregard the real incommensurability of products of labour as physical things and treat them as commensurable with respect to some 'suprasensible' property which they must be supposed to exhibit in equal quantities in order to be exchanged in regular proportions. By the same token, agents thereby treat as commensurable the diverse forms of labour devoted to the production of their goods: namely, inasmuch as organs of the total social labour. 'They are not aware of this,' as Marx puts it, 'but they do it.'[19] The concept of *value* is thus continually applied in the activity of exchangers and indeed it is only by virtue of the application of this concept that such activity is invested with both its economic sense and systematic coherence. Hence, whether or not it is properly understood, the concept of value must at least be 'precomprehended' by every participant in an exchange economy.

Much the same could be said for the concept of *money*. In order for the generalized alienation of the social product to occur, commodity-owners are compelled to express the relative values of their goods in a common standard. Again, this 'expression' is a *practical* accomplishment. As we shall see in detail below, that the value of commodities in general comes to be expressed in a common standard is a result of the fact that they are in fact regularly exchanged against that which serves as or represents this standard. Unlike, say, the concept of an electron, the concept of money is thus of the same age as the referent it determines.

The epistemological peculiarity of 'practical concepts' and their special significance for the explanatory procedures of economic science have been insufficiently appreciated, when recognized at all. This deficit has been no less conspicuous in the Marxist tradition than in that of 'bourgeois' social science. In an oft-cited passage from the *Grundrisse*, Marx commented that the 'correct scientific method' is to begin from simple abstract determinations, in order only thereafter to proceed to a knowledge of the 'concrete', viz. as a 'combination of many [such] determinations' (*Gr.*, 100–1/35). Following indications to be found in Althusser,[20] many recent interpreters of Marx have taken this remark as confirmation for the general philosophical view that scientific inquiry, being in this way dependent from the outset upon abstractions, lacks any 'pre-theoretical' mode of access to the empirical material representing the (real) object which it aims to apprehend. Since the 'raw material' upon which scientific practice works ('Generalities I' in Althusser's nomenclature) is, on this view, always already the result of some sort of discursive elaboration, the conclusion is usually then drawn – though it should be stressed that Althusser himself never drew such a conclusion – that scientific claims are ultimately non-adjudicable: every claim is relative to the 'problematic' from which it emerges.

This line of interpretation is not so much at odds with what Marx says as with what *he does* (and, in this sense, Althusser's own preferred citations have by now begun to function as 'famous quotations'). In fact the simple abstract determinations from which the science of political economy must begin are precisely what I have called 'practical concepts' of commodity exchange. To this extent, abstractions though they are, they are so far from being *opposed to* the 'empirical-concrete' of a capitalist economic system that they in fact *constitute* it: namely, with respect to its form. As Marx repeatedly emphasized, the very functioning of a generalized exchange economy depends upon abstractions *which are real*. Hence, that the science of political economy must start from these abstractions should, if anything, lead us to draw exactly the opposite conclusion from that usually drawn. Since its basic concepts are constitutive of its *real* object and not merely of a 'theoretical object' whose construction is requisite to grasping the latter, political economy must enjoy the good fortune that its claims precisely *are* adjudicable. (Of course, even in the case of sciences for which the 'real object'-'theoretical object' divide is not bridgeable by practical concepts, the protocols for deciding between competing theories are not so arbitrary as prevailing, ostensibly 'postmodern', views of science would lead one to believe. But to enter into such debates here would take us too far afield.)

What I am suggesting is that the practical concepts of exchange have in political economy a status rather like that which according to Kant's 1st Critique is occupied by the 'pure concepts of the understanding' in theoretical physics: a 'transcendental' status in effect. The application of the 'practical concepts' on the part of economic agents is a condition of the possibility of commodity exchange – even indeed of 'economic experience', one could say – just as the use of the 'categories' on the part of cognitive subjects is a condition of the possibility of sensible experience in general. Furthermore, just as from the 'categories' there can be derived certain 'axioms of the understanding' – which latter are, in effect, nothing more than explications of the meaning of the former – so too from the 'practical concepts of exchange' there can be derived certain 'axioms of exchange', so to speak: most notably, the very 'law of value' itself.

5 Property and Person (or the Birth of the Juridical Subject)[1]

To resume our findings from the previous chapter, the categories of social relation whose historical conditions of validity remain obscured in the analyses of the political economists are of the nature of 'practical concepts' of economic activity. That these 'practical concepts' are peculiarly susceptible to dehistoricization issues from the fact that they are not explicit but rather *covert* categories of social relation, since for the purposes of the economic agents who apply them, it is in fact sufficient that they serve to pick out specific sorts of physical thing. Paradoxically, however, these specific sorts are not essentially distinguished by any physical feature or features which the items belonging to them share in common, but rather by 'social properties' which, as we have seen, these items acquire by virtue of the role they play within the exchange system. (Here again, incidentally, the inappropriateness of an empiricist model of abstraction to the case of economic categories is made manifest.) Thus the reference to things which economic agents make in employing the 'practical concepts' of commodity-exchange is in fact accomplished under descriptions which only apply to such things to the degree that they mediate relations that economic agents enter into and reproduce precisely by owning and exchanging them. Practical concepts of economic activity which explicitly designate things while covertly alluding to relations obtaining among the individuals who own them are, then, the symptomatic expressions of a sort of social formation in which social relations are in general 'mediated by things'.

In what sense, however, is this 'mediation by things' a peculiarity of just those social relations which arise specifically on the basis of commodity-production? It could be objected, after all, that in a sufficiently broad sense *all* social relations are 'mediated by things'. If by 'social relations' we understand real relations of dependence among individuals (and not merely, for instance, the 'intersubjectivity' established through verbal communication), then social relations in general are in the last analysis always social relations *of production*. The interdependency of the *material* reproduction of the individual members of a society (of which cultural reproduction is an indispensable condition[2]) is the only criterion – the 'last instance' – according to which we are even able to assign them to a single 'society'. In this sense, it can be said that social relations as such always *concern* material things, since in all their various configurations they form the framework for the commerce of human beings with their natural environment, making the satisfaction of the individual's wants and needs a function of his or her subordination to the collective. Inasmuch as it is supposed to represent a principle of socio-historical research and in its most lucid formulations at any rate, this pre-eminent materiality of social life is the very point of Marx's 'materialism'.[3] ('One thing is clear,' Marx writes bluntly in *Capital*, 'the Middle Ages could not live on Catholicism, nor could the ancient world on politics' [*CI*, 176n./96n.].)

That the cohesion within a single social formation of activities performed by distinct individuals is determined in the last instance by their connection – whether of participation or dependence or both – to material production and reproduction can thus be regarded as a general rule, equally applicable to all forms of social life. In pre-capitalist social formations, however, the dominant social relations are established between individuals directly: either in the form of conscious cooperation in productive activities (as would largely be the case in tribal societies) or according to a hierarchy of functions which appear in the first instance extra-economic (for example, political, ecclesiastical or familial), though in practice they in fact serve to distribute individuals among the various functions of material production and reproduction and to regulate in turn the distribution of the social product among them.[4]

In a society based upon generalized commodity production, by contrast, the dominant social relations have the peculiarity that they, so to speak, simply do not appear as such. Rather, each given individual appears in the first instance as a legal person pure and simple, without any particular ties to any other such individual and with exactly the same rights and obligations as all the rest. The relations of dependence which obtain among these legal persons are realized and reproduced only *indirectly* via the exchange of material goods: which is to say, via the mutual transfer of the *legal claims* to property which the respective parties to such transfer as juridical subjects are all equally entitled to own.

In a society of generalized commodity production, viz. in a capitalist society, the basic formal relation which serves as the fulcrum around which the completed network of societal interdependencies gets articulated is thus that of *ownership*: not a relation of person to person but rather a relation of the socialized individual *to things* over which *as against other individuals* s/he possesses unique rights of use and alienation. Wherever commodity production takes place, and precisely proportional to the extent that it takes place, individuals are constituted as persons in relation to their property, whereas the relations *between* them are precisely *de*personalized.[5] Commodity exchange *is*, so to speak, a nexus of depersonalized social relations. Only insofar as labour becomes specifically *wage*-labour, however (that is, with the commodification of labour-power), is commodity production generalized, with the consequence that the *dominant* form of social relationship becomes the depersonalized one of ownership.

Marx's claim (which is widely corroborated by the ethnological literature) that commodity exchange in its earliest appearance occurs at the boundaries *between* communities is instructive in this regard. 'The exchange of commodities', he writes, 'begins where communities end, at their points of contact with foreign communities' (*C*I, 182/102). This relation of 'reciprocal foreignness', which characterizes the parties to commodity exchange precisely *in contrast* to the character of the relations they enter into *within* their respective communities, is then internalized to a given social formation with the emergence of an internal market and finally (viz. in capitalist society) generalized with the elevation of commodity exchange to the dominant mode of sociality. Under such conditions, the *positive* rights and obligations which bind individuals become wholly a function of the transactions which realize the transfer of property between them as legal persons.

The contrast between this situation and that which obtains in earlier forms of social life could not be more striking. This is not, of course, to say that ownership is necessarily absent from pre-capitalist social formations, but rather that even where it appears it remains itself subordinate to other relationships which take the explicit form of personal dependencies. Even in pre-capitalist social formations which manifest a sufficient degree of internal exchange to give rise to monetary economies (as was the case, for example, in the Athens of classical antiquity), so long as the direct producers are not 'free' in the 'double sense' described by Marx – that is, 'that they neither form part of the means of production themselves, as would be the case with slaves, serfs, etc., nor do they own the means of production, as would be the case with self-employed peasant proprietors' (*C*I, 874/742) – ownership remains a subordinate relation and the depersonalization of social relations throughout society as a whole does not occur. (One should, however, be sensitive to the irony of this fact in the case of the Athenian city-state: viz. that social relations as a whole remain personalized, despite the emergence of commodity exchange, only to the extent that an entire segment of the population is itself denied personhood.)

In pre-capitalist social formations, the title to ownership of the given individual is thus mediated by the place s/he occupies in a pre-existing structure of reciprocally determined (and normally hierarchical) personal definitions: for example, as suzerain or vassal, lord or serf, citizen or slave, priest or layperson, husband or wife, and so on. It is precisely not the case that each individual is equally entitled to possess property simply by virtue of their status as subjects under the law, since in pre-capitalist social formations *there is no* juridical subject as such.[6] Either property is exclusively the attribute of the community as a whole (and, in which case, the abstract right of the individual has not yet emerged) or, where private appropriation already takes place (as, for instance, in feudal societies or the ancient Greek city-states), there are rather distinct categories of legal subjects whose *differential* rights and obligations it is precisely the function of the law to codify. Equality under the law is (as Maurice Godelier has quite rightly put it) 'unthinkable' in such societies,[7] since, where it already exists in an explicitly codified form, the law *is* precisely the institutionalization of *in*equalities. Indeed the juridical person as the bearer of equal rights is a peculiarly 'bourgeois' creation: which is to say, it derives its very sense from the system of exchange. As Marx puts it, 'Equality and freedom are . . . not only respected in exchange based on exchange-values, but the exchange of exchange-values is the productive, real basis of all equality and freedom. As pure ideas they are merely the idealized expressions of this basis' (*Gr.*, 245/170).

It is thus only with the emergence of generalized commodity production, with generalized bourgeois right as its necessary juridical correlate, that *ownership* becomes the basic organizing principle of social relations in general. Up to this point, either property is communal, with the individual members of the community only ever enjoying provisional 'possession' of the material conditions it comprises,[8] or the legal order regulating private appropriation is an explicitly hierarchical one, and the individual's title to specific categories of property (for instance, and most importantly for our purposes, the objective conditions of production) is a function of his or her belonging to a specific category of legal person (that is, to a specific estate, caste and so on).[9] Where ownership is not simply communal, it is this prior structure of legally ordered personal relations which determines the parameters of ownership in pre-capitalist societies, viz. just *who* can own, *what* they can own, and even *how* they own what they own – or, in other words, which determines the limits of private appropriation.[10] If we define property in general as the regulated mode of appropriation by socialized individuals of their natural environment, then we can say that in pre-capitalist social formations, property relations (viz. the relations of persons to things) are mediated by social relations (viz. the relations of persons to other persons).

In capitalism, exactly *the reverse* is the case, which is to say, namely, that in capitalism social relations are 'mediated by things'. It should by now be clearer in what sense this mediation of social relations by things is peculiar to commodity-producing societies and pervasive in capitalist society as the generalized form of the latter. (In other words, in those pre-capitalist social formations where commodity production occurs but on a restricted basis, some subset of concrete dependencies are 'mediated by things'; in a capitalist social formation, the tendency is for the social product in all sectors of production to be drawn into the exchange-nexus, and hence for all social relations to be 'mediated by things'.) 'Mediated by things' means here: mediated by the private use and privately contracted exchange of *property*. It means that the relations of person to person are mediated by the relation of each to things *which s/he owns*.

This is so, in the first place, inasmuch as the exchange-nexus represents the mode of realization of material dependencies among individuals who within the exchange relation count for one another merely as the legal title-holders to alienable goods: the juridical persons of whom I wrote above. All other forms of societal integration coordinate the activities of individuals by placing them in some positive and enduring relation to one other. In traditional communal forms, for instance, they are not only as members of the commune or clan collectively subordinated to it (for example, in cooperative labour), but also singularly though mutually obligated to other members by ties of kinship (for example, in certain sorts of redistributive schemes). In explicitly hierarchical forms of integration, as we have seen, they are grouped into specific reciprocally-determined categories of persons with corresponding rights and obligations with respect to members of the other categories. In the exchange relation, however, regardless of the real interdependency of their activities (both productive and non-productive) which is expressed in the fact of exchange, each economic agent represents for every other, so to speak, merely a human barrier to the acquisition of the property of which s/he is the legitimate titleholder.[11] The formal equality between subjects (or '*Gleichheit*'), which, as noted above, is a necessary condition of the exchange relation, is at the same time an indifference among them (or '*Gleichgültigkeit*').

This is, if you like, the irony of the exchange relation: that through it each of the exchanging subjects is constituted as a person, but only in order then to be personally indifferent to one other. The mutual acknowledgement of personhood which is built into the relation between exchangers of commodities amounts in effect to – is indeed *exhausted by* – the mutual acknowledgement of their status as *owners*: of the legitimacy of their respective claims to property and their (equal) rights with respect to the use and alienation of what belongs to them. In short, in acknowledging the personhood of the other through exchange, I acknowledge the other's right: (1) to retain and/or consume what is his or hers (according to the dictates of his or her own will and provided s/he does not thereby infringe upon the property rights of others); (2) to alienate only what s/he chooses; and (3), assuming that the latter is wanted by others, to obtain for it a value equivalent (whether in the general form of money, if s/he is alienating a particular commodity, or the particular form of other commodities, if s/he is alienating money) in exchange.[12]

Apart from this relation to property through which s/he is constituted *as* person, all other personal attributes which specifically pertain to the individual are for me as party to exchange thoroughly irrelevant. As exchanger, what concerns me are the attributes *of the property* (whether in terms of value or use-value or both), not the attributes of the person (whether s/he happens to be a distinct biological individual or, at a more advanced stage, a *merely* legal person, viz. a corporation) who alienates it.[13] In Marx's words:

> The subjects only exist for one another in exchange as equals through the equivalents [i.e. the value-equivalents exchanged], and they establish themselves as such through the exchange of the objectivity in which the one exists for the other. Since they only exist for one another in exchange in this way, as equals, as possessors of equivalents and guarantors of this equivalence, they are as equals at the same time indifferent to one another. . . . (*Gr.*, 241–2/167–8)

6 The Objectification of Social Relations

> Whence derive the illusions of the monetary system? From the fact that it was not able to detect from looking at gold and silver that as money they represent a social relation of production, albeit in the form of natural objects with peculiar social properties. And modern economists, who sneer condescendingly at the monetary system, does not their own fetishism become tangible as soon as they consider capital?
>
> (Marx, *Capital*[1])

6.1 MONEY AS A SOCIAL RELATION

The equality and indifference of the parties to exchange as juridical persons is determined by the formal structure of the exchange relation which brings them into contact. But what makes this contact into the mode of realization of a more comprehensive interdependence of individuals is rather the *content* of exchange. It is the fact that the given individual acquires through exchange the means of satisfying some part of his or her wants and needs, and does so only insofar as s/he in turn alienates goods required for the satisfaction of the wants and needs of others, that provides commodity exchange, along with the entire set of its formal conditions, its social content. The parties to exchange are formally equal and personally indifferent. But as concrete individuals they in fact *need one another*: or, more precisely, they each need what the other has. This would be to say, under conditions of simple-commodity production, they each need what the other has produced and hence, in the last analysis, the other him- or herself as producer. Though, for the case of specifically capitalist conditions, we have to say rather: they each need what the other has appropriated (through whatever means, even if through the productive activity of yet other economic agents), and hence the portion of the total labour available to society whose results the latter controls.[2]

In any event, apart from this real interdependence the very assertion of the equality of individuals as persons would be otiose, since no social relation among them would exist.[3] One might as well have asserted the equality of individuals from entirely different historical epochs or members of wholly unconnected social formations. In such usage, 'equality' clearly becomes a metaphysical notion: as in the 'self-evident truth' of the US Declaration of Independence that 'all men are created equal'. Here we are left with the 'pure idea', but deprived of all reference to its 'real basis'.

Now, both the practical interdependence of the participants in the exchange system and their personal indifference to one another gain expression in the form of *money*. Money is the reified expression of the indifferent interdependence of the parties to exchange. It is the expression of the *indifference* of the parties to exchange, insofar as every economic agent in his or her capacity as *buyer* is merely the subjective representative – the 'personification' – of money for others. 'Each appears for the other', Marx writes, 'as the possessor of money, and even as money itself, insofar as the process of exchange [as a whole] is being considered' (*Gr.*, 246/171). It is the expression of their *interdependence*, insofar as all economic agents in their capacity as *sellers* are compelled to convert the social character of their productive activity or the productive activity at their disposal, its character as an activity for others, into the objective guise of money. Indeed, failing that, this activity *has no* social character and the agent (that is, in the juridical sense) has in turn no claim to participate in the consumption of the social product.[4] As seller, the party to exchange alienates commodities in their natural form: or, in other words, use-values. But the social existence of the individual implicit in this fact is made explicit only to the extent that the social utility of these goods – and by implication the social necessity of (at least some part of) the labour expended in their production – is confirmed through their realization as *exchange-value*, viz. in the *money-form*.[5]

Since it is essential to our further specifying the sense of the 'mediation by things' to which capitalist social relations are subject, let us examine briefly the character of the compulsion under which the exchangers of commodities stand to convert their social relatedness into the money-form. As already discussed, the commodity product as exchange-value is merely an index of the socially-necessary labour requisite for its production, and hence of the 'volume' (viz. measured in terms of labour requirements) of the product which its possessor is entitled to withdraw from the market in return for it. As exchange-value, it represents not an object with distinguishing characteristics but rather an objectification in an homogeneous (or, in the case of corporate or individual producers with diversified product lines, relatively homogeneous) use-value of the portion of the total labour of society which its production has required. (It should be understood that the notion of what is 'required' here carries the connotation of a norm to which the labour actually *empirically* expended is, so to speak, ideally adjusted.) Supposing that it can be sold – which is to say, that the labour expended upon it (or some percentage thereof) is confirmed as having indeed been socially required, as having been 'social labour' and not individual error – then this objectification in an homogeneous or relatively homogeneous use-value of a portion of the total social labour bestows upon its owner a claim to whatever heterogeneous assortment of use-values s/he chooses to obtain on the market which in sum represent an objectification of an equivalent portion.

In short, the product as exchange-value is for its owner *already*, though, as Marx says, in the first instance only 'ideally', *money*. In order that the owner of the direct product can, however, convert the ideal claim which it bestows upon him or her into a real assortment of other use-values, it must itself first be converted into the universally convertible form of the exchange-value which it represents: viz. *real* money. *Sale* is thus in a precise sense the *realization* of the product as exchange-value. That is to say, sale is both: (1) the confirmation that the product is *in fact* the exchange-value which it already was *in principle* (or, to use a Hegelian idiom, that it is *really* what it already was *ideally*, *actually* [*wirklich*] what it already was *potentially* [*der Möglichkeit nach*]); and (2) the transformation of the exchange-value which the owner of the direct product has 'ideally' in it, and which in conformity with this still merely ideal mode-of-being gets expressed as a price (viz. a symbol distinct from the product itself), into the real, i.e. material, form in which this exchange-value *exists* as exchange-value. Again to resort to Hegel, the commodity in its natural form is directly (*unmittelbar*) a use-value but only mediately (*mittelbar*) exchange-value; it must be converted into its real value-form, viz. money, in order to exist *directly* as exchange-value, such that it can now be exchanged against all other commodities without any further mediation.[6]

Now, in all social formations economic agents are, of course, concerned with the acquisition of use-values: which is to say only that they are concerned, in whatever form, with their own reproduction. Originally, i.e. in the most elementary forms of social life and in the first stages of social production in every social formation wherein the direct producers remain the owners of the means of production, this 'acquisition' is nothing other than labour itself.[7] Even at more developed stages, however, where (some) use-values are acquired by (some) individuals from others – say as tribute or through administered redistribution or barter – this does not as such imply a mediation of the social relations which individuals thereby enter into or confirm by the exchange-value represented in their products. Indeed it merely implies that they *do* in fact enter into social relations: that a real material dependency exists among their respective activities (though not necessarily a reciprocal one).

The acquisition of use-values indirectly, i.e. from others rather than through labour, occurs in various ways in various sorts of social formation. But only in a generalized system of commodity exchange is the acquisition of use-values placed under the condition of the acquisition of *exchange-value*, viz. not merely the acquisition of things *through exchange* but the acquisition of the independent form of the value which things have *in exchange*. In commodity exchange, the direct product of labour is not only exchanged in order to be realized as use-value (as might incidentally be the case, for instance, in barter), but rather it must first be realized as exchange-value – viz. through its sale – in order then to be reconverted into use-value.

The generalized exchange of property, of things owned by formally independent individuals in their capacity as juridical persons, which under conditions of commodity-production mediates the real interdependence of the reproduction of these individuals – or, in other words, their social connection – is thus itself in turn mediated by the circulation among them of that pre-eminently 'social thing' (*CI*, 165/86): *money*. In order that the exchange of the product of labour as personal property become the dominant mode of societal integration, it is necessary that there coalesce an objective token of the social character of expended labour which can *itself be owned and alienated*. This is the 'money-function' inherent to relations of commodity-exchange of which I wrote above, and with the maturation and normalization of exchange within the context of any given social formation this function comes to be impressed upon a particular species of exchangeable thing, which henceforth embodies this function as 'money itself'.[8]

We found previously that the so-called 'reification' of social relations – their representation as the objective features of things – only occurs to the extent that the things at issue in practice mediate the social relations. Now we find that where in general social relations are mediated by things, i.e. the relations of person to person by the relations of each to things which s/he owns, this mediation must in turn be particularized in a species of thing which comes to represent *the very social relatedness* of these persons in an alienated objective –

and hence *appropriable* – form. 'The individual', as Marx puts it, 'carries his social power, as well as his connection with society, in his pocket' (*Gr.*, 157/90).

6.2 CAPITAL AS A SOCIAL RELATION

It is possible, at least abstractly, to conceive of a society of generalized commodity production which would not be specifically capitalist – though such a society has surely never existed in fact and it is doubtful whether it could exist for any considerable length of time without becoming capitalist. Indeed, it is impossible *not* to conceive of a specifically capitalist society as *simply* a society of generalized commodity production, a 'market society', so long as we concentrate solely on the formal structure of the exchange relation. The very concealment of their specifically capitalist character which occurs in this instance suggests a third and final sense in which we can speak of a mediation of social relations by property relations under capitalist conditions. This is the case, namely, insofar as the concrete relations of domination and subordination in which individuals stand to one another within the process of social production as a whole, and likewise the disproportionality of their respective shares in the social product which corresponds to this hierarchy, are no longer a matter of explicit legal stipulation, but are determined as a function of their holding property or not in certain specific sorts of good. One should recall that in feudal society, for example, the direction of determination is precisely the reverse: an individual's entitlement to hold, or exclusion from holding, property in certain categories of good – most importantly, property in land – being a function of his ('his' simply in recognition of some other well-known restrictions on property-ownership under feudal conditions) legal status as member of a dominant or subordinate estate or 'order'.

Since the economically decisive category of good under capitalist conditions, viz. produced means of production, are only a source both of social power and revenue if owned in certain critical proportions (and indeed, with increasing mechanization, their most decisive element, viz. the instruments of production, are only even obtainable in ever increasing proportions), the real possibility of individuals holding property in them is in turn determined by the relative *amount* of property they are respectively able to control. As we will see in greater detail below, the more widely recognized, so to speak, 'qualitative' determination of the class structure of capitalist society (viz. by the sort of property controlled) reflects a still more fundamental '*quantitative*' determination. Furthermore, since the economically decisive goods under capitalist conditions are themselves products of labour – unlike under feudal conditions, where the economically decisive category of good is a naturally-given resource, viz. *the land* – what we are confronted with here is a kind of circle. The disproportionality in the distribution of the social product which is the result of the production process under capitalist conditions is predicated upon a disproportionality in the distribution of the social product which is its precondition.[9]

Now, before going any further, the vague notion of an 'amount' of property requires some commentary. For prima facie, if we regard the goods figuring as property just in their material aspect, it is not clear how such a notion could be specified. As articles of use, goods take various concrete forms which do not share any intrinsic unit of measurement nor lend themselves to any common unit, least of all an economically significant one. The 'amount' of a plot of land (measured, say, in acres) is not immediately comparable to that of a sheet of linen (measured in yards) or that of a bar of gold (measured in pounds) – to say nothing of produced goods whose intrinsic unit is just themselves (a car, a cup, a lathe, and so on). Indeed, even where a common physical measure is available (say, for two goods of the same kind), it does not necessarily provide an accurate index of the relative 'amounts' of the goods *qua* property. Regarded as an element of personal wealth, one plot of land of a given acreage will only exceptionally represent the same 'amount' of property as another plot of land of the same acreage, given differing fertilities and the variability of other geographical factors affecting their possible uses.

Under conditions of generalized commodity exchange, however, the 'amount' of property controlled by any given person is in principle *exactly* determinable: viz. by the sum of the market values (even if these cannot a priori be known, and hence in fact would have to be estimated) of the heterogeneous assortment of goods which they own plus the total value of their financial resources (which is, of course, known, since such are by definition already in the value form). The former constitute what might be called the 'real' or 'concrete' property of the person, as opposed to the, so to speak, 'ideal' or 'abstract' or 'general' property represented by monetary wealth. The universal alienation of the product of labour gives rise to a strictly social measure – viz. *value*, as expressed in quantities of the general equivalent – which is uniformly applicable to each and every good susceptible of exchange. The sum of the value of the 'concrete' and 'abstract' property of any given person provides an exact expression of the total amount of property that person controls. Needless to say, matters would be more complicated if we were taking account of credit relations. But the basic principle would remain unchanged.

It is important to notice that the 'control' over property which thus gains quantitative expression refers both to the definite things to which a person holds legal title *and* to the portion measured in value terms of the remainder of the, so to speak, 'exchangeable universe' to which that person can acquire title if he or she (or it, in the case of a corporate 'person') so chooses given his or her (or its) financial assets. It will be recognized at once that this division corresponds to the bifurcation of the product of labour into use-value and value, which, as we have seen, is a necessary condition of generalized exchange. It will be recognized too that it is only insofar as the use-values constituting 'concrete' property are themselves convertible into the real form acquired by value in exchange, viz. money, that the degree of control over property which they severally represent can be aggregated and summed together with the 'abstract property' already in the money form. The relevance of this value-measure for understanding the basis and perpetuation of specifically capitalist social relations is made more difficult to grasp, however, by the equally conspicuous fact that the elements of 'concrete' property might include goods which are not products of labour at all: hence goods which, though they might indeed have a market value (or, more simply put, a *price*), are not themselves values, in Marx's sense, since not reproducible. Land is the most obvious and least controversial example of such 'fictitious commodities'.[10]

6.3 A BRIEF DIGRESSION ON RENT

The anomalies created by the existence of property in non-reproducible goods can be handled theoretically in two different ways. One way is to ignore them. Unique goods which do not figure among the conditions of production or reproduction – works of art, historical artefacts, and the like – are of no systematic economic significance. For their owners, they might be a source of pleasure or prestige or what have you. Supposing they are sold, then they are an instant source of cash. But, unlike owned factors of production – whether products of labour or not – they are not an enduring source of *revenue*. In other words, *ownership* of such goods does not secure for their owners an income;

only *sale* of them does – that is to say precisely the forsaking of their ownership – and it does so (unlike in the case of labour-power) once and for all. Hence, the titles to 'rarities' of various sorts can change hands, but always on the assumption that the revenues with which they are purchased ultimately derive from other sources.

(This is at least so if we limit the application of the designation 'good' exclusively to *material* things. The juridical fiction of 'intellectual property', however, manages to construe whole categories of unique abstract objects – software programs, scientific formulae, musical compositions, and so on – as if they were appropriable in the manner of physical goods, and thus creates rents for their title-holders. Both the productive importance of abstract 'goods' and the growing distributional importance of their ownership in the contemporary global economy are undeniable. But the challenges posed to economic analysis – and indeed to the theory of value – by 'intellectual property' rights are so great as to require at least a digression, if not a treatise, of their own. So, in order not to get diverted from our present aims, it will have to suffice merely to have alluded to them here.)

Unlike cultural 'rarities', limited natural resources, such as arable land, are clearly of great economic significance and hence cannot be dismissed so easily. Above all since the natural resources they contain or constitute form conditions of production, though also inasmuch as simple inhabitable space forms a condition of individual reproduction, property in 'particular portions of the globe' (*C*III, 752/628) can generate revenues for their owners and hence secure for them a share in the social product. But the first thing that should be noticed is that ground-rents, like wages and profits, are then precisely claims upon a certain portion of the social product: the *real* shape, as opposed to the 'ideal' monetary shape, of rent is precisely that portion. Furthermore, the monetary or value measure of that portion, like the value measure of any portion of the product, serves as an index of the allocation of social labour requisite to its production. Such as to highlight their 'social content', Franz Petry has thus aptly described the distinct forms of revenue as so many 'forms of disposition over human labour'.[11] In the case of limited natural resources, then, ownership in non-reproducible goods has a distributional significance inasmuch as the goods themselves have a productive or reproductive significance, and the distributional significance of property in such non-reproducible goods is precisely that it secures for their owners as rent a claim upon produced ones.

Just how the quantitative level of rental incomes gets determined – the subject matter proper of the theory of rent as usually understood

– will not concern us here. But it is important for present purposes to notice too that land and other limited resources secure such incomes for their owners without the latter having to engage in any economic activity at all or – which amounts indeed to much the same thing under generalized market conditions – to enter into any real exchanges. The land, to take the most clear-cut example, is simply there, and even after it has been cultivated for however many seasons, it is still simply there: indeed the regeneration of its productive capacity depends precisely on *leaving it be*. It has neither to be reproduced and repurchased – like (constant) 'capital goods' – nor to be reproduced and resold – like labour-power – in order to secure for its owners an income.

Whereas, moreover, the totality of the transactions entered into by capitalists with wage-labourers bring about on the aggregate level a real exchange of goods between them, labour-power being exchanged against means of (individual) consumption; and whereas this exchange is the very basis of the revenues which the parties to it respectively obtain (and indeed, as we shall see, of the persistent inequality of those revenues); and whereas, finally, the transactions entered into by capitalists with one another even more obviously mediate a manifold of real exchanges among them (at any rate, if we exclude pure financial and speculative transactions from consideration) – whereas all of this is true for capitalists and wage-labourers, landowners give *nothing* in exchange and yet still obtain rents. In this sense, even under capitalist conditions, the revenues generated by landed property continue to have something of the character of *tribute*;[12] apart from the formality of contract, the only difference being that payment is normally made in money and the level of payment is regulated by definite economic laws (which laws it is, again, incumbent upon the theory of rent to clarify). It is for this reason that Marx treats rental incomes as a deduction from surplus-value, extracted *directly* by landowners from the capitalist class, who extract the total mass of surplus value from the working class, though in the latter case, unlike the former, only *indirectly* via the mediation of a definite sequence of exchanges.[13] Profits have to be *realized*, rent is simply *paid*.

It is for this same reason, finally, that the anomalies created by landed property can be safely ignored in analysing what I have called the 'quantitative' determination of capitalist social relations: viz. because they are precisely *anomalies*. Rental incomes are the economic form taken by remnants of feudal privilege in social formations otherwise dominated by the capitalist mode of production. This is by no means to suggest that a capitalist order ever could have arisen without the concentration of productive resources, on the one side, and the divestiture of all claim upon such resources, on the other, which was only possible under the legal mantle of private ownership in the land. Nonetheless, once such an order has come into being, the specific social relations which define it *as* capitalist in no way depend upon the existence of landed property. The basic structure of capitalist relations of production would continue to be what it is even if there was no landowning class: if, say, all natural resources were leased by productive enterprises from the state and housing stock was likewise exclusively a public good.[14] Indeed, such a hypothetical circumstance would conform more exactly to the, so to speak, 'pure form' of capitalist conditions, since all revenue-generating property, i.e. all property capable of securing for its owner an enduring claim upon some portion of the social product, would have then itself to constitute part of the social product.

Once we have posited such a circumstance in the manner of a simplifying assumption, there is no reason not to go still further and postulate that *all* property, without exception, is property in produced goods: either in the 'concrete' use-value-form of determinate products or the 'abstract' value-form of monetary command over the latter. Under this assumption, all property would have then to be *in fact* exactly what the abstract value measure of property represents it as *in principle*: viz. an objectification of some definite fractional allocation of the total labour requisite to the production of the social product. The practical irrationality of the existence of property in goods which are not products of labour in a system of generalized commodity exchange – Marx wrote of capitalism having brought about 'the reductio ad absurdum of landed property' (*C*III, 755/631) – is thereby eliminated by abstraction, and the immanent process of reproduction of the capital/wage-labour relation, wherein an unequal distribution of the social product figures as both precondition and result, can be grasped in its purity. The abstractive procedure here described is precisely that employed by Marx (apart from one crucial historical excursus) throughout the first two volumes of *Capital*. The fact that the empirical reality of capitalist social formations presents *three* classes and property in land did not prevent him from analysing the logic of a capitalist mode of production in which all exchangeables are products of labour and all exchangers, either capitalists or wage-labourers.

Of course, even under 'pure' capitalist conditions, a financial dependent of the juridical recipient of either profits or wages can appear as an immediate party to a market transaction, though, NB, only as *buyer*. In that case, however, the dependent functions economically as a kind of proxy for the juridical recipient in spending a portion of the latter's revenue. On the aggregate level, then, the encompassing exchanges, viz. of products, which are mediated by such isolated monetary transactions – 'partial metamorphoses' of commodities, as Marx would write – still occur between or among the juridical recipients themselves: viz. the sellers of those products. This essential relation is not altered by the fact that the revenues also underwrite consumption by financial dependents, whether non-earning spouses or children representing the next generation of capitalists and wage-labourers and non-earning spouses.

I have said that simply ignoring them is just one way of dealing with the anomalies created by the existence of property in non-reproducible goods. There is another. Insofar as such goods are accorded the legal status of property, they can be alienated; and insofar as they are alienable, the market value which they potentially represent can be converted into the independent equivalent form of value: viz. into a sum of money. Indeed, it was precisely this fact that made it necessary for us to consider them in the first place. We have seen that in the case of cultural 'rarities', the prices which they fetch in being alienated represent their one and only economic 'form of appearance'. But land too, insofar as appropriable, can be not only periodically leased, thus functioning as an enduring source of revenue, but also definitively sold. Indeed, the 'price of land' (this 'irrational category', as Marx called it[15]) ought, strictly speaking, to refer to its *sales*-price, not its rental-price, since, as just discussed, in renting a plot of land, its owner does not in fact enter into any real exchange. Now, the factors influencing the prices at which non-reproducibles exchange are of no importance for us here. In any event, those factors will be quite diverse depending on whether the goods in question are productive resources or mere 'rarities': being in the former case at least derivable from determinants governing the prices of 'real' (that is, produced and reproducible) commodities, and to that degree systematic, and in the latter largely fortuitous and, in effect, extra-economic.

What is important here is just that the 'imaginary' value of 'fictitious' commodities, just as much as the value of 'real' ones, is thus convertible into the *real form* of value: money. This allows us, for the purpose of analysing the class structure of capitalist society, to 'absorb', so to speak, property in non-reproducible goods, in spite of its qualitatively anomalous character, into the pure quantitative measure, viz. the *value* measure, of property in general. It does not matter that this measure is not immanent to them, as it is to the elements of the total commodity product. Its application to appropriable goods of whatever sort provides us the means for assessing the degree of their convertibility, via the intermediary of money, into appropriable goods of whatever other sort.

This enables us to formulate, and to be guided by, the following absolutely general rule: under capitalist conditions of production, there is some level of total assets which represents the minimum amount necessary to control some good or complex set of goods – whether produced or not – whose ownership will generate revenues sufficient to free its owner from the necessity of selling labour-power. This level of assets determines the dividing line between the fundamental classes of a capitalist order. All economic agents with assets below the requisite level figure among the producers of the total social product, whose claim upon at least some part of the portion of the latter necessary for their reproduction is mediated by the receipt of a wage. It is, of course, understood that the material requirements of reproduction are determined by some customary standard of living or 'subsistence norm', rather than any bare biological minimum, and hence that such requirements both vary historically and are continually subject to modification through political struggle. Furthermore, it is not excluded that for any given worker some percentage of his or her monetary income – this monetary income representing the limits of his or her abstract claim upon the product – will derive from sources other than the wage: viz. property rights in goods other than labour-power. It is only excluded that their non-wage income be sufficient to cover the full extent of their consumption requirements.

All economic agents with assets at or above the requisite level are able to maintain an at least 'normal' standard of living solely on the basis of shares which they claim in the remaining, 'surplus', portion of the total product: that is, the portion of the total product which remains when the part purchased against wages has been removed. The latter are entitled to these shares as a function of shares in the total surplus-value – that is, the value as embodied in money which remains from the gross value of the product when the value portion represented by wages has been deducted – which flow to them in the form of specific categories of revenue as a function in turn of specific sorts of property which they control. From the point of view of value-relations, it is immaterial whether this property has the concrete form of land (whose ownership yields ground-rent) or produced means of production (yielding industrial profit) or finished consumer goods (yielding commercial profit) or even if it does not have *any* concrete form at all – as with the interest obtained from controlling pure monetary resources of sufficient magnitude.

6.4 CAPITAL AS A SOCIAL RELATION (CONTINUED)

If, as I wrote above, under capitalist conditions the dominant social relations, the relations which determine the capitalist character of the social order, do not appear as such, this is because the formal apparatus of exchange (whose principles acquire systematic expression in bourgeois law) brooks no distinction among the parties to it: its 'subjects'.[16] Consequently, in the same measure as the very social relatedness of individuals is obscured with the generalization of commodity exchange, the definite and indeed hierarchical character of the social relations in which they in fact stand to one another – the *structure* of said relations – is as well. As juridical subjects, wage-labourer and capitalist have exactly the same status. Each enjoys equal protection under the law, which means that each is formally free to acquire whatever s/he pleases (viz. so long as s/he does so through the normal channels of exchange) and to use or alienate the property at his or her disposal as s/he will; and each is bound to respect the property rights of others and the sanctity of the contracts by which such rights are transferred.[17] In all formal juridical respects, exchanges between wage-labourers and capitalists are no different from the exchanges entered into by one capitalist with another or, for that matter, by petty-commodity producers. Hence Marx's observation that:

> The sphere of circulation or commodity exchange . . . is in fact a very Eden of the innate rights of man. Here alone reign Freedom, Equality, Property and Bentham. Freedom! – since both buyer and seller of a commodity, let us say of labour-power, are determined only by their own free will. They contract as free persons, who are equal before the law. Their contract is the final result in which their joint will finds a common legal expression. Equality! – since they relate to one another simply as commodity owners, and they exchange equivalent for equivalent. Property! – since each disposes only of what is his own. Bentham! – since each looks only to his own good. (*CI*, 280/189–90)

As exchangers of commodities, all economic agents are formally free and formally equal, they all dispose of their own property and strictly according to their own choices.

In the midst of all this formal juridical equality, however, the first clue to disclosing the *class relation* between capitalist and wage-labourer is the specific nature and use of the property which in fact falls to their respective share and the *real content* of the exchanges into which they consequently enter. Thus, whereas capitalists and wage-labourers are formally equal and independent inasmuch as owners and exchangers of commodities, they are not only *unequal* but placed in a definite and substantively unequal *relationship* inasmuch as the former own property in means of production, thus permitting them to extract surplus-labour from the latter, and the latter *lack* property in the same (or, more exactly, as according to the general formula just proposed, sufficient property in the same), thus compelling them to sell their labour-power to the former. This, as Marx put it on numerous occasions, 'separation' of the direct producers from the means of realization of their labour – a 'separation' which is only even thinkable under the aegis of private property rights and which has as its necessary correlate the conversion of those means into the property, viz. the *capital*, of a distinct class of individuals – forms, as I have said, the basic 'qualitative' determinant of the capitalist/wage-labourer relation.

Clearly, however, this 'qualitative' side of the relation, to the extent that the relation in question is viewed as an enduring one, has itself to be explained in 'quantitative', viz., as we have seen, *value* terms. No one, after all, is legally *prohibited* from holding property in means of production: the absence of such legal exclusions belongs to the very meaning of the formal equality of all economic agents as owners and exchangers. Whereas land, moreover, can be owned in perpetuity and still – so long, of course, as the economic order continues to be a capitalist one – retain its capacity to generate revenues for its owner, the same does not apply for means of production. Means of production only generate revenues for their owners to the degree that they are consumed – viz. *productively* consumed – and their being consumed implies precisely that they gradually cease to exist (that is, *qua* means of production). Hence, the capital investment which means of production represent can remain 'fructifous' only to the extent that it is periodically renewed, which is to say that the means of production themselves are periodically (viz. every production period in the case of raw materials and after some regular cycle of production periods in the case of instruments of labour) replaced. All of this is so even assuming just '*normal*' reproduction, i.e. no sudden devaluation of means of production through changing market conditions or technical change.

We will see how the distribution of concrete property-rights, the aforementioned juridical 'separation' of workers from the means of production, which forms the 'qualitative' basis of capitalist production (and of the class structure proper to it) is in turn reproduced through the very process of capitalist production. But that distribution *has* precisely to be reproduced: it is not given once and for all. Of course, some goods will be applied as means of production in producing goods of exactly the same kind. Hence their replacement will be a spontaneous consequence of their use and not require the mediation of exchange. In such cases, indeed, 'capital goods' take on some of the quality of landed property. Such cases are, however, clearly the exception. Abstracting from them, the reproduction in question entails that to the same degree as means of production are consumed in the current production period the capitalist enterprise obtains the means of exchange requisite for it to acquire *new* means of production to replace the consumed ones.

Now, it is no great mystery whence these means of exchange come. They are, in the first instance, nothing other than the product itself which has resulted from the consumption of the expended means of production. More exactly, they are just some portion of that product: whatever percentage of the total-value of the product is equal to the value of the consumed means of production, that same percentage of the total product itself represents the means of exchange requisite for the replacement of the latter. The product *qua* exchange-value is already, as we have seen, 'potential money'. Assuming the coincidence of supply and demand, the enterprise has, then, in the form of a portion of its own product, exchange-value in dimensions exactly adequate to the renewal of its investment in 'capital goods'. All that is needed is that this portion of the product be *sold*, such that the exchange-value which it potentially or 'ideally' represents get converted into the real form of exchange-value, viz. *actual* money.

Consequently, when capitalist production is viewed as a continuous process rather than an isolated event, the juridical control enjoyed over some particular set of means of production, while indeed a necessary condition for the generation of capitalist revenues, turns out to be a *subordinate* expression – a 'moment', as Hegel would put it – of the control over property in general represented by assets of a sufficient magnitude. It is the having of assets in the requisite amount – assets which in order to be preserved must continually alternate between the use-value form of commodities (as both elements and issue of the production process) and the independent value form of money – that represents the enduring 'quantitative' basis of the social power, collectively, of the capitalist class and, severally, of its members. The peculiar distribution of *concrete* property-rights which gives rise to the capital/wage-labour relation at the level of the enterprise is thus a function of a persistent inequality in the distribution of *abstract* property-rights, viz. of monetary command over the social product, which ensures that just certain persons will be able to control means of production in the requisite proportions and others will not.

Note that the 'quantitative' formulation of the basis of the capital/wage-labour relation has the advantage, as against the 'qualitative' one, of avoiding any appearance of rigidity, such as might invite the drawing of *too* exact analogies between, say, capitalist and feudal class structure. The ability to claim title in those forms of property which will allow the receipt of capitalist revenues – or, alternatively, where partial, viz. stock, ownership is concerned, to claim sufficient property so as to be relieved of the burden of having to sell one's labour-power – is a function of one's overall level of assets. Hence it is clear that, insofar as the latter can vary, the endurance of a capitalist class structure in no way excludes the movement of individuals between the fundamental positions it comprises. Here it is a question, as Marx put it in his only notable allusion in *Capital* to Hegel's famous 'law' of the 'transition of quantity into quality', of 'purely quantitative changes' that 'at a certain point turn into qualitative distinctions' (*C*I, 423/327).

There is one last reason for assigning precedence to the 'quantitative' determination over the 'qualitative'. For, even if we leave aside rental incomes, it is, of course, possible that the different phases of the capital circuit acquire formal autonomy as the special domains of different categories of capitalists or firms, thus giving rise to derivative forms of capitalist revenue (viz. interest and commercial profit) which are *not* in fact tied to direct ownership in means of production. The quantitative account allows us to handle such special cases without difficulty. It is, nonetheless, true that while the receipt of capitalist revenues is not predicated upon direct ownership in means of production, the very *availability* of surplus-value, whatever the proportions in which it ultimately gets distributed among the specific forms of capitalist revenue and rent, is indeed predicated upon the persistent (as we have seen, themselves 'quantitative') *barriers* to ownership in means of production which constrain workers to sell their labour-power. (Such barriers ensure that there will even be a distinct class of persons thus dependent upon the sale of labour-power and hence secure the existence of the *sine qua non* of capitalist production: a 'labour-market'.) It is not necessary to own means of production in order to claim a share in the total surplus-value; it is, however, necessary that the direct producers do *not* own the means of production which they apply in order for there even to be a pool of surplus-value from which shares can be claimed.

For ease of presentation, then, let us here adopt another one of the elements of the regime of assumptions maintained by Marx in volume I of *Capital* and regard all the functions necessary to the completion of the capital circuit (financing, production and sale) as being united in every capitalist firm.[18] In other words, we will be abstracting from the existence of formally autonomous financial and commercial capital. Making this abstraction will allow us to set in sharp relief just how the 'separation' of workers from the means of production, once it has come into being and thus given rise to capitalist production, is in turn the immanent result of the latter. Now, since what is meant by a 'separation' here is, as already indicated, just a definite distribution of concrete property-rights, clearly this 'separation' cannot result from the process of capitalist production considered simply in its material aspect as a production process. Rather it must result from the latter by virtue of the specific juridical conditions under which it gets carried out and which make it precisely a *capitalist* production process: by virtue, that is to say, of its 'form'.

For the sake of a touch of realism with respect to contemporary economic conditions, and since our presentation will not be excessively burdened by doing so, we will employ here the example of a firm, rather than that of an individual capitalist as is Marx's custom. The firm represents the juridical amalgamation of all the individuals with participating shares in it. The material elements of the production process, means of production and labour-power, having been purchased by the firm, they comprise the property of the latter and it ('it', again, as – in principle at any rate – the agent of the collective will of its shareholders) enjoys the exclusive right to their use. Hence, in turn, the products of the productive combination of these elements belong likewise to the firm, which consequently enjoys the exclusive right likewise to their use or, what is more relevant here, to their *alienation*. According to the norms of commodity-exchange, the firm (supposing, of course, a market exists for these goods and, for simplifying purposes, a coincidence of supply and demand) will, then, be able to receive in exchange a value-equivalent in the money-form for the entire value they 'ideally' represent. Of this latter sum of value, it will owe to the workers it employs, viz. in the form of the wage, only a portion equal to the value of the commodity, viz. their labour-power, which it purchases from them.

Now, the value of labour-power, like the value of all other commodities, is regulated by the socially necessary labour-time requisite for its production. In this case, however, unlike that of any other commodity, the labour-time requisite to the production of the product resolves itself without remainder into the labour-time requisite to the production of its '*means of production*': which are here just the consumption goods (broadly understood) required to reproduce the labourer (both individually over a working-life and inter-generationally) in a 'normal' condition.[19] Consequently, the receipt of the wage provides workers with means of exchange just sufficient to realize the value of said goods, hence to obtain the portion of the social product which they require to reproduce themselves and thereby their labour-power, but not sufficient to acquire the additional portion which would be required for their labour's independent realization.

The juridical 'separation' of workers from the means of production which they apply (viz. at the behest of the owners of such means) thus proves to be self-perpetuating, and so too does workers' dependence upon wage-income. Of course, individual workers may be able over time, through, say, exceptional industriousness or abstinence, to accumulate monetary assets (that is, in amounts exceeding those needed for merely provisional 'savings') and hence gradually to reduce and even finally to surmount their dependence upon the wage. The margins for inter-generational class mobility are typically even somewhat greater. This in no way contradicts the fact, however, that other things being equal the spontaneous outcome of the capitalist production process is to reproduce the wage-dependency of the members of the working class.

If we abstract from the existence of share-capital, as Marx does in volume I, and we assume that all commodity production is capitalist in character, then it follows that the monetary-income of workers will consist of the wage and nothing else. In other words, it will not be possible to own just 'a little bit' of capital and hence to be, so to speak, just 'a little bit' of a capitalist, apart from being a worker. Under our own present assumptions, however, this is indeed possible. It is only excluded that wage-workers in general are able to claim non-wage income in sufficient magnitude to relieve them altogether of having to sell their labour-power – otherwise, there could be no stable market in 'labour' and hence no capitalist production at all.

As for the firm, once the wage-bill has been deducted, it will be left with a sum of value in the money-form comprising both a portion equivalent to the value of the means of production which have been used up in the production process *and* – supposing, namely, that the labour-time necessary for the reproduction of the labour-power it purchases is less than the socially necessary labour-time realized by the same in the production of the product it sells – a *surplus-value*. The former portion will, by definition and as noted above, be sufficient to renew the firm's investment in 'capital goods' (viz. *constant* capital), which, as we have seen, represents the 'qualitative' basis of its ability to exploit labour-power and hence to generate capitalist revenues. The latter portion – precisely the aggregate 'pool' from which those revenues are drawn – will, assuming for present purposes just simple reproduction, flow to its shareholders severally in the form of dividends. To the degree that their percentage participation in the firm's total assets is the juridical grounds for their claims upon an equivalent percentage of the profits that those assets generate, these shareholders then take on the guise of capitalists. As Marx puts it, 'the economic character mask of capitalist only attaches to a man insofar as his money continually functions as capital' (*C*I, 711/591).

It needs to be stressed, however, that whereas the 'character mask' of capitalist might 'attach to a man' no matter how meagre his investments, only those investors whose aggregate holdings generate an income sufficient to free them altogether from the necessity of wage-work belong, strictly speaking, to the capitalist class. Here again the 'quantitative' line of demarcation between the fundamental classes of a capitalist society has to be insisted upon. The corporate allocation of stock to employees surely makes of the latter in some sense 'divided souls'. But, however significant it might be on the aggregate level, worker participation in stock ownership is clearly for most individual workers nothing more than a covert form of wage-dependency. The inequality of economic power between pure owners and 'employee-owners' is much the same as that which has customarily obtained between the former and pure workers.

Whether, then, the social relation in question is reciprocal and functional (as is the case, for instance, with respect to the real interdependence of exchangers 'expressed' in the category *money*) or hierarchical and exploitive (as with the category *capital*), within the nexus of commodity-exchange specific social relations come to be 'represented in' specific categories of things: viz. of things owned by individuals who through exchange enter into those relations. Furthermore, just as we found in the case of money that the sort of material thing in question acquired new 'social properties' by virtue of the relations it mediates, so too with capital. It is only the fact that purchased means of production are applied under the specific juridical conditions described above that impresses upon them the social character of being *capital*: means not only of *production*, but also means for the appropriation of surplus-value.

Herein lies the actual substance of Marx's mature critique of the political economists: namely, that the latter managed theoretically to 'naturalize' and hence 'eternalize' capitalist production by confusing social form and the material bearer upon which qua private property that form gets impressed. Marx says just this in numerous passages of exemplary clarity, in which it is manifestly not a question of his having employed any special 'method' in order to expose this error, but rather of the political economists having employed a peculiarly fallacious 'method' in order to commit it. Here, in closing, is an example:

> The folly of identifying a specific *social relationship of production*, which gets represented in things, with the thing-like [*dingliche*] natural property of these items themselves is what strikes us most forcibly whenever we open the first best textbook on economics and read right on the first page how the elements of the production process, reduced to their most general form, are land, *capital*, and labour. One might just as well say that they were *landed property*, knives, scissors, spindles, cotton, grain, in short the *materials* and *means of labor*, and – *wage-labor*. On the one hand, we name the elements of the production process combined with the *specific social characteristics* peculiar to them in a given *historical* phase, and on the other hand we add an element which belongs to the *labor process* independently of any particular social formation, as an eternal process between man and nature. . . . it is evident at once that this is a very convenient method by which to demonstrate the eternal validity of the capitalist mode of production or that *capital* is an *immutable natural element* in human production as such. (*Res.*, 998/25–6)

7 An 'Idealism of Matter'

As I suggested at the outset of this part, there is in fact another direction in which Marx's early criticisms of political economy could be taken, besides that which issues in his mature critique. This other direction is indeed the direction in which Marx himself took his criticisms in elaborating upon them at the time, and even much later he was often prepared to say that this was the direction in which he had actually gone – though I have tried to show that in fact he went along a completely unrelated route, which led to realizable ends, instead of imaginary ones. In any event, I think this is surely the direction along which one finds everything which is most specious and unrewarding in the Marxist tradition.

Let us inspect once more Marx's celebrated remarks from the *Poverty of Philosophy*:

> The economists express the relations of bourgeois production, the division of labor, credit, money, etc., as fixed immutable, eternal categories. . . . The economists explain how production takes place in these given relations, but what they do not explain is how these relations themselves are produced, that is, the historical movement which gives them birth.

Now, I noted above that Althusser in quoting this passage annexes to it a fragment which in fact belongs to the following section of Marx's text: 'these categories are as little eternal as the relations they express. They are historical and transitory products'. Quoted in this way, it would seem that the antecedent of 'these categories' in the latter remark is the 'fixed immutable, eternal categories' in which – or rather 'as' which – Marx has earlier accused the economists of 'expressing the relations of bourgeois production': a reading which, apart from its other problems, makes Marx into the perpetrator of a rather blatant contradiction. If we restore this fragment to its place in Marx's original text, however, we find that the actual antecedent is to be found rather in the sentence which immediately precedes it: 'The same men who establish the social relations conforming to their material productivity, also produce the principles, the ideas, the categories conforming to their social relations'. This is preceded in turn by the following all-too-familiar contention:

> In acquiring new productive forces, men change their mode of production, and in changing their mode of production, the manner of earning their livelihood, they change all of their social relations. The windmill will give you the society with the suzerain; the steam engine, the society with industrial capitalism. (*PP*, 109/119)[1]

From the context, then, it is abundantly clear that the categories which Marx wants to expose as 'historical and transitory products' are not merely the categories specific to political economy, but quite simply *all the categories of human thought*. Furthermore, the proof of the historical status of the latter derives from nothing more compelling than the unrelentingly expressive model of causality which Marx insists upon as the principle of his 'materialism': proceeding as it does from the (ever developing) productive forces to social relations (or 'social relations of production') and, finally, passing through forms of political organization in order to arrive at the realm of 'ideas' or 'consciousness'. In other words, the alleged historicity of the categories in question is not so much first made accessible through, but, I am suggesting, entirely *an artefact of* the 'inversion' of speculative idealism which Marx had already announced (at any rate, which Marx and Engels had announced to themselves) in *The German Ideology*:

> In direct contrast to German philosophy which descends from heaven to earth, here we ascend from earth to heaven. That is to say, we do not set out from what men say, imagine, conceive, nor from men as narrated, thought of, imagined, conceived, in order to arrive at men in the flesh. We set out from real, active men, and on the basis of their real life-process we demonstrate the development of the ideological reflexes and echoes of this life-process. The phantoms formed in the human brain are also necessary sublimates of their material life-process, which is empirically verifiable and bound to material premises. (*GI*, 47/26)

This is, of course, the very same 'inversion' which Marx would later allude to in his 'famous quotations', and which was supposed to result in the creation of 'his' 'dialectical method'. 'My dialectical method', Marx writes in his 1873 'Afterword' in well-known words which are strikingly similar to those from *The German Ideology*:

> is, in its foundations, not only different from the Hegelian, but exactly opposite to it. For Hegel, the process of thinking, which he even

> transforms into an independent subject, under the name of 'the Idea', is the demiurge of the actual, and the latter is only the external appearance of the former. With me the reverse is true: the ideal is nothing but the material transposed and translated in the human head. (*C*I, 102/26)

The problem with such an 'inversion', however, is that it leaves wholly unaltered the structure of relations it 'inverts': hence its result is, in effect, indistinguishable from that upon which it operates. We will have here to anticipate some of the subject-matter of the following part. Thus if we begin with the Hegelian model of a self-developing system of thought untouched by materiality (viz. 'logic') which, 'without the assistance of any foreign material or stuff',[2] *determines itself* as an actually existing (that is, *temporally* existing) world of objects, then when we venture to 'invert' this structure, we will end up with the presupposition of a 'reality' understood as an inwardly subsisting realm of material processes which are only passively 'reflected' in the conceptual 'phantoms' of thought. In the 'idealist' original, the development of the concept into a systematic whole is, in the first instance, a *pure logical* development, which is only thereafter by virtue of thought's own resolve and activity *reproduced* as a temporal succession of historical forms. In the inverted 'materialist' facsimile, the realm of material immediacy becomes the self-moving mover, whose development, in being opposed to the systemic self-diremption of the concept (through which nothing comes-to-be or ceases-to-be[3]), is thereby determined as temporality itself. The consequence of this 'inversion' cannot be that the real material development is thereafter supposed to be reproduced as a parallel development in the 'realm of ideas', since *there simply is no* 'before' or 'after' except as calibrated by the stages, indeed by every fleeting instant, in the former process of development. The autonomous development of the material world must, then, rather *in each of its moments* be reproduced as an ideal image: that is to say, so long as the instrument of this 'sublimation' – viz. the 'human head' – is present.

This qualification, incidentally, only further reveals the perfection of the symmetry obtaining between Hegel's idealism and the 'materialism' which only succeeds in thinking itself at all as the 'inversion' of the latter. For, in each case, *human cognition* serves as the vehicle through which the correlation of thought and being gets established: human cognition is, so to speak, the indispensable axis without which the articulation of the two could not even occur. If a relation of priority of whatever sort is to be established between the material world and the process of thinking, it is, of course, essential that thought and matter both *be present* such as to be able to be placed in relation. For Hegel, this is not so much of a problem, since thought is complete as a system in itself, independent of its temporal actualization, and the priority of thought as against the material world consists precisely in the fact that the latter is *nothing other than* the former, although in the condition of alienation. It is thought as '*Geist*' or *Logos* which 'gives itself flesh' in the material world. This objectification of '*Geist*', however, would remain otiose and indeed only incompletely realized if '*Geist*' did not come to *know itself* in its alienation: namely, to know the objective world as but its own form of manifestation.

The process of human cognition, beginning with the stage of sense-certainty in which the object in its immediacy appears in opposition to the subject which would know it, is precisely this process of subjectivity's withdrawing the opposition and coming to consciousness of itself in its 'other-being'. Particular cognizing individuals, as part of the material world which stands in opposition to the universal, are thus in fact essential to the latter's achievement of self-knowledge. In this sense, as Colletti has quite rightly pointed out, the empirical human individual is in Hegel's presentation made a predicate of thought, rather than thought being a predicate of the human individual.[4] As the immediate subject of cognition, the human being is the vehicle whereby thought, which is complete unto itself prior to its objectification in the world, overcomes this alienation and re-establishes by way of 'absolute knowledge' its self-identity. If all of this seems somewhat opaque, I hope it will become clearer in the chapters to follow. For the moment, however, it is easy enough to see that human cognition is assigned *exactly the same role*, though with the terms reversed, in the would-be 'materialist inversion' of idealism. It is only insofar as the primary material process of development itself gives rise to an existing organism capable of cognition that the former can then be 'transposed and translated in the human head'.

Finally, since the revelation of the historicity of the categories of thought was supposed to be the very achievement of the 'inversion' of speculative idealism, we need to examine just what sort of 'achievement' this in fact is. Whereas in 'idealism', temporal existence, being merely the existent form of 'the concept' ('*der daseinde Begriff*'), was deprived of any independent effectiveness; in 'materialism', thought, being merely the ideological 'reflex' of material life, is equally so attenuated. In either case, however, it should be emphasized that thought remains *in itself ahistorical*: in the 'idealist' original, because it is already complete as a system independently of its resolve upon temporal existence; in the 'materialist' facsimile, because temporality as such is a monopoly of the material to whose transformations thought only passively responds. Hence the extremity of the conclusion to which Marx and Engels will be led by the above-cited reflections from *The German Ideology*: 'Morality, religion, metaphysics, all the rest of ideology and their corresponding forms of consciousness, thus no longer retain their semblance of independence. They have no history, no development . . .' (*GI*, 47/26–7). Marx's claim here is in fact a perfect image of the position for which he would take Hegel to task in *The Poverty of Philosophy*: viz. that *history itself* has no autonomous principle of development, but is merely a temporal instantiation of forms of development already elaborated in the realm of logic – 'There is no longer "history according to the order of time", there is only the "succession of ideas in the understanding"' (*PP*, 109/118).

The categories of thought are only thus 'historicized' through the 'inversion' of idealism to the extent that they are denied any history *of their own*, being rather set in motion by a 'material life-process' which is opposed at every point to its ideal reflection. The so-called 'materialism' which is the doctrinal product of this 'inversion' has become an unshakeable point of honour for much of the Marxist tradition. We can see now with what justification it should be called rather an 'idealism of matter'.

Part III

'Dialectical' Contradiction and the Logicization of the Empirical

8 Two Principles of Contradiction

The work accomplished in the first part of this volume was largely a work of destruction: the destruction, namely, of the historicist model of Marx's 'dialectics'. We saw there, however, at least in a preliminary way, that the historicist model is as misleading with regard to the character of the 'dialectical method' in its archetypal (at any rate, for the purposes of Marxist discussions 'archetypal') Hegelian context as it is with regard to the actual norms governing the conduct of Marx's mature economic analyses. The mere destruction of the historicist model does not, then, per se exclude the possibility that the former might still be relevant to understanding the latter, albeit in some other manner than that suggested by historicism. So the question remains: just what, if anything, is 'Hegelian' in the discourse of *Capital*? As already indicated, if, having once cleared away the obstacles presented by the historicist model, we are now going to be able to resolve this question, we will have first to examine just what in general is distinctive about a Hegelian mode of argumentation as opposed to any other. We will need to know, in effect, just what is distinctively 'Hegelian' *in Hegel* before we can say what is 'Hegelian' in Marx. Furthermore, if, as I have suggested it does, this question is to bear upon the *legitimacy* of Marx's economic analyses, then we cannot stop at asking just what is distinctive about a 'Hegelian' mode of argumentation, we will need to establish whether that mode of argumentation is in general valid or not. The moment has come, then, when we have, as Roman Rosdolsky once put it, 'to bite into the sour apple' of Hegel's *Logic*.

However much particular logical systems, from Aristotle to the truth-functional calculi of modern formal logic, may differ in detail, logic in the customary sense is founded upon the axiom of identity and its correlate the principle of non-contradiction. It is for this very reason that 'logic' in the Hegelian sense is *sui generis*. For if anything is conspicuously distinctive of Hegelian 'logic', it is the denial of these two allegedly universal 'laws of thought' and their replacement by Hegel's own 'law of contradiction': viz. that '*everything is in itself contradictory*' (*SL*, 439/II, 74). Whereas in both ancient and modern logic, the principle of non-contradiction serves as the very canon of argumentative validity (or, as Kant puts it, of 'analytical knowledge'), Hegel challenges the principle by attacking what he takes to be the *onto*logical presuppositions it involves. Such 'laws of thought' are, Hegel suggests, at once *judgements* which have as their subject *everything which is* or, in other words, anything which could serve as the subject of some more particular judgement. Thus, according to Hegel's interpretation, the principle of non-contradiction implies that A, where 'A' stands for anything, cannot be both what it is and what it is not, both 'A and not A':[1] it implies that while judgements concerning things can be contradictory, *the things themselves* cannot be. Hence, indeed, since there are no 'real contradictions', but only discursive or logical ones, the appearance of contradictions of the latter variety is supposed to entail the need for theoretical revision – or, alternatively, to serve as the proof of a conclusion if they arise on the assumption of its negation.

As against this entire conception, Hegel's 'law of contradiction' suggests not only that there are contradictions which are *real*, but that *reality is contradictory*. Whereas the axiom of identity holds that everything is just that which it is, and hence entails the traditional law of non-contradiction, namely (and crudely, for the moment), that it cannot be what it is not, Hegel writes:

> The truth is rather that a consideration of everything that is, shows that *in its own self* everything is in its self-sameness unlike itself and self-contradictory, and that in its difference, in its contradiction, it is self-identical, and is in its own self this movement of transition of one of these determinations into the other, and this for the reason that each [i.e. each of the determinations] is in its own self the opposite of itself. (*SL*, 412/II, 40)

We should in fact be suspicious of the swiftness with which in a passage such as this one Hegel moves from difference (*Verschiedenheit*), then paratactically to contradiction (*Widerspruch*), and finally to opposition (*Gegensatz*). In the sequel, we will attempt carefully to distinguish what Hegel manages here rather to conflate. For present exegetical purposes, however, and precisely to bring out the (albeit slippery) connection between these terms in Hegel's own usage, we can summarize the distinctively Hegelian conception by way of the famous formula of the 'identity of opposites': viz. that everything is in itself identical with its opposite and hence 'contradictory'.

The Hegelian (or 'dialectical') logical canon is, then, exactly the reverse of the customary (or 'analytical') one. Whereas according to the latter a discourse succeeds in grasping its object only to the degree that it avoids contradiction (this is, of course, a necessary condition though not a sufficient one), according to the former a discourse grasps its object only *by* precisely exposing the object's essential contradictoriness: hence by itself *pronouncing contradictions*. This is, of course, also not supposed to be a sufficient condition (though, as we shall see, unlike the case of the analytical principle, the insufficiency in this case is not then supposed to have the implication that the logical criterion of knowledge must be supplemented by some additional criterion). The 'dialectical' exposition of the object does not stop at the generation of contradictions (which is, according to Hegel, rather the programme of scepticism[2]). Having once shown that the object abstractly considered cannot be grasped in its determinacy without implicating what it is not, the exposition then goes on to 'sublate' (*aufheben*[3]) this opposition (or first 'negation') in some more concrete determination of which the opposites are now revealed to be 'moments' or aspects.

This more concrete determination represents the 'truth' of the '*aufgehoben*' opposites. Hence what is initially taken as the object of investigation – say, for instance, 'pure being' in the *Logic* or sense certainty in the *Phenomenology* or abstract right in the *Philosophy of Right* – is revealed in the course of its apprehension not in fact to have been an independent object at all, but merely a subordinate determination *of something else*. Thus, for example, Hegel identifies *becoming* as 'the third' in which the abstract opposition of being and nothing gets 'sublated': 'This third is an other than they; they subsist only in an other, which is equivalent to saying that they are not self-subsistent' (*SL*, 92/I, 95: compare *En.L*, §88). (Hegel also in fact identifies '*determinate being*' [*das Dasein*] as 'the unity of being and nothing'. The reasons he offers for giving two 'unities' of these opposites need not be gone into here.)

With each new, ostensibly more concrete determination obtained in this way the same procedure is then repeated, until finally, propelled by the motor of the contradictoriness of the merely partial determinations considered in themselves, the totality is reached of which all of them are but vanishing 'ideal' moments. Since *every* merely partial determination – which is to say, at least according to Hegel, everything *finite* (though there is in fact a crucial ambiguity concealed here) – only is as such a 'transition into its opposite', and hence is only graspable by way of the more comprehensive determination which represents the unity of these opposites, in the final analysis the totality to which they belong is always the same: viz. what Hegel calls, variously, the 'true infinite', the 'universal', the 'idea', or '*Geist*'. It is the latter, Hegel writes, 'which reveals itself as the concrete and final supreme truth of all being' (*SL*, 71/I, 70). By the same token, each specific domain of objective or 'revealed' '*Geist*' will have to constitute a partial totality in its own right, and hence the knowledge of the phenomena peculiar to that domain will be subject to the same canon as knowledge in general or 'absolute knowledge'.[4]

Such is the logical canon laid down by Hegel's doctrine of 'dialectical' contradiction. It is quite another matter, of course, whether Hegel actually follows the described procedure in his exposition, and we will have to return to this question below. For the moment, however, it should be recalled from our earlier discussion that Marx located the rational contribution of 'dialectic' in its articulation of the moment of negation inherent to what he called simply '*das Bestehende*' – 'that which is'. As can be appreciated from the foregoing, the remark is in effect just a faithful restatement of the doctrine of 'dialectical' contradiction. The famous 'rational kernel' which Marx thought he had succeeded in extracting from the 'mystifying shell' of the Hegelian system is, then, clearly supposed to be this doctrine. This means that 'dialectical' contradiction as a logical canon ought to be separable from its idealist context, and hence applicable to the investigation of a range of objects (any object?) which would *not* have in each case to turn out to be just so many objectifications of '*Geist*'. The viability of such an 'extraction' and materialist application of 'dialectical' contradiction has, of course, been the target of forceful criticism.[5] And it has so with good reason, since for Hegel the inherently contradictory nature of '*das Bestehende*' was supposed to serve precisely as the demonstration of the 'illusory' character of the being which belongs to the 'merely' finite or immediate – or, in other words, to the objective elements of the material world, which thus gets degraded *as a whole* to but the 'realm of appearances' in which '*Geist*' externalizes itself. The principle of the contradictoriness of the finite is, then, indeed a very strange principle to choose for any 'materialist' application whatsoever.

If Marx managed to avoid this problem in his methodological resumés – or at least those of his methodological resumés which have had the greatest influence on the subsequent Marxist tradition – this is only due to the fact that, as we have seen, he gave the 'negativity' to which the doctrine of 'dialectical' contradiction refers a mundane interpretation. Hegel makes a *logical* claim, viz. that any given 'determination' only is that which it is by virtue of involving its specific negation (or 'opposite'). He interprets this claim as having metaphysical implications, viz. that everything must then be 'in itself' contradictory or 'the opposite of itself'. In Marx's treatment, however, this logical claim suffers a banalization whereby it gets converted into the *empirical* claim that the real object under investigation, whatever its specific determinacy, *will be* 'negated', i.e. will *cease to be*.

As we have also noted, however, Hegel was not himself immune to such a banalization of his doctrine of contradiction. Since the Marxist tradition has unwittingly found itself burdened with its consequences, we need to examine how and why this banalization occurs in its original Hegelian context. By giving the 'negativity' at the core of 'the dialectic' a mundane interpretation, Marx, in effect, employed the logical term 'negation' as but a metaphor for an empirical process. Here we have yet another 'inversion' of Hegelian procedure: since, as will be seen directly, in Hegel it is rather empirical processes which are made to serve as the tropes for logical forms.

9 The Word Made Flesh or Hegel's Incarnation of Logic

9.1 'LOGIC' AS *PARS TOTALIS* OF THE HEGELIAN SYSTEM

It is fair to say that in principle the *entirety* of the Hegelian system is or, at any rate, is supposed to be contained implicitly in the *Logic*, that, in effect, the entirety of the system *is* the *Logic*. The *particular* division of the system which bears the name 'logic' is supposed to provide the exposition of the pure 'determinations of thought' or *Denkbestimmungen* in their 'dialectical' self-development. Again, the putative character of this development as a *self*-development has to be stressed (though not naively credited, of course). Beginning with the most simple abstract determinations, those which are allegedly just 'there before us' when nothing else is presupposed[1] – viz. *being* and *nothing* – the totality of the determinations constitutive of 'pure thought' is supposed then to produce itself in a necessary movement, governed, namely, by precisely that principle of self-transcending contradiction which is here in question.

As the completed system of these determinations, 'logic' comprises, then, according to the Hegelian mode of expression, the science of 'the concept' as 'the idea' still merely *in itself*. The passage from this 'logic' in the narrow sense to the subsequent stages in the system, viz. the sciences of nature and then 'spirit', is, however, supposed to resume the necessary movement whereby the 'pure' *Denkbestimmungen* *give themselves* actuality – that is to say, it is supposed to be just a *phase* in the same 'self-development' of thought which forms the object of 'logic' as such. Hence it is the very same 'idea', the very same *Denkbestimmungen*, albeit at (allegedly) ever greater levels of concretization, which continue to form the object of the other 'philosophical sciences' as well.

Recall that according to the principle of 'dialectical' thought, any new determination which arises in the course of a valid scientific exposition can only be *either* the opposite into which a given determination necessarily passes (hence in fact *not* a 'new' determination, but 'in essence' coeval with the 'prior' one) *or* the resolution of the contradictory identity of these opposites, the 'unity' in which they are 'sublated' (and hence, again, *not* in fact a 'new' determination at all). Nothing *external* to thought is supposed to be simply *adduced* in order to provide its content, but rather thought as universal 'form' is supposed to provide its own content, to concretize *itself*. If this principle is to be consistently applied, it follows that the object of the entire system, which in the end should get grasped in the totality of its determinations, will be nothing different from that which as simple immediacy provided its point of departure. (This is, of course, just the same conclusion which we came to above: viz. that every merely partial determination must, in the end, turn out to be a determination of one and the same 'self-mediating' totality.) 'The beginning of philosophy,' Hegel writes, 'is the foundation which is present and preserved throughout the entire subsequent development, remaining completely immanent in its further determinations' (*SL*, 71/I, 71).[2]

An examination of the final section of the 'Logic', in any of its variants, bears witness to Hegel's commitment to respect this principle in presenting the conclusion of 'logic' as the necessary and immanent transition into the philosophy of nature. (Again, whether this transition or, for that matter, any of Hegel's transitions are in fact so immanent as he suggests they ought to be is a separate question.) 'Because,' Hegel writes,

> the pure idea of cognition is so far [viz. in the 'sphere' of *logic*] confined within subjectivity, it is the *urge* to sublate this, and pure truth as the last result becomes also the *beginning of another sphere and science*. . . . The idea, namely, in positing itself as absolute *unity* of the pure concept and its reality and thus contracting itself into the immediacy of *being*, is the *totality* in this form – *nature*. (*SL*, 843/II, 572–3)[3]

The material world (or, in other words, the specific object of the philosophy of nature) thus proves to be but the actuality acquired by 'the idea' in its 'alienation' or 'otherness'; and the 'spiritual' or *geistige* world (namely, the object of the philosophy of 'spirit') in turn, but the self-conscious forms which 'the idea' acquires in returning from out of this alienation and recognizing itself in its 'other'.

Indeed, the 'necessity' attaching to the self-alienation of 'the idea' in the form of immediate being turns out to consist in nothing more than the indispensability of this objective form for the purpose of mediating its acquisition of self-consciousness (hence the form of 'subjective freedom') in 'spirit': 'the idea' as 'infinite subjectivity' must give itself objective form in order to be able to recognize itself therein. (The appearance of this 'necessity' at this point – a 'necessity' of something 'for the purpose' of something else – should, incidentally, already begin to raise some doubts for us concerning the alleged immanence of Hegel's exposition.) Thus Hegel, in the final sentence of the 'greater' *Logic*, concludes:

> . . . in this proximate resolve of the pure idea to determine itself as external idea, it thereby only posits for itself the mediation out of which the concept ascends as a free existence that has withdrawn into itself from externality, that completes its self-liberation in the *science of spirit*, and that finds the supreme concept of itself in the science of logic as the self-comprehending pure concept. (*SL*, 843–4/II, 573)[4]

'Logic', Hegel writes elsewhere, 'exhibits the elevation of the *idea* to that level from which it becomes the creator of nature and passes over to the form of *concrete immediacy* whose concept, however, breaks up this shape again in order to realize itself as *concrete spirit*' (*SL*, 592/II, 265).

Now, it is clear from all of this that the subject-matter of logic ought for Hegel to turn out to be identical with the subject-matter of the completed system of knowledge as such. Or, in other words, the 'subjectivity' of knowing should turn out to be identical with the 'objectivity' of that which is known (wherein is supposed to lie the 'absoluteness' of such 'absolute knowledge'). Thus, in summarizing the relation of logic, as the science of the pure forms of thought, to the 'concrete sciences' of nature and 'spirit', Hegel observes:

> As contrasted with these concrete sciences (although these have and retain as their inner formative principle that same logical element, or the concept, which had served as their archetype), logic is of course a formal science; but it is the science of the *absolute form* which is within itself a totality and contains the *pure idea of truth itself*. This absolute form has in its own self its content or reality; the concept, not being a trivial, empty identity, possesses in its moment of negativity or of absolute determining, the differentiated determinations; the content is simply and solely these determinations of the absolute form and nothing else – a content posited by the absolute form itself and consequently also adequate to it. (*SL*, 592/II, 265)

There should be no mistaking what Hegel is here contending: namely, that the subject-matter of the sciences of nature and 'spirit' is, in effect, *the content of logic*. It is symptomatic in this regard that Hegel chooses to describe that specific part of his system which bears the title 'logic' as 'the science of the idea in and for itself' (*En.L*, §18). Above, I said that 'logic' in a narrow sense was rather the science of 'the idea' *in itself*, since, as the subsequent development of the system shows, 'the idea' only becomes *for itself* to the degree that it passes through the moment of its alienation and recuperates its self-identity (now – of course – 'mediated with difference') in 'spirit'. Hence, it is rather *the entirety* of the system which comprises 'the science of the idea in and for itself'. We can appreciate, however, that there is in fact, at least by Hegelian standards, no inconsistency here: the 'logic' is at once part of the system *and* its entirety. It is, in short, a *pars totalis*.

This means that it is an absolute *requirement* of Hegel's systematic construction (and indeed it is this very requirement of Hegel's systematic that we encountered above appearing *within* the system under the title of 'necessity') that the 'pure' determinations of thought which provide the subject-matter of 'logic' will then *somehow and in some form* be rediscovered in the spheres of nature and 'spirit'. 'Logic' provides, as Hegel puts it in the passage just cited, the 'archetype' (*Vorbild*) for the latter, just as in their further development it continues to function as their 'formative principle' (*Bildner*).[5] Now, Hegel not only explicitly acknowledges this requirement – he even goes so far as to suggest that the entire interest of the other 'philosophical sciences' will consist in our being able to 'recognize' just these same determinations of thought in their material and 'spiritual' 'modes of expression':

> If in pursuance of the foregoing we consider logic to be the system of the *pure* determinations of thought, then the other philosophical sciences, the philosophy of nature and the philosophy of spirit, appear, so to speak, as an applied logic, since logic is the soul which animates them. The interest of the remaining sciences is then only [sic] to recognize the logical forms in the shapes [*Gestalten*] of nature and of spirit – shapes which are only a particular mode of expression of the forms of pure thought. (*En.L*, §24, add. 2)

Of course, any particular 'mode of expression' with which nature or 'spirit' endow the forms of 'pure' thought will only in fact be particular to the extent that it is precisely '*im*pure'. This point is crucial to a correct appreciation of the character of Hegel's 'system' as a whole. If 'the concept' is 'the universal' – and cleansing this claim of the typically Hegelian accretion of hypostatized logical categories, it becomes the more plebeian observation that concepts as the element of thought are 'universal', viz. *general*, relative to the particulars which they subsume – then the particularity of the particular will consist in its alloying 'the universal' with extraneous and accidental elements which fail in their immediacy to correspond to it. This is what Hegel calls the 'impotence [*Ohnmacht*] of nature', which 'brings with it the inability to represent the logical forms in their purity' (*En.L*, §24, add. 2).[6] Now, it will be noticed that while, on the one hand, Hegel attributes this '*Ohnmacht*' specifically to *nature*, on the other hand, *both* the natural *and* the 'spiritual' mode of expression of the logical are supposed to be affected by it. This apparent inconsistency is explained by the fact that, though the 'shapes' acquired by the logical forms in 'spirit' are likewise unable to represent the latter in their purity, nonetheless the 'spiritual' shapes only suffer from this '*Ohnmacht*' to the degree that they are burdened precisely with the taint of naturalness – or, in other words, of immediacy (recalling that the 'sphere' of nature as a whole represents, according to Hegel, 'the concept contracted into the immediacy of being').

Everything merely *particular*, whether in the 'sphere' of nature or that of 'spirit', is characterized by such a 'natural' mode of being; whereas *universality* is the essential element of *thought*, precisely in contrast to immediate being. Hegel also calls such a particular which exists in opposition to the universal, and hence which is sensuously perceived rather than intellectually comprehended,[7] an 'immediate' or 'natural' (sometimes too a 'sensuous') 'individual', in the sense of being a separable and delimitable one among others (or, in other words, a 'unit'). 'The distinction of the sensuous from that which is thought lies in this,' Hegel writes,

> that the determination of the former is *individuality* [*Einzelheit*], and insofar as the individual (abstractly, the atom) also exists in connection with others, the sensuous is an *outside-of-one-another*, whose further abstract forms are *alongside-of-* and *after*-one-another. (*En.L*, §20)

The entirety of nature is supposed to be composed of 'individuals' of this sort, and so too is every human being such an individual insofar as it individualizes *itself* in acting through and upon such natural objects (and to this degree and in this respect the human being is itself *part of* nature, rather than 'spirit').[8] This natural 'individuality' is not to be confused with what Hegel calls the 'individuality of the concept': the former is the determination of the particular in *opposition to* the universal; the latter is rather the universal 'reflected into itself' from out of a range of particulars which, no longer having the 'appearance' of independence, have been exposed as but so many of its own functions or 'moments'. 'Natural' individuality is then *particularity*, whereas the 'individuality of the concept' is rather the universal expressly posited as the *totality* of its determinations: it is not an 'outside-of-one-another', but rather a 'being-in-and-for-itself'.[9]

In the realm of '*Geist*' there will be residues of natural individuality to the degree that there are many particular subjects or 'souls' (*Seele*) which are not in the immediacy of their existence identical with the 'absolute subjectivity' of '*Geist*' as such.[10] As suggested above, it is precisely the involvedness with a domain of natural objects, defined as outside and independent of it (as, namely, *Gegenstände*), that makes the subject in its activity a natural, i.e. empirical, individual. The particular subject or 'soul' thus represents a kind of intersection between the domains of nature and '*Geist*': the particular subject is at once nature invested with 'spirit' and 'spirit' embodied in nature. 'The soul', Hegel says, 'is as it were the middle term between corporeality and spirit or the bond between them. The spirit as the soul is immersed in corporeality, and the soul is what animates the body' (*En.L*, §34, add.).

9.2 THE UNIVERSAL AND THE PARTICULAR IN '*GEIST*'

An example from the *Philosophy of Right* (the material of which figures in the arrangement of the *Encyclopedia* under the heading of 'objective spirit') can help us to grasp the character of the relation which is supposed to obtain between natural individuals and 'the universal' in '*Geist*'. (Indeed, as we will see, this relation in '*Geist*' will ultimately serve Hegel as the model for the relation which is supposed to obtain between *all* particulars and their 'concepts'.) The object of the science of 'right' as a whole is to be understood, according to Hegel, as the will, which he defines as 'thought translating itself into existence' (*Ph.R*, §4, add.); and the existence which thought thus acquires under the aspect of its activity in the world is precisely the completed system of 'right'. It should be stressed that Hegel gives this term a very broad signification, such that it ultimately comprehends not only juridical forms in the narrow sense, but also all the processes of social integration which are regulated by them.[11] Hegel distinguishes, however, between the will of particular subjects (which represents, so to speak, the immediate form of existence of the will) and the 'absolutely free will' which belongs to – or rather, in a speculative sense, 'is' – '*Geist*' itself. The former he calls the 'natural' will.

This 'natural' will is free 'in itself', but since its content and object exist outside it as some given thing (recall that we found 'reciprocal externality', which here appears as the reciprocal externality of subject and object, to be the defining feature of 'natural' individuality), it does not yet have *itself* in this object – 'the subjective side is still other than the objective' – and hence is not yet free 'for itself' (cf. *Ph.R*, §11 and §15). As we will see, such 'natural' wills in their restricted particularity provide a necessary condition for the actual*ization* of the concept of the 'absolutely' free will, but they do not *as such* represent the actuality of the latter. The sort of freedom which the subject in the form of the merely particular or *natural* individual can enjoy is rather what Hegel calls '*Willkür*' – 'arbitrariness' or 'caprice' – which is the analogue in the 'spiritual' world to *accident* in the strictly natural one (it is, Hegel says, 'contingency manifesting itself as will' [*Ph.R*, §15; and cf. *En.L*, §145]).

Since it consists only in a subject's being able to choose from among a range of possibilities which are determined independently of him or her, *Willkür* is, so to speak, merely freedom in the abstract (and its purest form of expression is thus constantly being just *at the point of* choosing, since the definite choice once made implies precisely the *restrictedness* of such a subject). '*Substantial*' or 'concrete' freedom, by way of contrast, can only be enjoyed by a will whose object is identical with itself and which is thus *un*restricted. *Substantial* freedom is then an attribute – indeed *the* attribute – of '*Geist*'. The subject as natural individual can at best *participate in* such substantial freedom: namely, by *forsaking his or her individuality* and acting, not according to caprice, but rather according to the dictates of reason as such, hence by '*willing the universal*'.[12]

There are then traces of natural individuality in the domain of '*Geist*', in the form, namely, of particular subjects whose will remains at variance with 'the universal'. Nonetheless, since, as noted, the completed 'shapes' of the 'spiritual' world are supposed to be precisely the forms of self-consciousness acquired by 'the idea' in returning to itself from its 'alienation' in nature, the domain of '*Geist*' as a whole is conceived as but the incessant stripping away of the immediacy with which the logical forms are burdened in their natural incarnation. Hence, '*Geist*' represents the recuperation of the purity which these forms had sacrificed in order to gain existence – *existence* being a function precisely of *particularity*. In other words and very schematically: *logic* constitutes the completed system of the pure determinations of thought, but as yet *unrealized*, merely 'in themselves'; the *philosophy of nature* (and indeed *nature itself*) displays these same determinations now *existent* (*daseiend*), since precisely *particularized*, though, as a consequence of this particularization, in impure form; and, finally, the *philosophy of spirit* displays the very same determinations developed or rather developing into actuality, insofar as they prove themselves to be the abiding essences of the particular modes of existence they had previously acquired. 'Spirit' is, then, the process whereby 'the idea' returns from out of its alienation, and recognizing itself in its 'other-being' in nature, comes to be '*for itself*'. 'Spirit' is the universality of thought viewed from the perspective of its having acquired reality in nature and its 'knowing itself' therein.

Now, if we examine this structure, it becomes clear that, however much Hegel may disparage nature on account of its '*Ohnmacht*', it is only by virtue of the impure particularity of the incarnation which nature gives to the pure 'determinations of thought' that the latter are able to gain actuality at all. If the given particular coincided in every detail with the 'universal' under which it falls – in other words, its 'concept' – then it would quite simply *be* that universal and hence *not* in fact a particular. In this way, however, one would never depart from the sphere of logic: the logical would remain purely logical, which is to say, it would *not* succeed in 'giving itself' reality. The 'reality' of universals and the concomitant 'nothingness' or 'illusoriness' of particulars, upon which Hegel places such great emphasis (and which, as we have seen, constitutes the core principle of idealism in the sense in which he uses this term), consists rather in the fact that the 'universal' or 'concept' asserts itself (*setzt sich durch*) in the field of particularity.

The way in which this occurs in '*Geist*' is through precisely the *particular* will's diverging from the *general* will (this is what Hegel would call the 'first negation'), and then being *corrected* by some instance representative of this latter, which thus in this act of correction (by, namely, 'negating this negation') '*setzt sich durch*' and gains actuality. We can see this more concretely by returning to our example from the *Philosophy of Right*. While, as noted, the particular subject can participate in the 'substantial freedom' of '*Geist*' by acting according to the dictates of rationality as such[13] or, in other words, the principles of abstract right (which for Hegel are – or, at any rate, ought to be – embodied in the constitution of the state), it is in fact essential for the realization of these principles that the merely particular subject precisely *not* always do so. In other words, it is essential that particular subjects '*contradict*' the demands of the 'general will' and 'do wrong', since it is only insofar as the particular will fails to correspond to the general that the former demonstrates its real independence from the latter; and it is only insofar as the particular will demonstrates such independence that the 'general will' is able to abandon its merely abstract mode of being and *realize itself* by in practice *bringing* the particular into correspondence with it – viz. through the institutions of state power.

The 'general will', in Hegel's words,

> first posits itself in the opposition between the general will in itself and the single explicitly independent will; and then, through the supersession of this opposition (through the negation of this negation), it determines itself in its *existence* as a will, so that it is a free will not only in itself but for itself also. . . . (*Ph.R*, §104)

In this subordination of the particular will, the independence it had demonstrated in the doing of 'wrong' is now revealed as a mere 'show', a 'nullity', and the 'universal' is revealed as the power which stands over the particular and constitutes its 'truth'.[14]

9.3 THE UNIVERSAL AND THE PARTICULAR IN NATURE

This last example illustrates how the 'universal' or the 'concept' – in this case, the concept of the will – is supposed to 'realize itself' concretely in the 'administration of justice': it realizes itself *at the expense of particulars*. But the pattern of the universal's alleged realization is in fact everywhere the same throughout Hegel's system, whatever the specific subject-matter under examination happens to be. The 'concept' only acquires actuality at all by virtue of 'releasing itself' to existence in a range of particulars. To the extent, however, that the latter as such fail to correspond to their 'concept' – which is precisely what constitutes their particularity – they are then *qua particulars* condemned in turn to *cease to exist* (they are mere 'appearances', in the Hegelian sense, because they will *dis*appear). Everything in the particular which *makes it* particular is 'thus', i.e. through its passing, exposed as 'untrue', a 'show' (*Schein*), and, conversely, the truth and 'essence' of such particulars is revealed to lie in their abiding 'concept' and, ultimately, *the* 'concept'.[15] The truth of the particular is the general: which is to say, according to the Hegelian system of equivalences, that the truth of being is thought; the truth of nature, 'spirit'; the truth of the empirical, the logical.

Now, as we have just seen, in the case of the, so to speak, 'moral' world or, in Hegelian terms, the world of objective '*Geist*', it is *the universal itself* which, through the agency of some existent proxy (for example, the monarch or the court), is supposed to bring about the 'decease' of the particular which is at variance with it. This does not mean, of course, that every 'wrong' volition has to be punished by the death of the 'natural' individual whose volition it is (though for Hegel certainly some such volitions ought to be so punished), but only that, whatever the punishment happens to be, in its being accomplished the universal – here the 'general will' – eliminates the discrepancy of the particular and so demonstrates the reality of its power over the particular. It is an evident weakness of Hegel's systematic construction, however, that he is not able to provide any analogous instance demonstrating the real existence of universals in nature as such. As noted, Hegel merely relies on the alleged fact that the 'natural' individual of whatever sort ceases to exist.

Leaving aside the question of the accuracy of this observation for inorganic nature (and it is doubtful that it in general even makes sense to speak of 'individuals' of kinds in inorganic nature), it is at least uncontroversial that the specifically *biological* individual, the organism, does indeed die. But, in this case, the universal of which the particular individual is an instance does not actively intervene in bringing about such an outcome. Hegel, of course, says things like: 'The living dies, because it is the contradiction of being *in itself* the universal, the species, while immediately existing only as individual. In death the species proves itself to be the power over the immediate individual' (*En.L*, §221, add.). Hegel *says* such things, he *asserts* (repeatedly) that the individual declines 'because of' the non-correspondence of its existence with its 'concept'.[16] But he nowhere *shows* that in nature the universal actually exhibits this 'power' which he attributes to it.

Again, the contrast with what Hegel has been able to accomplish in interpreting the constituents of the political organization of society is crucial here. One need not concede to him, of course, that in a constitutional monarchy the monarch *really is* the representative of the general interest of society as such. Nonetheless, he has been able to show that there is indeed, at least according to the *principle* of the political constitution, a representative instance of universality in the political realm, and, furthermore and most importantly, that this instance (whether or not its function conforms to its principle) does indeed make its dominion over the individual *real*. Wherein, however, consists the reality of the dominion which the *species* is supposed to enjoy over the individual organism?[17]

Hegel's importing of the moral category of *obligation* – of 'the ought' (*das Sollen*) – into the discussion of finite existence and particularity as such is symptomatic of his efforts to conceal this lacuna in his presentation by simply transferring characteristics of '*Geist*' into nature. Thus, just as the particular *moral agent* in 'doing wrong' demonstrates the discrepancy between its actions and the principles of right in general – demonstrates in effect that it does not do what it '*ought*' to do (and again, this is at least an acceptable description of what occurs from the perspective of the prevailing legal system, if not much more than that) – so *everything* merely particular and finite is supposed, according to Hegel, to be constituted by the 'obligation' to overcome its limited existence and 'return' to the universal. The problem, however, is that if the biological individual is in its existence at variance with its 'concept' and hence not what it 'ought to be', it is not at all clear in what sense *by dying* it manages to overcome this 'defect' and *become* 'what it ought to be'. Hegel has not shown that in the case of biological demise there is any disturbed union of the particular with its universal which gets re-established. The particular legal subject who in committing some 'wrong' deviates from the, so to speak, prevailing 'universal' (Hegel, of course, would leave out the modifier) is in the act of 'correction' then *brought back* to it, either insofar as s/he thereafter *wills* just what s/he 'ought' or insofar as the merely particular will is unable to prevail over the 'general will' and in fact the reverse takes place.[18] In *dying*, however, the individual organism *simply* ceases to exist as such; it does not become reunited with some 'universal' from which it was severed in living.

Or *at least* it does not do so as long as we refrain from ascribing to life and death a significance which transcends their simple biological meaning. If, however, we maintained that the 'essence' of the natural individual is rather its 'soul' – which, though it gets individualized through the corporeal existence to which it is bound, is not thereby *identical* with this bodily individuality – we might then arrive at different conclusions. And this is precisely the Hegelian scenario. As we have already noted, the 'soul' is, according to Hegel, supposed to be the conduit between the universality of '*Geist*' and the particularity of bodily existence: it is 'the concept . . . realized in a body, with respect to whose externality the soul is the immediate self-relating *universality*, just as it is *particularization* with respect to the concept' (*En.L*, §216).

In this case, while death would remain the demise of the biological organism, it would at the same time represent the 'soul's' shedding of this its biological mode of existence, hence too of its particularity, and its reunification with '*Geist*'. The 'universal' to which the natural individual is supposed to 'return' in death is not then its *kind* or species, as Hegel's discussion of the biological organism would seem to suggest. Indeed, it is not even exactly the natural individual as such which 'returns' to the 'universal', but rather the '*soul*' which does, since, as nothing other than the universality of '*Geist*' particularized in the form of the natural individual, in so doing the 'soul' rejoins the unity whence it came. It is precisely *the* 'universal', the *absolutely* unlimited, the 'true infinite' – viz. '*Geist*' – to which the 'soul' returns.

Here, as elsewhere, Hegel exploits the ambiguity of the German *Allgemeinheit*, which does double-duty for the significations easily enough distributed in English between 'universality', having the dominant connotation of the *absolutely* inclusive, and 'generality', having the connotation of the relatively *more* inclusive (as is, for instance, the generic term relative to the specific).[19] If we ignore the paralogical flourishes which this ambiguity permits him, Hegel's reasoning in concluding that the individual organism dies as a result of its non-correspondence with its kind (even though, as we have just seen, it does not thereby 'return' to its kind), and, more generally, that the existing particular 'ceases to be' as a result of its non-correspondence with its concept, is clearly analogical in character. The individual is to the kind as existence is to the concept as nature is to 'spirit' as *body* is to *soul*. 'It is *the definition of finite things*,' Hegel writes:

> that in them concept is different from being, that concept and reality, soul and body, are separable and hence that they are transient and mortal; the abstract definition of God, on the other hand, is precisely that his concept and his being are *unseparated* and *inseparable*. (*SL*, 89–90/I, 92)

It is often suggested that the appearance of such theological categories in Hegel's discourse is somehow extraneous to the actual development of his argument: that *soul* and *body*, for example, and even *God*, serve merely as convenient figures for logical categories, the character of whose systematic relation has been demonstrated quite independently of any appeal to the content of the theological ones. On this reading, Hegel would merely have mined the categorial resources of Christian doctrine; but he would have invested the theological terms with a strictly *logical* significance. Our analysis shows, however, that in fact exactly *the reverse* is the case: it is rather the logical concepts which Hegel invests with *theological* significance, and it *is* precisely this theological significance that converts the logical categories into the 'essences' of the real forms of existence to which they are meant to apply, that gives them, in short, a *substantial* character. Thus, as we have seen, the conclusion Hegel arrives at concerning the substantiality of the relation between the particular and the 'universal' – which precisely as a consequence of this conclusion becomes a relation not only between categories, but between *that which is* particular (viz. what exists) and *that which is* general (viz. thought) – *depends upon* his annexing to the logical categories the theological significations of *body* and *soul*.

'God alone', Hegel writes, 'is the true correspondence of concept and reality; all finite things, however, involve an untruth: they have a concept and an existence, which, however, does not conform to their concept. Therefore they must perish . . .' (*En.L*, §24, add. 2). We too as merely particular subjects are, like all the finite things of the world, burdened with corporeal individuality, and hence at variance with our 'concept'; and so, Hegel reminds us, it is 'our affair': 'to lay aside our immediate subjectivity (to put off the old Adam) and become conscious of God as our true and essential self' (*En.L*, §194, add. 1). The open secret of Hegel's entire systematic construction is a Christian *theological* one. This would make it rather surprising that generations of would-be 'dialectical materialists' have seen fit to follow his example in attributing to logical forms a mundane existence – if it were not for the other open secret that though Hegel may have retained quite a few 'Marxist friends', he has not so many Marxist readers.[20]

10 The ‘Reality’ o Contradiction

10.1 TRUTH AND FALSITY IN AN EX

‘Logic’, Hegel writes, ‘is the all-animating
determinations of thought as found in logic
§24, add. 2). The theological scenario sketch
context for what I have called the ‘banaliza
trine of contradiction undergoes in the cours
his system. Hegel leaves no doubt that it is p
study of pure thought, that we achieve the ra
But since God as ‘essence’ is ‘the infinite gc , that lets its own show freely issue into immediacy and grants it the joy of existence’ (*En.L*, §131, add.), it is necessary to know God as well in the concrete forms of manifestation or *Erscheinungsformen* of this essence: to discover ‘His’ truth in the *untruth* of everything which is not ‘Him’.[1] Thus, just as God who is infinite ‘spirit’ animates the entire universe of merely finite modes of existence, so too *logic* as the science of infinite form is the ‘spirit’ which ‘animates’ all merely finite sciences. Whatever determinations are to be found in logic, or in thought which is as yet without content, *must* then be *re*discovered – as I said above, somehow and in some (namely, finite) form – in the investigation of the concrete contents which thought ‘gives itself’ in reality. Such determinations must be shown themselves to *have* reality.

In conformity with this requirement, Hegel goes about dutifully projecting into the world (or, as Hegel says, the ‘so-called world’! [see note 18 below]) categories whose application is usually restricted to ‘thought’ or discourse concerning a world: he gives *meta*theoretical or ‘second-order’ categories, in other words, a ‘first-order’ use. Consider, for instance, the opposition of *truth* and *falsity*. In its customary logical application this opposition is taken to characterize propositions in their relation to some object or objective condition which they are supposed to be about. This does not exclude the possibility that the object to which the given proposition relates might itself in whole or in part be constituted by other propositions (we can, for example, make true or false statements concerning an argument or a discussion or a text, and so on). But, in any case, the property of being true or false belongs to *the proposition* and, furthermore, it does so only *by virtue of* the quality of the proposition's relation to its object. (This is, incidentally, supposing we continue to credit the distinction, as much the case for propositions whose truth or falsity can be decided upon in an analytical manner as for propositions of a synthetic sort.) The property *is* in fact the quality of the proposition's relation to its object.

For Hegel, however, the theoretical scene is quite different and indeed exactly the reverse of the aforesaid. For him, it is rather *objects* which are 'true' or 'false'. They are so as judged by the standard of their 'concept', since their 'concept', however they may exist, constitutes what they essentially *are*. Here, then, is an example of the Hegelian style of discourse:

> that a person is sick or someone has committed a theft may well be the case. But the content is untrue. A sick body does not correspond with the concept of life, and likewise theft is an action which is not congruent with the concept of human conduct. (*En.L*, §172, add.)

Indeed, as we have seen, every form of merely finite existence will, according to Hegel's criterion, turn out to be 'untrue', since in corresponding to its 'concept', and hence gaining 'truth', the finite loses precisely the character of its finitude.[2]

Hegel is always happy to find examples in colloquial discourse of the transfer of the designations 'true' or 'false' to extra-logical objects, thus confirming his own usage: as when someone speaks of a 'true friend', for instance.[3] Nonetheless, the property of being true or false in a logical sense (and this logical sense has at least *become* the primary acceptation of these terms in English, as well as of their semantic equivalents *wahr* and *falsch* in German) belongs, as I have suggested, to what we can call a specific sort of logical entity: namely, propositions or judgements. (We will be using these terms interchangeably, though Hegel sometimes, if not consistently, distinguishes between *Sätze* and *Urteile*.) Judgements have other sorts of property too: for instance, the property of being universal or particular in scope. There are also other logical entities – for instance, concepts or inferences or arguments – and these other logical entities have still other logical properties: in the case of inferences or arguments, for instance, the property of being valid or invalid. Now, Hegel not only attributes logical properties to empirical objects, he also – which should come as no surprise in light of the foregoing discussion – treats empirical objects as 'in essence', or in 'truth', logical ones.

We are already familiar with the basis of this practice: viz. the claim that the 'truth' of that which is lies not in the particularity of its existence but rather in the generality of its 'concept'. 'Everything', Hegel writes, 'is concept' (*En.L*, §181) and 'the concept is ... the principle of all life' (*En.L*, §160, add.). Hegel, however, does not stop at the substantialization of the 'concept', but insists on attributing substantial being to other logical forms as well. Hence: 'all things are a judgement' (*En.L*, §167); and even 'everything is a syllogism [or "inference" – *Schluß*[4]]' (*En.L*, §181) and 'the living is the syllogism' (*En.L*, §217).[5] As we have seen, Hegel invests logical categories with *theo*logical significance, which has, then, the consequence in turn that he substantializes the logical or, what amounts to the same thing, *logicizes* the empirical.

10.2 HEGEL ON JUDGEMENT

In its execution, Hegel's logicization of the empirical results in what can only be described as some of the purest quackery imaginable. That such quackery has of late acquired renewed credibility in (thankfully small and for the most part German) academic circles should not compel us to take it any more seriously than it deserves. It would not be worthwhile to prolong our discussion of Hegel solely for the cause of doing battle with dilettantism. Nonetheless, it is important for present purposes that we acquaint ourselves, so to speak, with the tenor of such quackery. For not only have Marxists and Marxism by no means remained unaffected by its fascination,[6] but, indeed, as I will try to show, the supposed 'reality' of contradiction, which so many Marxists have even taken to be the 'rational kernel' of their 'dialectical method', is in the original Hegelian context just another instance of precisely the same genre of nonsense.

'All things are judgements', then, in the Hegelian universe, because 'they are *individuals* which are a *universality* or inner nature in themselves, or a *universality* which is *individualized*' (*En.L*, §167). Now, of course, we already are supposed to know what Hegel here claims about the nature of 'all things' from the prior development of 'logic', even before Hegel comes to address the specific topic of *judgement* as such. What we learn in the discussion of judgement is just that this logical form allegedly 'expresses' this content: namely, the identity of the individual and the universal. Such, Hegel claims, is the very meaning of the form of judgement (and it is evidently, in the first instance, *categorical* judgements that Hegel has in mind), apart from any more specific meaning that might accrue to some determinate judgement.[7]

'The abstract judgment', Hegel writes, 'is the maxim: "the individual is the universal"' (*En.L*, §166). If the content of a given judgement so happens to deviate from this meaning which its form is supposed to express, then that is to be regarded as a defect of the judgement in question and a measure of its 'untruth' (see *En.L*, §172). In light of the fact that, as Hegel himself is forced to concede, this will turn out to be the normal fate of judgements – such, for Hegel, is the 'contradiction' contained in judgement: namely, that 'the subject is the predicate' and yet 'the predicate should *not* be what the subject is' (*SL*, 630/II,310) – it might with greater justification be regarded rather as evidence of the defectiveness of Hegel's interpretation.

Hegel claims, for instance, that all 'qualitative' or 'immediate' judgements – that is, judgements which contain a 'singular term' as their subject expression – are 'untrue' in the sense outlined, and he gives as an illustration the judgement 'this rose is red':

> If we say, 'this rose is red', then it lies in the copula 'is' that subject and predicate correspond with one another. The rose, however, as something concrete is not only red: it has an odour, a specific form, and many other determinations not contained in the predicate 'red'. The predicate, on the other hand, as an abstract universal, does not apply to the rose alone. There are other flowers and in general other objects which are red too. The subject and predicate in the immediate judgement thus touch, as it were, in a single point, but do not cover each other. (*En.L*, §172, add.)

What Hegel describes here, however, as a special defect of the 'immediate' judgement – namely, what we could call an 'excess' of determinations on the side of the subject and an 'excess' of extension on the side of the predicate – will in fact be characteristic, even constitutive, of all the other sorts of judgement which he discusses as well. Hence, for example, it is no less true in what Hegel calls a 'judgement of necessity' (such as 'Gold is a metal') or even what he calls a 'judgement of the notion' (namely, *normative* judgements, as when we judge some aesthetic object to be beautiful or some action to be good) that the subject implies determinations which are absent from the predicate and that the predicate is of wider extension than the subject.

Indeed, if it were not for a special class of judgements, which we could call 'judgements of identity',[8] we would have to conclude that *all* judgements have this 'defect' and that it is indeed precisely this 'defect' that makes them judgements. (A *definition* employs the form of judgement, but lacks the content, since it contains no real knowledge or knowledge-claim, but merely stipulates a rule for distributing signs over things.) Hegel acknowledges this elsewhere, leading him to the more frank assessment that the form of judgement must then simply be inappropriate for the expression 'truth' in his peculiar sense.[9]

10.3 THE HEGELIAN 'SYLLOGISM' AND THE SYLLOGISM

Analogously to his remarks concerning judgement, Hegel explains that 'Everything is a syllogism', because:

> everything is concept, and its existence is the distinction of the moments of the concept, such that its *universal* nature gives itself external reality through *particularity* and thereby, and as a negative reflection-into-self, makes itself an *individual*. Or, conversely, that which is actual is an *individual* which through *particularity* raises itself to *universality* and makes itself identical with itself. (*En.L*, §181)

Or, as in his more concise formulation from the 'greater' *Logic*: 'Everything is a *syllogism*, a universal that through particularity is united with individuality' (*SL*, 669/II, 359). Again, Hegel's account of inference or the 'syllogism' adds nothing to our knowledge of inference as a logical form. In fact Hegel is openly contemptuous of formal syllogistics. His purpose in considering the traditional figures of the syllogism and other rules of inference is merely to confirm the character of the relation between the more basic 'determinations of thought' whose 'self-development' allegedly issues in them. As with his treatment of judgement, if the syllogistic forms prove unsuitable for this purpose, then this will have to be attributed to some defectiveness on *their* part.

A case in point is Hegel's reaction to the fact that the so-called 'middle term' or *Mitte* of the second figure of the syllogism does not bear the same relation to its extremes as is the case in the first figure. In fact Hegel – who was of the opinion that the investigation of the various 'moods' of the syllogism, being strictly mechanical and 'intrinsically meaningless', had been 'justly consigned to oblivion' (*En.L*, §187) – seems not to be aware that it is just the first *mood* of the first figure that connects its extremes in the manner to which he accords the status of the 'general schema' of the syllogism as such (cf. *SL*,

667/II, 355).[10] In this first mood of the first figure, or the so-called syllogism in *Barbara*, the 'middle term' is the subject connected to the 'major term' in the 'major premiss' and the predicate connected to the 'minor term' in the 'minor premiss'. Hence it is of lesser extension than the 'major term' and greater extension than the 'minor' one, as in the textbook example:

> All men are mortal,
> Caius is a man,
> Therefore Caius is mortal.

It is this sequence of decreasing orders of generality as one moves from 'major' term to 'middle' to 'minor', or increasing orders if we reverse the sequence, that Hegel has in mind in describing the inference or 'syllogism' as 'a universal that through particularity [*Besonderheit*] is united with individuality'. 'Individuality,' Hegel elaborates,

> unites with universality through particularity; the individual is not universal immediately, but through the medium of particularity; and conversely the universal similarly is not immediately individual but descends to individuality through particularity. (*SL*, 667/II, 355)

Hence, Hegel symbolizes the 'general schema' of the syllogism as 'I-P-U' (or, in the original German, 'E-B-A' for '*Einzelheit*, *Besonderheit*, *Allgemeinheit*').

As the example makes clear, incidentally, it would often be more faithful to accepted logical usage to render Hegel's '*Besonderheit*' by 'specificity', rather than the 'particularity' typically favoured by his translators. Hegel's own usage of '*Besonderheit*' is, however, systematically ambiguous between the senses of 'specificity' and 'particularity' and indeed – analogously to what we found above with respect to his usage of '*Allgemeinheit*' – the course of his exposition frequently depends upon his paralogically exploiting this ambiguity.

In any event, after our previous discussion, it will not be hard to see how Hegel's schematic depiction of the syllogism suits his purposes. There is, however, in the first place, nothing which requires the minor premiss to be precisely a *singular* judgement. It is, yet again, merely *convenient* for Hegel to exploit what is in fact a fortuitous feature of the textbook example in order to identify the minor term with individuality. Leaving this first difficulty aside, the gravest problem with Hegel's schema is that it simply is not applicable to the actual structure of most syllogisms. Even in the first figure, the sequence of increasing orders of generality from minor to middle to major term only necessarily obtains on the condition that both the major and minor premiss are universal in scope (a singular judgement being a special case of a universal) and affirmative in quality. Thus, if the minor premiss is merely particular in scope, for instance, we get a syllogism such as 'All philosophers like syllogisms, Some Greeks are philosophers, Therefore some Greeks like syllogisms'. What this tells us is that the set of all Greeks and the set of all friends of syllogistics *intersect*, *not* that the former is a *subset* of the latter.

If, now, we move on to the *second* figure of the syllogism, in which the middle term serves to mediate not the *affirmation* of a connection between the major and the minor term but rather the *denial* of such a connection, the application of Hegel's 'general schema' leads to patent absurdities. Consider the following example of a syllogism in the second figure and the mood of *Cesare*:

No dog is literate,
All Oxford graduates are literate,
Therefore no Oxford graduate is a dog.

Hegel's 'general schema' implies that the major term in a syllogism subsumes the minor by way of the middle. If we were to insist upon the relevance of the schema to the cited instance, however, and *notwithstanding* the negative quality of the conclusion – the 'schema' is, after all, supposed to be 'general' – then it would follow that the set of all Oxford graduates must be a *sub*set of the set of all dogs.

Hegel acknowledges the problem. In his more elaborate discussion of the syllogism, he even gives some evidence of awareness that the conclusion in the second figure is a negation, and hence implies no 'unity' of the universal and the individual at all. But he does not treat it *as* a problem. 'The true meaning of the fact that this syllogism [that is, the second figure] does not correspond to the general form of the syllogism,' he writes, 'is that the general form has passed over into this syllogism since the truth of that form consists in its being a subjective and contingent connecting of terms' (*SL*, 676/II, 367). A more obvious conclusion to draw would be that the 'general form' of the syllogism is quite simply not what Hegel says it is. Such analyses have justly earned Hegel the wrath of modern logicians. And when Hegel turns to the consideration of inference schemata – for example, *modus ponens* – which do not contain any recognizable 'middle term', the paralogical acrobatics which he undertakes to indicate the relevance of his 'general schema' become more strenuous still.

10.4 'REAL' SYLLOGISMS AND 'LIVING' JUDGEMENTS

Hegel does not, however, merely make the general observation that, given what he claims is the basic structure of judgements and syllogisms and given what we are supposed already to know about 'everything that is', it (happily) turns out that everything 'is' a judgement and a syllogism, he also adduces some examples of *specific* things which are supposed to be 'syllogisms' and 'judgements'. In other words, he adduces some alleged empirical *exemplifications* of just *how* things 'are' syllogisms and judgements. There is a rather obvious inconsistency involved in Hegel's doing this: for if indeed only *some* things are suited to exemplifying the point, then it would seem rather that such instances serve in fact to *disprove* it. It would in general appear ill-advised to attempt to lend support by way of an inductive procedure to a claim which is supposed to hold apodictically of everything. Nonetheless, this does not stop Hegel from trying. I want simply to cite some of Hegel's examples here without much commentary, since in them we receive what is surely the fullest measure of the aberrations to which what I have been calling his 'logicization of the empirical' can lead.

Thus, recalling the status of the 'middle term' in Hegel's interpretation of the syllogism, it turns out that nature offers an albeit 'impotent' and 'naive' representation of the syllogism in the form of the *magnet*: 'which in the middle [*in der Mitte*], in its point of indifference, brings together its poles, which thereby in their difference are immediately one' (*En.L*, §24, add. 2; and cf. *En.*, §312). Systems of physical bodies held together by gravitational force in relations of strictly mechanical interaction are also 'syllogisms', with the central body (for instance, the sun in a solar system) representing the 'absolute middle term' (bodies orbiting around the centre constituting in turn 'relative middle terms' with respect to their own satellites).[11]

Hegel's attempt to elaborate upon this allegedly 'syllogistic' structure in his 'greater' *Logic* sets in particularly sharp relief the connection between such usage and his own peculiar realism of universals. Thus he writes:

> In the material world it is the *central body* that is the *genus* [*die Gattung*], but it is the *individual* universality of the single objects

> and their mechanical process . . . In the *spiritual* sphere the centre and unity with the centre assumes higher forms; but the unity of the concept and its reality, which here, to begin with, is mechanical centrality, must there too constitute the basic determination. (*SL*, 722/ II, 423–4)[12]

The bizarreness of Hegel's here identifying one object among others as the 'genus' – the 'individual universality' (*individuelle Allgemeinheit*) – of the rest is the sort of thing that usually remains unremarked by Hegel *aficionados* (whose attitude toward Hegel is often not unlike the attitude which Hegel claims is that of the 'ordinary man' toward nature: namely, wonderment). The secret of such mysteries is not, however, so hard to discover for those with the desire to know it. For, if not in physics, in Christian theology there is indeed a universality which takes shape as one individual among others: namely, the *Christ*.[13]

'Like the solar system' (this is Hegel's phrase) in the sphere of external nature, so too the *state* (understood as the unity of the citizen and civil society) in the sphere of objective '*Geist*' is supposed to be 'a system of three syllogisms', with each term taking the role of middle and then being relegated to the extremes, though the state itself (as *pars totalis*) represents here the one 'substantial middle term' (*En.L*, §198).

Returning to nature, we find that it offers evidence not only of 'real universals' and 'real syllogisms', but also of the 'reality' of judgement – for instance, in the 'shape' of a plant:

> the seed of a plant contains its particular, such as root, branches, leaves, etc., only this particular is at first only present in itself and is first posited insofar as the seed sprouts, which is to be considered as the judgement of the plant. (*En.L*, §166, add.)

Finally, both 'spirit' and nature are drawn upon by Hegel in order to illustrate the distinction between the simple negative judgement and the so-called 'negatively infinite' judgement. Again, it has to be remarked that what Hegel has to say concerning this distinction in its 'narrowly' logical significance is not only idiosyncratic, but opportunistic. It is, as always, the demands of 'the concept', of the *absolutely* unlimited, which his interpretation obeys – even if at the expense of grossly distorting the *specific* phenomena, in this case, the specific logical forms, which provide the supposed (at any rate, 'immediate') object of that interpretation. Thus Hegel insists that a simple negative judgement leaves the connection of subject and predicate undisturbed, while merely denying some particular 'determination' of the predicate; whereas the 'infinitely-negative judgement' represents the 'complete incompatibility of subject and predicate'. But this is utter nonsense. The negative quality of a negative judgement lies precisely and obviously in the fact that the connection of subject and predicate gets denied. Hegel tries to suggest that this is not the case by citing the example 'The rose is not red'. In such a judgement, Hegel points out, 'we merely deny the particular color of the flower, but not its color in general' (*En.L*, §173). Of course, he is right! Unfortunately, what gets predicated of the rose in *this* judgement is precisely the property of being *red* – this 'particular color' – and hence indeed it has been quite completely denied.

Presumably, if we instead denied of the rose the property of having any colour at all, this would, according to Hegel's criterion, constitute a 'negatively-infinite judgement' – as in 'The rose is not coloured'. But in fact this latter judgement, formally considered, is a simple negative judgement just like the prior one. There are surely not likely to be many roses of which this particular judgement will be true. But this is a function of the judgement's *content*, *not* its form.

In any event, Hegel is clearly more impressed with the alleged real 'modes of existence' of these logical forms than with the forms themselves. Consider the following series of observations:

> Crime may be considered as an objective example of the negatively-infinite judgment. Whoever commits a crime . . . does not . . . deny merely the particular right of someone else to one particular thing, but rather the other's right in general. . . . The civil-law suit on the contrary is an example of the simple negative judgment where merely the particular right is violated, while law in general is so far acknowledged. . . . Similarly, death is then a negatively-infinite judgment, as distinguished from disease, which is a simply-negative judgment. In disease, merely this or that function of life is checked or negated: whereas in death, as we ordinarily say, body and soul part, i.e. subject and predicate utterly diverge. (*En.L*, §173, add.)

I think that should be enough. As I have suggested, most of this amounts to little more than quackery and, though it might claim a place of great honour in a museum of philosophical curiosities, the reader might with some justification wonder what place it could possibly have in a study which is supposed, after all, to concern the logical structure of the Marxian theory of value. Prima facie nothing could be more foreign to Marx's theoretical project than Hegel's writing of logic into the world. Consequently, the almost universal practice of commentators on the 'Marx–Hegel relation' has been simply to avoid these more embarrassing traits of the Hegelian 'system' – the readily available alibi being, of course, the thesis of the separability from the latter of Hegel's 'dialectical method'. But the commentators have only sought to avoid such embarrassment at their own risk: at the risk, namely, of making Hegel's embarrassment their own. For, as will be seen directly, the doctrine of 'dialectical' contradiction is no 'materialist' kernel waiting to be extracted from the idealist shell of the Hegelian system: 'dialectical' contradiction is entirely of a piece with Hegel's idealism.

10.5 THE BASIC PRINCIPLE OF MATERIALISM

Having learned how in Hegel's logicized universe all things 'are' judgements and everything 'is' a syllogism (even if only some things turn out to be judgements and syllogisms in an exemplary fashion!), I hope it will now be easier to appreciate how the doctrine of 'dialectical' contradiction adheres to this same pattern. When Hegel enunciates his own 'law of contradiction' as against the traditional one, to the effect that 'everything is in itself contradictory', the stated maxim no less involves the projection of a logical category into the world than 'all things are a judgement' and 'everything is a syllogism'.[14] Whereas the ascription of real existence to syllogisms and judgements might seem like a mere eccentricity, however, the ascription of real existence to *contradiction*, or, more fundamentally, of contradictoriness to reality, is of far greater consequence.

The most straightforward and precise formulation of the traditional law of non-contradiction is that of Leibniz: every proposition is either true or false.[15] Note that such a formulation does not make any allusion to 'things' at all. Nonetheless, Hegel is quite right: this law is not *only* a logical principle, but also by implication an *onto*logical one. This is not to say that it prescribes anything *about* that which is: it tells us nothing – not even anything completely general, as in the case of Kant's 'principles of the pure understanding' – concerning what the objective world is 'like'. Nor does it commit us to admitting the existence of any particular or specific sort of object. The law merely, so to speak, serves notice that there *is* an objective world: a world which is completely independent of, because indeed *discontinuous from*, 'thought' or discourse, such that it can no more be a simple 'emanation' of the latter than the latter can be an 'emanation' of it.

In this sense, the law of non-contradiction should be regarded as the basic principle of all materialism, insofar as 'materialism' is here understood as a distinctive philosophical position. (Though it is frequently confused with philosophical 'materialism', Marx's, so to speak, socio-historical 'materialism' – or, in other words, his 'materialist conception of history' – is an entirely separate issue.[16]) Note that this implies a certain ecumenicism. The use of the law as our standard of what should count as 'materialism' selects out a broad family of doctrines. Kant's so-called 'transcendental idealism', for example, would qualify as a member – which should come as no surprise, since it was Kant, after all, who pronounced idealism a 'scandal to philosophy' and claimed as a special merit of his first *Critique* its having provided the 'refutation' of the latter.[17] The philosophical doctrine which is customarily described as 'materialism' within the Marxist tradition, however, clearly *would not*. It is precisely because the latter 'materialism', in strict analogy to the 'idealism' which it 'inverts', construes the material and the discursive as being continuous with one another – just which is made the epiphenomenon or attribute of the other is of no particular importance – that I have said it is more aptly described as an 'idealism of matter'.

To establish non-contradiction as a logical canon, as a norm to which discourse must conform in order to have objective validity (again, this is a necessary, but not sufficient condition), is to admit that there is something *apart from* discourse which is just what it is. This holds for the entire domain of the objective as such: which, to use Hegel's own idiom against him, has then the character of a '*Beisichseiende*' or 'self-enclosed existence' (though in this case that 'self-enclosed existence' is not thought but rather precisely the other of thought). And it holds likewise for any parcel or aspect of the objective which might be made discursively thematic by way of some linguistic classification. The latter can only be shown to *belong* in fact to the domain of the objective on the condition of its being accorded the general character of the objective – on the condition, that is, of its being accorded the character of objectivity. Supposing that this condition is fulfilled, then we can, of course, still say many things about a given theme which are false. But we are, at least, treating that theme objectively: we cannot say just anything about it that we please. In this sense, incidentally, the 'intra-discursive' criterion of logical consistency is not opposed to but rather coordinate with the demand that the 'truth-content' of a discourse be judged by its relation to *something else* which it is supposed to be about (though this is not to say, of course, that the relation in question should be one of 'correspondence').

To project contradiction into the material world is, then, to withdraw from the material world the aspect of its thought-independence: namely, to *idealize* it. The being which belongs to the finite things of the world is thus degraded to the status of a merely 'illusory being' or '*Schein*'; and '*veritable* being' ('*wahrhaftes Sein*' – and the significance of the appeal to 'veracity' in this context should by now be familiar to us) is reserved rather for thought, the 'true infinite', which 'shows itself' in this material 'world of appearances'. We will recognize in such a formulation, in contrast to the principle of philosophical materialism, the very counter-principle of Hegel's idealism – indeed the principle which Hegel claims is the principle of all idealism: viz. that which asserts the *nothingness* of the things of the world. The Hegelian 'law of contradiction' is but its necessary correlate. Though his Marxist sympathizers may not always be so lucid, Hegel himself was unequivocal about this. 'The absolute is,' Hegel writes, 'because the finite is the self-contradictory opposition, because it is *not* . . . [T]he inference runs thus: . . . the non-being of the finite is the being of the absolute' (*SL*, 443/II, 79).[18] The implication of all this with respect to the reception of Hegel in the Marxist tradition is obvious enough: the expression 'dialectical materialism' is an oxymoron.

10.6 WILT AND DIEGO: ON THE 'IDENTITY OF OPPOSITES'

Before going on to see in what empirical shape contradiction is supposed to be manifest in the world, I want first to examine in greater detail what Hegel has to say concerning his 'law of contradiction' in its general statement. In the *Encyclopedia* variant of his discussion of contradiction, the Hegelian maxim becomes 'everything is opposite', and gets stated in a polemic against the so-called 'Maxim of the Excluded Middle'. Though the terms of this polemic will already be quite familiar to us, it will be useful for what follows to cite a somewhat lengthy fragment of it here:

> Instead of speaking according to the Maxim of the Excluded Middle (which is the maxim of the abstract understanding), we should rather say: everything is opposite [*entgegengesetzt*]. Neither in heaven nor in earth, neither in the world of spirit nor that of nature, is there anywhere such an abstract 'either–or' as the understanding maintains. Everything that is anything is concrete, and thereby in itself different and opposite. The finitude of things consists then in the

> fact that their immediate existence does not correspond to what they essentially [*an sich*] are. Thus, in organic nature, for example, the acid is in itself [*an sich*] at the same time the base: i.e. its being is only this, to be related to its other. Hence, the acid is not, however, the tranquilly fixed thing of the opposition, but rather strives to posit itself as that which it is. Whatever moves the world, that is contradiction; and it is ridiculous to say that contradiction is unthinkable. (*En.L*, §119, add. 2)

In considering this passage, we should note, to begin with, the ambiguous 'then' in the sentence concerning the 'finitude of things'. We have already seen what is supposed to constitute the defectiveness of things in their immediacy: namely, that they fail to correspond to their 'universal'. But Hegel's reasoning here is at best completely circular (and, I suppose it has to be added in this context, in a strictly pedestrian way). The inherent contradictoriness of that which exists is apparently meant to serve as proof that things in the immediacy of their existence are 'untrue' and only 'true' in conforming to, or, more precisely, joining with, the 'universal' which is their essence. But that *wherein* this 'contradictoriness' is supposed to consist is left opaque. If we search elsewhere for clarification, we come across passages such as that cited above on the death of the living organism, which 'is the contradiction of being *in itself* the universal, the species, while immediately existing only as individual'. The alleged 'contradiction', then, only appears on the condition that we accept Hegel's conclusion as already proven: viz. that the individual 'is' in essence the species and hence *qua* individual not what it 'ought' to be.

Hegel endeavours to overcome this deficiency in his argument by appealing to a specific example: viz. that of the implicit identity of acid and base. Of course, as we have already noted, in the case of a claim which is supposed to hold apodictically, such a procedure by its very nature only serves to confute the claim it is called upon to support – in effect, it makes the deficiency of Hegel's argument still more glaring. But, even apart from this fact, it is evident that Hegel's example cannot bear the burden of demonstration which he places upon it. A base is only determinable *qua* base in opposition to acidity. This certainly does not imply, however, that the base must then 'in itself be the other of itself', as Hegel suggests. It merely implies that the *determinations* – not the *things* so determined – are wholly functions or, to use Hegel's idiom, 'moments' of their opposition.

Hegel's use of the acid–base example is characteristic of his argument more generally. He repeatedly appeals to reciprocally-determinate polar opposites – positive–negative, left–right, east–west, father–son, above–below, and so on – as putative evidence on behalf of his 'law of contradiction' and against the traditional one. But such an appeal is blatantly specious. Opposite determinations such as these do not 'demonstrate' that 'everything is in itself the opposite of itself', because they do not pertain to 'things' at all, but rather to relations in which things – in some cases, specific *sorts* of things, in others not – either stand to one another, supposing they are given, or can be placed, supposing an agent of comparison.

For example: if we take a particular axis as reference, then everything existing (let us just say for the sake of simplicity) in my field of vision is either to the right of that axis or to the left of it, and apart from the axis which separates and opposes them there is indeed no right or left as such. But this does not mean that *that which* happens to be to the left of me is thereby 'in itself its opposite', much less that its opposite is *that which* happens to be to my right, much less that the former must then 'pass into' the latter which it allegedly 'in itself' is! Since the determination *tall* is entirely a function of its opposition to the determination *short*, and is indeed no determination at all apart from its opposite, we could with as much justification claim that Wilt Chamberlain (being a tall person) is implicitly Diego Maradona (being a short person and hence Wilt's 'opposite'), and that Wilt must then '*im Diego übergehen*': Wilt and Diego are, to cite Hegel, nothing but 'the incessant transition of the one into the other'.

10.7 THE PARALOGICAL HINGE OF HEGEL'S EXPOSITION

I have not wanted here to ridicule Hegel simply for the pleasure of so doing. Though, in fact, given the vastness of Hegel's influence and the intellectually crippling effect that it has had, above all in the Marxist tradition, I think it is important that we not shield such nonsense behind the veil of a sobriety and respect which is supposed to be the due of all 'great philosophers'. Our examples, however, do not only expose Hegel's argument as nonsensical, they clearly reveal what is *the source* of the nonsense involved: Hegel makes no distinction between the *intension* of a term or 'determination' and its *extension*.

The consequences of this omission are compounded in some of the specific cases under examination by the fact that purely-relational opposite terms do not strictly speaking *have* any extensions. They can be *used* on particular occasions as components of referring expressions – as in 'the ceiling above me' or 'the door to the right' – but, unlike general empirical concepts, they have no extensions simply as such: there is no *class* of 'things which are to the west' or even, for that matter, of 'tall things' as opposed to short ones. The latter example clearly involves complexities which the former does not, since the term is subject to what linguists working within a transformational-grammar approach would call more severe 'selection restrictions'. In other words, whereas anything physical can be located with respect to other things in abstract space, only *some* things can be tall or short with respect to others. Nonetheless, the point remains: *nothing* is 'in itself' tall or short, hence *a fortiori* there is certainly not any tall or short thing which could 'in itself' be its opposite.

In contrast to such pure-relational opposites, what we could call 'empirical-relational opposites' present a somewhat different case. The acid–base opposition is an example of empirical-relational opposition: an example, as Hegel says, taken from the domain of inorganic nature. Father–son (obviously mother–daughter or, more generally, parent–progeny would work just as well, though Hegel's interest in the gospel no doubt predisposed him to the first) is an example from that of organic nature. We could also gather examples from the sphere of, so to speak, social being. Some of these are discussed by Hegel himself at various junctures, though curiously (and I suspect not accidentally) his treatment of them does not make allusion to the 'identity of opposites': such, for instance, are the oppositions of master/slave and sovereign/subject. Others, though not treated by Hegel, could have special importance for us: for instance, the opposition wage-labourer/capitalist.

In each of these examples, the relation involved is not, as was the case for the 'purely-relational' variant of opposites, merely a consequence of the placement of the things related in abstract space or of their comparison on the part of some subject of cognition external to them. Things can *be related* through the employment of purely-relational opposition, but the relation does not exist as such: to use a Hegelian idiom, it is a product merely of 'external reflection'. In the case of empirical-relational opposites, however, the relation is itself an existent relation. It is not only a relation *for us*, but it is a relation that bears upon the things themselves so opposed. In this sense, we could say that the opposition is 'internally-reflected' as a positive characteristic of the things which stand in the relation specified: that is to say, it is a positive determination of them (and for them, in the case of at least explicitly political relations, such as sovereign/subject, though not necessarily all social relations) so long as they stand in that relation. As a consequence, empirical-relational opposite terms do indeed have extensions. Thus, whereas it would be meaningless to speak of the set of all 'things to the east' as such, we can at least meaningfully speak of, say, the set of all 'acids' or that of all 'daughters' or that of all 'monarchs'. The latter sets might on some given occasion prove to be empty, but the former simply does not constitute a set at all.

This does not imply that if Hegel had limited his appeal to opposites of an empirical-relational sort he might have been on more solid ground. Indeed we first encountered Hegel's conflation of intensionality and extensionality in examining precisely the acid–base example. If we examine any other pair of empirical-relational opposites, we will be led to the same conclusion. It is, of course, true, for instance, that a parent is only a parent by virtue of the relation in which s/he stands to his or her child and, vice-versa, the child is only a child by virtue of the relation in which s/he stands to his or her parents: just as with other pairs of opposites, each of the opposed terms is a function of their opposition. Neither has any sense – and *sense, nota bene*, is a matter of *intension* (we are not speaking here, as Hegel would, of 'existence') – apart from this opposition. But this certainly does not mean, as Hegel seems to suggest, that some individual *who is*, for example, a father is thereby the 'opposite' of some individual *who is*, for example, his son,[19] much less that the two are 'identical' in their opposition.

Again, the expediency of such a conflation for Hegel's purposes is obvious: for in Christian doctrine *God the Father*, who is universal 'spirit', is identical with Himself in the particular form of his Son, the Christ. Marx, having 'leafed through' his Hegel[20] and possessing an evident literary flair, was happy enough to make use of this metaphoric in a pivotal passage of *Capital* explaining the distinction of capital-value from value as such.[21] Nonetheless, as it pertains to the more mundane sorts of fathers and sons, the claim clearly has very little application.

My contention is that the conflation of intensionality and extensionality represents not only an occasional error which happens to arise in the course of Hegel's exposition, but the paralogical hinge around which that exposition in general moves. As we have already had occasion to note, Hegel in fact regularly exploits ambiguities in the terms of his discourse: the most ample source of conceptual slippages throughout his exposition being precisely the three component terms of the 'syllogism'. Such ordinary conceptual slippages are easy enough to spot and they have been frequently pointed out, especially by critics of Hegel from the tradition of 'analytical' philosophy. But what we could call the endemically paralogical quality of Hegel's argumentation – the cause for the nausea which any but the most superficial reader of Hegel will know too well – does not derive from such ordinary conceptual slippages. This endemically paralogical quality does not derive from the occasional conflation of two senses of some given term, but rather from the continual conflation of sense and *reference* in the Hegelian treatment of virtually *any* term or 'determination'. It is the collapsing of this distinction that allows Hegel to slide effortlessly from claims which are quite legitimate as concerns the determinacy of *concepts* (for example, that the latter is a function of systematic differences and, at least in the case of certain special classes of concepts, opposition) to quite preposterous conclusions concerning the determinate existence of *things* (for instance, that 'everything is in itself contradictory'), thereby lending the aura of demonstrability to his idealism.

We discussed above the character of the method which Hegel claimed to have followed in the development of his system; or rather, the character of the method which as 'absolute form' is supposed to develop *itself* into that system. But just as with Marx, with Hegel too we have to be suspicious of methodological indications. Whatever Hegel may have said or thought on the matter, in fact the regime followed by his argument is constituted not so much by a unique logical canon as by a distinctive *para*logical tendency.

Let me be more precise. It would be too strong a claim to suggest that *all* of Hegel's 'transitions' are paralogical in character. A serious defence could even be made of the alleged immanence of the first systematic 'transition' from abstract being to abstract nothingness: in other words, of the validity of Hegel's demonstration of the identity of these supposed opposites. I want to suggest, however, that thereafter all those 'transitions' are paralogical in Hegel's exposition which give even just the mere appearance of being logical at all. Otherwise – and this is the aspect of Hegelian argumentation which has been more widely acknowledged and condemned – Hegel's 'transitions' exhibit an unmistakeably *teleological* character. We already have noted the teleological appeal made in the 'transition' from the 'idea' in itself to the 'idea' in its externality: or, in other words, from the 'sphere' of 'logic' to that of nature.[22] In such cases, the alleged 'necessity' of the transitions in question is always just an expression of the requirements of 'absolute subjectivity': namely, that it should gain objective form *in order to* know itself therein and thus realize its 'freedom'.[23]

10.8 THE OPPOSITE OF LIMITATION

Let us return for a moment to Hegel's example of the acid–base opposition. I have tried to show that such an example is not in fact, as Hegel suggests, indicative of the inherently contradictory quality of finite existence. Suppose, however, we simply *grant* to Hegel that base and acid are each implicitly the other, and even that each is thus compelled in reality to 'pass into' its other. *Still* such an example would not be adequate to the task which Hegel assigns it. Remember that the inherent contradictoriness of things was supposed for Hegel to serve as evidence that in their immediacy (that is, in their particularity) they are not what they 'ought to be'; and what they 'ought to be' is, namely, 'the universal' which allegedly constitutes their essence. I criticized Hegel above for applying the moral category of obligation to material things in order to assert the 'power' of 'the universal' over them, and in the 'greater' *Logic* it is in fact precisely in his discussion of 'the ought' that Hegel first alludes to the acid–base example.

But what exactly does such an example prove? If a base has 'passed into' acid, then it is *acid*, and if it has passed back into base, then it is *base*. No 'sublation' of the merely finite determinations is brought about through such oscillation: the limitation of the base has not been 'overcome', as Hegel insists it should be, but merely traded in for the opposite limitation. Perhaps it will be suggested that in all this passing back and forth Hegel has in mind just *logical* transition. But in such examples Hegel expressly does *not* have in mind *merely* logical transition. 'If . . . in the case of such general propositions framed by the understanding, such as that limitation cannot be transcended,' Hegel warns, 'thought will not apply itself to finding out what is implied in the concept, then it can be directed to actuality, where such propositions show themselves to be the most unactual' (*SL*, 134/I, 145).

The problems with the example, however, are greater still. Suppose, now, that we simply granted to Hegel not only that acid and base 'pass into' one another, but even that in so doing they shed their limitations and resolve themselves into 'the universal'. What 'universal' exactly would *that* be? Opposite determinations do not even in any obvious sense *have* a *genus* to which they belong. This is precisely a peculiarity of them as against general empirical concepts (or, in other words, concepts of 'natural kinds'), and it is indeed a correlate to the observation we made above to the effect that their pure-relational variety per se have no extension.[24] What, for instance, is the 'universal' of east and west? North? Perhaps it will be pointed out in Hegel's defence that what he calls '*the* universal' is not simply *a* universal. And, as we have seen, this is right. But since Hegel chooses to call the absolutely unlimited 'the universal', just like *a* universal (leaving aside that there are strong reasons to object to this treatment of the unlimited under the category of 'universality'), he creates for himself the opportunity of conflating the two. This is precisely what occurs, for instance, in the argument we have examined concerning the finitude of living things, where *a* universal, viz. the species, is used to represent the 'power' of '*the*' universal vis-à-vis the individual biological organism.

What, then, exactly is the point of Hegel's appealing to the acid–base example? How is it even supposed to relate to the claim on behalf of which he adduces it? Well, the resolution of this mystery consists in yet another conflation: a petitio principii of even more imposing ornateness than those upon which we have already commented. Consider the following passage which precedes Hegel's appeal to the acid–base opposition in his discussion of 'the ought' (once again, Kant is the obvious antagonist here):

> great stress is laid on the limitations of thought, of reason, and so on, and it is asserted that the limitation *cannot* be transcended. To make such an assertion is to be unaware that the very fact that something is determined as a limitation implies that the limitation is already transcended. For a determinateness, a limit [*Grenze*], is determined as a limitation [*Schranke*] only in opposition to its other in general, that is, in opposition to its *unlimited* [*sein Unbeschränktes*]; the other of a limitation is precisely the *being beyond* it. (*SL*, 134/I, 145)

Now, the concept of the limited or the determinate is fully a function of its opposition to the concept of the *un*limited or *in*determinate. There is not, of course, anything which could be given in experience corresponding to this latter concept, nor even anything which could be related to something else by virtue of its application on some particular occasion. In this sense, the opposition in question is not a relational opposition at all, neither empirical nor pure. Indeed, for this reason, it might be better to call the opposite of the concept of the limited not a 'concept', but rather, following Kant, a 'transcendental idea'. We can *think* the absolutely unlimited: namely, by generalizing the procedure whereby we can think some specific limitation as absent (whereby, that is to say, we can abstract from the latter). But thinking *every* possible limitation as absent, there is no longer any *object* which can thus be thought. Whereas we can, then, oppose the *concept* of the limited or determinate to the *idea* of the absolutely unlimited, this does not imply that there is some *class* of things which are limited and determinate as opposed to some *class* of things which are unlimited and indeterminate (no more than the fact that difference is the opposite of identity implies that there is some class of things which are 'identical' as opposed to some class of things which are 'different').

To the degree that Hegel seems to suggest the contrary, he is confusing intension and extension. Hegel is right that the determinacy of the concept of the determinate in general consists in its opposition to the indeterminate – but this tells us nothing at all about what the determinacy of *some specific* determination might consist in. If we consider some thing simply under the aspect of its being *in some way* limited without specifying that limitation, of its simply somehow being determinate without specifying the determination – in short, of its being *finite* – then the opposite of the aspect under which we are considering it will clearly be the 'condition' of being *beyond* limitation as such, of being, in short, *infinite*. (I place the word *condition* in quotes for the obvious reason that such a 'condition' could only be the 'condition' of being *un*conditioned.) But the same does not apply to anything considered under the aspect of some *specific* limitation which makes it some specific *sort* of finite thing (it being understood that any given thing can in fact be classified into various sorts). Now, suppose we consider some thing under the aspect of some specific determination by virtue of which it belongs to some specific sort, rather than considering it simply as a specific thing of *whatever* sort. Under this supposition, it is not even necessary, first, that the determination in question will have any 'opposite' and, second, if it does, that *specific* opposite cannot be the 'unlimited' as such (it will have in fact to be some sort of empirical-relational opposite) – hence the speciousness of Hegel's treating the 'unlimited' as the opposite of *a*, i.e some specific, limitation: as 'its unlimited'.

It is this conflation of the opposite of finitude as such, viz. infinity, the opposite of *every* specificity, viz. the 'absolutely' universal, with the opposite, so to speak, of some *specific* specificity, that sustains Hegel in the otherwise unthinkable logical feat of identifying *acidity* with unlimitedness! '*Since*' the base as something merely particular is constituted by the 'obligation' to overcome its limitation, hence it 'passes into' its opposite, namely acidity, but, 'since' the 'opposite' of the base simply *qua* some limited, i.e. finite, thing is the absolutely *un*limited, hence this serves as sufficient proof that the base is 'in itself' identical with 'the universal'.[25] In the event that his readers have not succeeded in following the subtleties of his reasoning, Hegel concludes his argument by recapitulating it in much blunter form. 'The reference to the wholly abstract universal', he writes, 'suffices against the equally abstract assurance that limitation cannot be transcended, or, again, even the reference to the infinite in general suffices against the assurance that the finite cannot be transcended' (*SL*, 135/I, 147).

10.9 'CONTRADICTION' BEFORE JUDGEMENT

Even if we leave aside the question of the *legitimacy* of Hegel's 'law of contradiction' (and I take this question to be settled), what is especially conspicuous about Hegel's presentation of the 'law' is the logical slipperiness of its formulation. Indeed, the very fact that this alleged 'law' is given two quite distinct statements in the *Science of Logic*, on the one hand, and the *Encyclopedia*, on the other – in the 'greater' *Logic* being formulated with reference to contradiction proper ('everything is in itself contradictory') and in the *Encyclopedia* with reference to contrariety ('everything is opposite') – is symptomatic of the slipperiness I have in mind. In both of the passages expounding upon the 'law' which we have cited, Hegel begins by associating whichever of the terms he includes in its general statement with *difference* (either paratactically, as we have seen in the passage from the 'greater' *Logic*, or merely disjunctively, as can be verified by conferring the *Encyclopedia* variant) and ends with a remark employing the other term.

In the *Encyclopedia*, having exchanged contrariety and contradiction in this way, Hegel then makes a rather feeble attempt to give this slippage the mantle of systematic rigour by designating 'contradiction' as 'posited opposition' (whereas in the 'greater' *Logic* he writes instead of opposition becoming 'posited contradiction' [*SL*, 439/II, 75]). *Outside* of the Hegelian context, however, the categories of *contrariety* and *contradiction* are not normally so easily substitutable for one another – or at least they are not where there is any interest in distinguishing what is meaningfully distinct. Even where logical precision is not of any special importance, neither at any rate is normally substitutable for *difference*!

Now, it could be suggested in Hegel's defence that the subject-matter of his treatment of the so-called 'determinations of reflection' or 'essentialities' is precisely the sequence of dialectical 'transitions' among these categories: *identity* 'passes into' its opposite, viz. *difference*, and this opposition is then 'sublated' in the category representing the 'unity of identity and difference', viz. *opposition*, which finally then yields to *contradiction* (let us say, in a generous spirit, as 'posited opposition'). A 'Hegelian' might, then, conclude that in light of the conceptual 'development' which precedes it and allegedly even issues in it, Hegel's employment of the categories as interchangeable in his treatment of contradiction is entirely justified.

Well, in the first place this conclusion does not follow: even if Hegel has indeed been able to demonstrate the 'necessity' of the 'dialectical transitions' among the categories, it does not follow that we ought then to be able to *apply* them interchangeably. In the second place, if such a conclusion did follow, clearly it would depend upon the legitimacy of the 'transitions' in question. A detailed examination of these 'transitions' would confirm that they are no less specious than Hegel's other alleged 'transitions'. Readers whose appetite for unpacking intricate nonsense is not yet satiated are invited to refer to the appendix to this chapter for an analysis of the first 'transition' in the series: viz. that from identity to difference. In any event, the very fact that *contradiction* is even just *included* in this series is symptomatic of the slippage with which we have been here concerned.[26] For *concepts* or 'determinations' considered simply *in themselves* ought not even to be susceptible of 'contradicting' one another. It is only by their being attributed to a common subject – namely, in *judgements* – that concepts might give rise to contradiction. But Hegel derives his alleged 'law of contradiction' before even discussing judgement.

10.10 THE 'REALITY' OF CONTRADICTION

Now, according to the protocols of what I have called Hegel's substantialization of the logical, we know that a given logical form is supposed in the realms of nature and 'spirit' to acquire empirical forms of manifestation. Like the syllogism and judgement, contradiction has to be shown to have reality in the 'so-called world': the contradictoriness which is alleged to affect all finite *concepts* ought to be detectable in that *to which* such concepts refer. We have already repeatedly come across the empirical form in which the allegedly contradictory character of 'the finite' is supposed to be manifest: namely, in the fact that it *perishes*.[27] Whether the finite thing in question is, as in the realm of 'spirit', the individual 'natural' will at variance with the 'general will' or, as in the realm of nature, the particular biological organism 'at variance with' its species – or even, it will be recalled from Chapter 3 above, the individual point in abstract space! – everything merely finite is not what it 'ought' to be and 'hence', at the very least, it cannot remain what it is. The 'reality' of contradiction is, in short, identified by Hegel with the phenomena of change. 'We are aware that everything finite,' he writes,

> instead of being stable and ultimate, is rather mutable and transient, and this is nothing else than the dialectic of the finite, by which the finite, as in itself the other of what it is, is forced beyond its immediate being and turns into its opposite. (*En.L*, §81, add. 1)

We have already discussed at length all the paralogisms condensed into this one bewildering statement and I will not rehearse them yet again. I merely want to call attention to the fact that this banality in which Hegel's doctrine of 'dialectical' contradiction issues is none other than the banality from which 'Hegelian Marxism' of an historicist sort departs. That said, and given what we have discovered here concerning the significance and consequences of the doctrine of 'dialectical contradiction' when regarded strictly as a logical canon, it would, if anything, have been a far worse fate – and this is a fate which I fear is being tempted by the more sophisticated versions of 'Hegelian Marxism' which have arisen in recent years – had Marx in fact developed his economic theory according to the requirements of such a canon.

Nonetheless, I want now to suggest that if Marx was guilty of 'misrecognizing' the order of his own analysis under the title of 'dialectics', this misrecognition was not simply a mistake. There are reasons why Marx found himself 'coquetting' with a Hegelian 'mode of expression': especially so in his analysis of the value-form. These reasons have to do not with any 'methodological' choice or predisposition, nor even with simple flirtatiousness, but rather with the peculiar character of the objectivity which belongs to economic value: with the character of what Marx called the 'value-objectivity' – the '*Wertgegenständlichkeit*' – of commodities.

APPENDIX: HEGEL'S 'TRANSITION' OF IDENTITY INTO DIFFERENCE

Hegel often presents a linguistic paradox as sufficient refutation of some position against which he is polemicizing: in other words, he claims the position is untenable because it is 'unsayable'. This is the tenor, for instance, of his critique of the distinction between pure being and nothing: 'It is the common opinion that being is the sheer other of nothing and that nothing is clearer than their absolute difference, and nothing seems easier than to be able to state it. But it is equally easy to convince oneself that this is impossible, that it is *unsayable*' (*SL*, 92/I, 95). It is likewise the strategy he follows in the famous critique of the certainty of sense-data or 'sense-certainty' in the *Phenomenology*. The alleged 'transition' of *identity* into *difference* involves an analogous procedure. Thus, as against the adherents of the maxim of identity, who, according to him, 'are given to stating that identity is not difference, but that identity and difference are different', Hegel writes:

> They do not see that in this very assertion they are themselves saying that *identity is different*; for they are saying that identity is different from difference; since this must at the same time be admitted to be the nature of identity, their assertion implies that identity, not externally, but in its own self, in its very nature, is this, to be different. (*SL*, 412/II, 41)

All that this amounts to, however, is the fact that *identity* and *difference* are what I have been calling 'pure-relational opposite concepts': they are indeed, to be more precise, what we could call 'pure relational opposites of the understanding', since their application (unlike say, right/left or above/below) is not dependent upon the conditions of sensible intuition. Nothing is identical *in itself*, no more than anything is different *in itself*: rather something is self-identical only *relative* to that which it is different *from*, and its being self-identical *means* precisely that it cannot be the same as that which is different from it.

In his remarks, Hegel is again clearly confusing the intensional content of the concept of identity with the meaning of its *application* on some occasion. The fact that the *concept* of identity is different from the concept of difference in no way implies that some object identified as such will, besides being identical with itself, also be 'identical' with *that which* is different from it. Nor does it *even* imply that the property of its self-identity will be 'identical' with its property of being different from that which is different from it. Now, the latter claim happens to be *true*: it follows from the character of the determinations identity/difference as relational opposites, in conjunction with the fact that difference is a specifically *symmetrical* relation. The contrast with a pair of relational opposites which are *not* symmetrical should help to clarify this point. Thus: if A is a parent, then this implies that there is at least one other thing, B, which is the offspring of A, but *not* that A is in turn the offspring of B. If, however, there is something, A, which is different from some other thing, B, then B must in turn be different from A. The identity of A will consist precisely in its being different from whatever is different from it.

Hegel's claim, then, interpreted as a claim concerning the reciprocally-determinate properties of identity and difference, is correct. But what is conspicuous is that the argument he makes on its behalf is, nonetheless, specious. If we apply the opposition identity/difference to the concepts of *identity* and *difference* themselves (in other words, exploiting the self-reflexive possibilities of discourse, the character of these concepts will be the objective theme of the claim we are about to make), then it turns out that the *concept* of identity has the (relational) property of being different from the *concept* of difference: as Hegel says, 'identity is different from difference'. This is in fact a rather pathetic and uninformative observation, since the concept of identity also has the properties of being different from the concepts of, say, *charity*, *sugar* and *baseball*. But, in any event, this observation certainly does not prove (though, in fact, other considerations do) that the (relational) *property* of being identical or identity is 'in itself' the same as the (relational) property of being different or difference. Hegel can only propose such a deduction by virtue of his characteristically bizarre procedure of attributing to objective conditions the properties of the concepts by which we allude to them. In this case, happily, the results are not too damaging, since the claim happens to be true. In other cases, however, as when Hegel, for instance, concludes that 'the understanding' falsifies the nature of the infinite by opposing it to the finite, hence presenting it as a 'finite infinite',[28] or when he concludes that the 'universal' is a particular species of itself, since it is particular as against the particular,[29] the consequences are more distressing.

Part IV

The Objectivity of the Economic

> Here we are right in the middle of Germany! Even while speaking political economy, we are going to have to speak metaphysics.
>
> (Marx, *The Poverty of Philosophy*)

11 A Fortuitous Theoretical Isomorphism

'Money', Marx writes, 'is God among commodities' (*Gr.*, 221/148). This is to say that money is nothing other than a *real universal*: a generality, viz. the common character of all commodities as 'exchange-values', which has acquired independent existence in the form of some determinate commodity or 'use-value'. It is an ideality 'realized' in material shape. More precisely, what is implied by Marx's comment is that money is the 'Christ' of the commodity world. It is 'objective spirit': the 'supra-sensible' essence of commodities become sensuous nature as itself a commodity, exchange-value become use-value – like God become man, the 'God-man' of the Gospels. The universal value-character of commodities is manifest in their similarity to money, 'just as the sheeplike character of the Christian is manifest in his similarity to the Lamb of God' (*CI*, 143/66).[1]

The metaphor of the Christ is in fact only perfectly suitable to specifically *commodity*-money, which is the sort of money that Marx – whether for essential or merely historical reasons will not occupy us here – clearly regards as basic. The increasing, so to speak, 'attenuation' of money's physical presence, viz. first in the form of token-money and then so-called 'credit-money', will be touched upon below. Though I will argue that money cannot serve to release value, the 'spirit' of commodities, from their diverse bodily enclosures without itself acquiring at least some material incarnation. Hence the gospel of the money-commodity reveals an economic truth which, however remote it may seem from the technical complexities of modern currency systems, remains relevant for understanding these too.

It is not so surprising, then, that Marx drew upon the resources of Hegel's 'logic', an esoteric philosophy with deep roots in Christian mysticism, when elaborating his value theory. For between the Hegelian 'idea' and the real form of economic value, viz. money, there is an unmistakable isomorphism. The value phenomena which constitute the immediate object of Marx's theory happen to exhibit just that structure which Hegel treats as constitutive of objectivity as such. This is a remarkable *accident* – and nothing more than that. To borrow some language from biology, the apparent similarities between the Marxian analysis of value and the Hegelian exposition of 'the concept' are analogical in character, not homological. This is to say that they are not the external sign of any intrinsic relation.

Of course, a formal similitude between theories which would be judged accidental according to immanent criteria, might itself be explicable on some other level – just as in biology anatomical 'analogies', while not explicable by genetic kinship, are normally explicable in functional terms. If we cared to engage in historical speculations, it could then be suggested, as Marx indeed suggests in various places, that the ideological dominance of Christian doctrine is precisely a consequence of its capacity to provide a suitably mystified representation of certain essential features of commodity production. Thus the theological motifs which govern Hegelian 'logic' would be but alienated ideological 'reflections' of the real alienation of subjective capacities which occurs under conditions of commodity-production and which achieves objective expression precisely in the form and power of money.

If this were so, it would turn out that the fundamental similitude is in fact between the structure of the imaginary Christian cosmos – above all, by virtue of its monotheism and its, in Marx's words, 'cult of man in the abstract' (*C*I, 172/93) – and the real world of commodity exchange. The similitude of the Hegelian and Marxian discourses would only be an incidental effect of the latter.[2] To pursue Marx's hypothesis of an adaptive 'fit' of Christianity to commodity production, we would have to return to indications from his early critique of Feuerbach.[3] Let it just be noted in passing here that both the recent spread of Christianity to areas newly subordinated to the rule of the market – of which the astonishing influence of evangelical groups among indigenous peoples in contemporary Peru is an instance – and its revival in areas where the rule of the market has been recently restored lend clear prima facie support to such an hypothesis.

In any case, whatever explanation might be given for the formal similarity between the Marxian analysis and Hegelian exposition, such similarity does not have any *cognitive* significance. This is what is crucial for our purposes (and this is what needs to be kept in mind in order correctly to evaluate the air of importance which recent pronouncements on the matter have tended to assume). In suggesting that the isomorphism between the two is theoretically fortuitous, I certainly do not mean to be so rash as to deny the massive evidence of the influence which Hegel's writings exercised over Marx, including, as has been frequently noted, during the period of his mature economic investigations (though it should not be forgotten that simply assembling the evidence of such influence tells us nothing at all about its effects). Indeed, the merely analogical character of the relation in question is made all the more difficult to recognize precisely by the real and immediate historical connection between the theoretical corpora being compared – whereas the analogical character of any similitude between, say, Buddhist philosophy and Derridian 'deconstruction' might be more readily conceded (though perhaps I am being overly optimistic in this regard).

To say that Marx's value-analysis and Hegel's exposition of 'the concept' merely exhibit a certain analogy, is to say that while Marx indeed makes use of logical formulae bearing an unmistakable Hegelian stamp, nonetheless the *content* of these formulae has been fundamentally transformed by the use which Marx makes of them.[4] Indeed, I will argue here that it is only in the use which Marx makes of them that these formulae for the first time *acquire* an unambiguously rational content – whereas in Hegel's usage, either (as with the 'unity of opposites') they oscillate between a rational 'second-order' sense and a mystical 'first-order' one or they are strictly mystical in connotation.

The presence of apparently Hegelian logical formulae in Marx's value-analysis does not, then, entail that the 'logic' of this analysis in general – much less the entire 'logic of *Capital*' – is 'Hegelian' or 'dialectical' in character. In light of the findings of the previous chapter, it should not now be difficult to appreciate the dire consequences this would have for Marx's analysis were it so. It has become something of a minor vogue of late to attempt to 'reconstruct' *Capital* as an unbroken series of intertwining 'dialectical syllogisms': as if the discourse of proof in *Capital* would be incomplete and insufficient without appeal to some 'logic' which is not to be found precisely in that discourse itself; and as if Marx's analysis were constrained to follow a conceptual ordering determined by the requirements of this 'logic', rather than the conceptual ordering proper to the analysis (in this sense, its own immanent 'logic') being determined by the requirements for grasping its specific subject-matter. The intellectual poverty of such exercises lies in just that sort of formalistic ordering of pre-given materials which, ironically and as we shall see further on, inspired Marx's explicit rejection of Hegelian philosophy in the first place.

I propose to call the emerging current of academic opinion on the 'Marx–Hegel relation' to which I have just made allusion the 'new' Hegelian Marxism: viz. in contrast to the 'old' or traditional Hegelian Marxism of the historicist variety discussed in Part I. In order to set in relief the difference between my own account of the substance of this relation and the account offered by the 'new' Hegelian Marxists, it will be useful to distinguish between, on the one hand, what I have been referring to thus far simply as Hegelian '*formulae*' and, on the other, Hegelian *patterns of argumentation*. As for the latter, despite the exertions of the 'new' Hegelian Marxists to demonstrate the contrary, Marx does not, thankfully, employ them much in *Capital* and not *at all* in any theoretically decisive context. The alleged 'dialectical transition' from money to capital – widely celebrated and indeed, inasmuch as *Capital* is concerned, wholly contrived by the 'new' Hegelian Marxists – is a case in point. As for the former, I am proposing that it is precisely in the use of certain expressions and certain formulations, even what we might call a certain *syntax*, that Marx's discourse exhibits a definite similitude with Hegel's. In other words and simply put, it is in the way that Marx says what he says, *not* in his manner of *justifying* it, that the similarity to Hegel is to be detected. In this connection, Marx's remark about 'coquetting' with Hegel's 'peculiar mode of expression' is in fact very much to the point.

Given what has been written directly above and in chapter 4 concerning the distinctive objectivity of value and the money-form, the Hegelian formulae which are here in question will not be difficult to surmise: the formula of the 'unity of opposites', for instance (though, *nota bene*, not that of the '*identity* of opposites' which Marx rarely if ever employs as such[5]), that of 'real universality', and that according to which – and here it is a matter precisely of a certain syntax and not just of an isolated expression – 'the particular' (or some particular) is but a 'form of appearance' or 'realization' of 'the universal' (or some universal). What is perhaps difficult is to comprehend how formulae whose mysticism in their original Hegelian context we have just finished exposing should be given a rational scientific employment in the discourse of Marx's value analysis. But in light of what I am suggesting is the transformation undergone by the content of these formulae through Marx's employment of them – in light of the fact that in Marx's analysis they are given precisely a *specific* content, that they are related to a *specific* object – the legitimate usage which Marx makes of them in no way entails the legitimacy of their original Hegelian usage. Indeed, it entails the contrary.

The very significance attaching to these formulae in the Hegelian context depended upon their application precisely *not* being restricted to any particular object domain. They were supposed, after all, to capture essential features of the '*absolute*'. This is why they are introduced by Hegel precisely in '*logic*', in the science of the *pure* 'determinations of thought'. When they subsequently reappear in the concrete sciences of nature and 'spirit', this is because the objects of those sciences are supposed to be revealed as but so many objectifications of thought and hence such objects are in their own nature supposedly bound to reflect the determinations of the latter. Indeed, the putative demonstration that objects in their specificity fulfil this obligation constitutes nothing less than the Hegelian manner of 'explaining' them.

This basic pattern will already be sufficiently familiar to us from chapter 9, though we should recall in somewhat greater detail the solidarity of the formulae here in question with it. This will help us then to bring out more clearly the nature of the transformation they undergo when removed from this context by Marx. The fact that the pure 'determinations of thought' are, according to the Hegelian conception of 'philosophical science', supposed to be rediscovered in every object domain is just the converse of the fact that these 'determinations' are in Hegel's treatment of them given an *ontological* or *metaphysical* interpretation. That this should be so, for instance, with regard to the most basic 'determinations' expounded in the first subdivision of the *Logic* is uncontroversial enough, since, as the title of the first subdivision, 'The Doctrine of Being', implies, its immediate subject-matter is nothing other than the traditional subject-matter of ontology. But that it should likewise be so with regard to the more complex 'determinations' covered in the *third* subdivision, 'The Doctrine of the Concept', is more peculiar, since it is precisely and only in fact there – indeed, it is only in the first subsection, entitled 'The Subjective Concept', of the third subdivision – that Hegel in *his* 'Logic' presents the elements of what is customarily called 'logic': viz. concepts (or, as Hegel puts it, 'the concept as such'), judgement and inference (or 'the syllogism').

As we have seen, however, he does not present them in the customary way. Thus, instead of analysing these logical forms, he simply takes their formal analysis for granted (indeed, as we have also seen, his argument, such as it is, frequently depends upon taking *too much* for granted) and interprets them as in each case bearing a metaphysical significance. Strangely enough, it turns out that they are all supposed, in effect, to bear the very *same* significance. This monotonic – one is tempted to say 'monomaniacal' – reduction of the heterogeneity of the logical material considered is itself a symptom of the mystical character of Hegel's treatment: all the logical forms, as indeed all determinate forms without exception, are called upon by Hegel to testify to one substantial – to *the* one substantial – 'truth'.[6]

Resuming our findings from the last part, we can summarize this 'truth' to which the logical forms testify as follows: *everything* is a universal which by manifesting its dominion over a field of particulars makes itself into an individual. (Here 'individual' is presumably to be interpreted in the sense of the '*Beisichseinde*': in other words, of a 'self-enclosed' totality. Though, as with so much else in Hegel's exposition, his usage of 'individual' [*das Einzelne*] and 'individuality' [*Einzelheit*] is systematically ambiguous and his argument frequently depends upon the exploitation of this ambiguity – as is indeed confirmed by the properly Hegeloid inference to follow.) Every existing individual – here now presumably in the, so to say, *dominant* connotation of the '*Auseinander*' (or, in other words, of 'bare' particularity) – is thus in essence universal.

This was, it will be recalled, precisely what Hegel claimed to be the basic 'meaning' of judgement as such, considered in abstraction from the determinate content of any given judgement: viz. 'The individual is the universal'. The formal structure of 'the syllogism' only added to this the aspect of mediation between universality and individuality: namely, by way of the slippery '*Besonderheit*'. It is indeed on account of the lack of such mediacy in the form of judgement – the '*Starrheit*' or 'rigidity' of the copula *is* – that Hegel disqualifies the latter as an appropriate vehicle for expressing 'the truth', declaring the form of judgement to be 'contradictory' (because in its immediacy the individual is *not* the universal) and 'dialectical' (which is to say here, inherently unstable). Hence – viz. according to the peculiar order governing the Hegelian discourse – judgement must pass over into 'the syllogism' as the more adequate form and indeed its own 'truth'.[7]

Invested with the metaphysical significance here indicated, the 'moments' of the syllogism are supposed to lay down the very structure of actuality. Hegel's substantial construal of the 'unity' and/or 'identity' of opposites belongs to this same arrangement:[8] since whatever specific oppositions might be constitutive of specific sorts of thing (and specific oppositions are indeed thus constitutive in the case of what I have called 'empirical-relational opposites'), these specific opposites are in Hegel's exposition assimilated to the allegedly fundamental opposition which is supposed to be inherent in finite things simply as such, viz. the opposition between their particular forms of existence and their universal 'essence'.[9] This is why, according to Hegel, it is not only the case that everything is 'opposite', but also that everything is 'contradictory': since the existence of things necessarily deviates from their essence.

Insofar as it is in fact the identity of *sorts*, an *intensional* identity, which is at issue, the former claim could be given a, so to speak, *profane* interpretation (even if it would require some modification before it became a defensible one). The latter claim, however, is pure mysticism – as the consequences which Hegel draws from it make clear. Things in their empirical existence, viz. as particulars, not being what they 'ought to be', they are – 'thus' – destined to *lose* their particular embodiment: to 'perish' (*zugrunde zu gehen*) or to 'return to their ground' (*zuruck in Grund zu gehen*), viz. 'the universal'. In so doing, they bear witness to the fact that only the latter, the 'true infinite', enjoys 'intrinsic being' and that their apparent independence was all along merely a 'show'. And so on. That whatever coherence such 'logical' formulae have in Hegelian discourse is inseparable from the thoroughgoing idealism of the Hegelian system should not require any further demonstration. As we have had numerous occasions to confirm, the reality of 'universals' in the Hegelian context strictly entails the *ir*reality, the 'nothingness', of the particulars in which they gain existence or 'appear': which is to say that the actuality of 'the idea' entails the 'nothingness' of the material world; the actuality of the singular object of *Geist* (viz. itself), the nullity of the manifold objects of sensuous intuition.[10]

Now, as is well known and as has already been touched upon here, Marx's youthful response to Hegel's mysticism was, in effect, to take the Hegelian formulae as is and 'place them on their feet'. This procedure of 'inversion', as it has come to be known – though it would be more exact to say '*re*-inversion', since it is in Hegel precisely that the correct order of things is, according to Marx, supposed to be represented in inverted form, viz. as 'standing on its head' – has, of course, been the subject of extensive commentary. This commentary has, however, for the most part been so generic in style, rarely venturing beyond paraphrase of Marx's own words, that it has obscured the actual heterogeneity of theoretical forms taken by Marx's work of 'overturning' Hegel in his early philosophical texts. These forms range from demystifying critical analysis of Hegel's treatment of a specific subject-matter (viz. in the *Critique of Hegel's Doctrine of the State* of 1843, to which we will return momentarily); by way of positive epistemological pronouncements of a Feuerbachian tenor, which in their straightforward simplicity often bring Marx's early 'materialism' dangerously close to a naive empiricism (for example, in certain passages of the *1844 Manuscripts*[11]); to the full-blown programmatic 'materialism' of Marx's so-called 'works of the break'. (Althusser places under the heading 'the works of the break' – presumably in the interest of chronological precision! – just Marx's theoretical output of 1845, viz. the 'Theses on Feuerbach' and *The German Ideology*, the latter in fact completed in 1846. As judged according to thematic criteria, however, *The Poverty of Philosophy* clearly forms a common set with the writings mentioned.) This programmatic 'materialism', as we have seen, in its most dubious (and, regrettably, also most influential) expressions assumes a structure representing such a perfect 'inversion' of Hegel's idealism that it is in fact nearly indistinguishable from the latter.[12]

The ambivalence of these early philosophical results, all arrived at *prior to* the great bulk of Marx's scientific investigations, has presented a major obstacle to understanding the role played by Hegelian formulae in the elaboration of Marx's economic theory. This is due in no small measure to Marx himself, who, even after those scientific investigations had been largely completed, continued to treat the earlier results as canonical in reflecting upon his own relation to Hegel. Thus, as we have seen, in the 'famous quotations' from the 1873 'Afterword', he is content simply to allude synoptically to the earlier 'inversion', privileging indeed its most speculative formulation. Once having done this and, furthermore, identified the 'inverted' relation between them as precisely – and, it would seem, exhaustively – what distinguishes 'his' 'dialectical method' from Hegel's, Marx is left to conclude that the relevance of Hegelian philosophy to the pursuit of his economic analysis must, then, lie in some general distinctiveness of such a 'method' (its 'rational kernel') which both Hegel's and his own alleged application of it share in common.

But this whole conception of the 'Marx–Hegel relation' – even if Marx's own – is pure confusion and, as we have seen in detail, its consequence has been unceasingly to sow confusion. It is confusion and has sown confusion because the attempt to detect a common 'method' in two fundamentally so disparate theoretical enterprises as Hegel's exposition of 'the concept' and Marx's critique of political economy has given rise to a methodological phantasm which has about as little to do with the one as with the other. But this conception is not only misleading in that it *diverts* attention from the actual basis of the 'Marx–Hegel relation', it positively *precludes* comprehension of the latter. It is, so to say, *perfectly* deceptive. This is because – contrary to all talk of the need to 'overturn' Hegel's idealism – the relevance of Hegelian philosophy to Marx's analysis consists *precisely* in the peculiar logical formulae which Marx takes over from it (and not in any 'method') and the distinctiveness of these formulae, as well as their usefulness for Marx, consists precisely in their *inverted* character. The whole riddle of the 'Marx–Hegel relation' consists in nothing other than this: which is to say, that it is precisely and paradoxically the *mystical* formulae of Hegelian 'logic' for which Marx finds a *rational* scientific application.

The key to the solution of this riddle lies in the very way of being or, to speak philosophical German, '*Seinsweise*' proper to the object of Marx's inquiry: in its peculiar 'objectivity', as I have put it. (Indeed, the key to the solution of this riddle *must* lie in the peculiar 'objectivity' of his object if Marx's application of the formulae in question is to possess the scientific validity which I am suggesting it does.) For in examining the phenomena of economic value – all of which are, in effect, *monetary*-phenomena – Marx made the curious discovery of an object domain in which the inverted relation between the universal and the particular which constitutes the distinctive principle of Hegelian metaphysics *in fact* obtains. Though the 'famous quotations' from the 1873 'Afterword' obscure this, so to speak, 'ontic' peculiarity of his chosen subject-matter, there is at least one text in which Marx acknowledges it explicitly. This is the appendix to the first (1867) edition of *Capital*, entitled 'The Value-form'. This appendix disappears from the second edition, with its materials instead being selectively incorporated into the revised first chapter of the text. In it Marx writes:

> Within the value-relation and the value-expression it comprises, the abstract-universal does not count as the property of the concrete, of the sensate-actual [*des Konkreten, Sinnlich-Wirklichen*]; but, on the contrary, the sensate-concrete counts as but the form of appearance or the determinate form of realization of the abstract-universal.

A little further on, he continues:

> This *inversion* [*Verkehrung*], whereby the sensate-concrete counts only as the form of appearance of the abstract-universal, and not, on the contrary, the abstract-universal as a property of the concrete, characterizes the value-expression. At the same time it makes the understanding of the latter difficult. If I say that Roman law and German law are both systems of law, this is self-evident. If, however, I say *the* law, this abstraction, *realizes itself* in Roman law and German law – these concrete systems of law – then the connection becomes mystical.[13]

The Hegelian overtones of what Marx writes in these passages will not be missed by readers who have followed our discussion up till this point. The illustration, moreover, with which Marx concludes, such as to underscore the peculiarity of the relation obtaining between universal and particular in the value-expression,[14] is especially significant for our purposes, since it not only brings to mind Hegel's *Philosophy of Right*, but, indeed, in substance strongly recalls the young Marx's above-mentioned critical commentary on the final section of the latter entitled 'The State'.

12 The 'Subject–Predicate Reversal': an Excursus on Marx's *Critique of Hegel's Doctrine of the State*

12.1 'THE ILLUSION OF REAL KNOWLEDGE'

The bulk of Marx's *Critique of Hegel's Doctrine of the State* is devoted to the task of exposing the mystification suffered by an otherwise mundane subject-matter through Hegel's 'logicizing' treatment of it. The mechanism of such mystification, as Marx shows in his painstakingly detailed paragraph-by-paragaph commentary, consists in the distinctively Hegelian procedure of 'explaining' empirical objects or circumstances as attributes of concepts which they allegedly serve to 'realize'. (A table of contents which Marx appended to the manuscript, but left uncompleted, contains the single entry: 'Concerning Hegel's Transition and Explication' [*CHDS*, 198/333].) This is not as simple a matter as might be supposed at first glance, since, as we have seen, every determinate concept is in Hegel's treatment presented as but a stage in the concretization of '*the* concept', and 'the concept', as we know, is itself articulated into three functional 'moments'.

Hence so too must every more determinate concept be thus articulated, and, just as Hegel announced in the *Logic* would be the case in the more 'concrete' sciences (see chapter 9, section 1 above), his whole effort in considering some empirical subject-matter – here, the institutions of 'the state' – is devoted to finding empirical aspects of it ('existents', as Marx says) which can be regarded as fulfilling this 'logical' requirement. Consequently, in treating empirical subject-matters Hegel's exposition increasingly forgoes the specific sort of paralogical manoeuvre which we found to be so abundantly in evidence in his treatment of 'logic' as such. Instead, it tends to rely even more heavily than in the *Logic* upon overtly teleological appeals, which are especially called upon to motivate the 'transitions' between categories (though it should be added that pun-making on the terms of the 'syllogism' is about equally employed in both the *Logic* and the more 'concrete' sciences as a, so to speak, 'ancillary' element of Hegel's argumentation).

The outcome of the procedure just described is, in effect, to *justify* the empirical 'existents' or, more simply put, *matters of fact* selected for discussion: converting the latter into nothing less than necessary features of 'the idea'. This is what gives to Hegel's philosophy as a whole (and not only to his philosophy of history, as he himself admits) the character of a *Theodicy*, and it is also what makes for the essentially apologetic tendency of Hegel's, and indeed Hegelian, political philosophy.[1] Thus, as Marx repeatedly points out, '*the* state', which according to Hegel is supposed in its totality to represent the empirical realization of the very concept of 'freedom', turns out distinctly to resemble – if not in *every* detail, at least even in many quite minute ones – the *Prussian* State.[2]

In light of the attempts alluded to above at reviving the Hegelian style 'dialectic of concepts' as a canon of scientific inquiry and doing so, moreover, in the name of defending Marx's political economy, it bears stressing that Marx himself was completely unequivocal *already in 1843* concerning both the nature and, just as importantly, the *speciousness* of Hegelian 'explanation'. Thus he writes, for example, in commenting on paragraph §262 of the *Philosophy of Right*:

> . . . the empirical reality is taken up as it is; it is also declared to be rational. However, it is not rational by virtue of its own reason, but because the empirical fact in its empirical existence has a meaning other than itself. The fact which serves as a starting-point is not grasped as such but as a mystical result. The actual becomes a mere phenomenon, but the idea has no content besides this phenomenon. The idea, moreover, has no goal besides the logical one to 'exist for itself as infinite actual spirit'. In this paragraph we find set out the whole mystery of the *Philosophy of Right* and of Hegel's philosophy in general. (*CHDS*, 63/207–8)[3]

and again, in a passage which strikes at the very heart of Hegelian 'philosophical science':

> An explanation which fails to supply the differentia specifica is *no* explanation at all. The sole concern [viz. of Hegel's exposition] is simply to re-discover 'the idea', the 'logical idea', in every element, whether it be the state or nature, whereas the real subjects . . . are reduced to mere *names* of the idea, so that no more than the illusion

of real knowledge [*der Schein eines wirklichen Erkennens*] is at hand. (*CHDS*, 67/210–11)

After continuing with a detailed analysis of the paragraph which provides the immediate occasion for these last comments (namely, paragraph §269), Marx repeats this charge: remarking that through Hegel's pseudo-logical argumentation 'the illusion arises, as if a *definite* content has been elucidated' (*CHDS*, 69).[4] This remark can serve us finally as emblematic for Marx's judgement of the cognitive value of Hegel's exposition in general. And much the same could be said too, I am afraid, as concerns most of the results produced by the 'new' Hegelian Marxists in their would-be 'dialectical' expositions of economic categories – except that the illusions devised by the latter are not often so beguiling as the finely-woven creations of their philosophical hero.

Now, it is precisely in the midst of his attempt to articulate the source of the mystification created by Hegel's exposition that, here in the 1843 *Critique*, the 'inversion' thematic first appears in Marx's writings. Adopting some of the language of Feuerbach's Hegel-critique, Marx repeatedly denounces the Hegelian procedure of 'explanation' just described as a 'reversal [*Umkehrung*] of subject and predicate'.[5] It is a 'reversal of subject and predicate' because the given empirical reality which constitutes the real *object* of knowledge, and hence presumably should also constitute the ultimate 'subject' of any network of propositions, any *discourse*, aspiring to the status of knowledge, in Hegel's exposition gets presented rather as a dependent characteristic of general determinations, viz. concepts, which might be truthfully predicated of it. What is to be known, so to say, is presented as an attribute of what could be known of it.

Marx's use of the logical category 'subject' in this context, especially in light of the Feurbachian background, tempts an empiricist reading. It also, however, bears comparison to Kant's logical explication of the concept of substance in the *Critique of Pure Reason*. 'If I leave out permanence (which is existence throughout time),' Kant writes, 'nothing remains in the concept of substance save only the logical representation of a subject – a representation which I endeavor to give reality by representing to myself something which can only occur as subject (without being a predicate)'.[6] Marx's charge against Hegel is indeed that he treats predicates as substantial and the subjects to which they are ascribed, on the contrary, as merely phenomenal: which is to say that in Hegelian discourse – and herein lies precisely its distinctiveness

– general determinants in fact *usurp* the logical place of the subject and depose empirical reality to that of the predicate. Of course, the ultimate generality of which all more specific determinations are presented in turn as dependent expressions in Hegel's exposition is the *absolutely* unlimited: the pure form, so to say, of generality (or 'universality'). Here again, the contrast with Kant is instructive: since per Kant's 'materialism' (in the sense in which I have defined materialism in chapter 10, section 5 above), it is rather pure formless particularity – even though it can never be known as such – which is the ultimate 'substrate' of all more general determinations.

12.2 AN EXAMPLE: THE HEGELIAN 'DERIVATION' OF THE MONARCH

In order better to appreciate the grounds for Marx's charge, we need to observe Hegel's 'subject–predicate reversal', so to say, *in action*: which is to say, as it operates in the *details* of his exposition. An example is, then, in order. An especially conspicuous one is supplied by paragraph §279 of the *Philosophy of Right*, in which Hegel brings off the interesting feat of deriving the existence of the monarch – not of *monarchy*, mind you, but of some biological individual who is monarch! – from the concept of the sovereignty of the state. Paragraph §279 reads as follows:

> Sovereignty, at first simply the *universal* thought of this ideality [viz. the ideality of the particular powers and departments of the state], *exists* only as subjectivity certain of itself and as the will's abstract, and to that extent ungrounded, *self-determination*, in which lies the finality of decision. This is the individual aspect of the state as such, in which alone it is *one*. Subjectivity, however, only exists in its truth as *subject*, personality only as *person*; and in the constitution which has developed into really-existing rationality, each of the three moments of the concept has its separate form of existence which is actual for itself. Hence this absolutely decisive moment of the whole is not individuality as such, but *an* individual, the *monarch*.

Here, in part, is Marx's comment:

> If Hegel's point of departure would have been real subjects as the basis of the state, he would not have found it necessary, to let the

state subjectivize itself in a mystical way. This too is a mystification. Subjectivity is a determination of the subject, personality is a determination of the person. Instead of grasping them as the predicates of their subjects, Hegel makes the predicates autonomous and then lets them transform themselves into their subjects in a mystical way.... Because Hegel starts with predicates of universal determination rather than with a real Ens (ὑποχείμενον, Subject), and indeed a bearer of these determinations must exist, the mystical idea becomes that bearer. (*CHDS*, 80/224)

The significance of this last passage for our present purposes is somewhat obscured by the circumstance that in it 'subject' gets used indiscriminately in two in fact quite distinct senses: namely, on the one hand, in the sense of *human* subjects – indeed, read in this way Marx's comments anticipate his discussion of human subjectivity and 'alienation' in the *1844 Manuscripts* – and, on the other, in the sense of *propositional* ones.[7] It is only the tendency of the passage which gets set in relief by construing 'subject' in the latter sense that is relevant to our present concerns. On this reading, the gist of Marx's comments is that by 'reversing subject and predicate' Hegel's account of the monarchical principle – or rather, more precisely, of 'the monarch' – serves to 'reverse' the rational order of cognition.

That an empirical individual gets invested with the power of the sovereign – that this individual in his or her relations with other individuals exhibits the attribute of sovereignty – is, of course, a social fact. Let us suppose that the sovereignty which the empirical individual enjoys is that of a modern constitutional monarch, as indeed is Hegel's supposition. (Princely authority is 'derived' by Hegel as a moment in the development of the 'concept' of the constitution.) The theoretical clarification of such a fact would, then, at least require an analysis of the particular form of the state which prepares the place of the sovereign to which the empirical individual accedes. But this is not all. For however much scope there may be for various forms of the state, the clarification of the very fact that there *is* a state – in the sense of a distinct complex of political institutions – would require in turn an analysis of that particular mode of social organization which necessitates the formation of the state as a condition for its own existence. It is indeed one of the most notable substantive insights of Marx's 1843 *Critique*, even if it remains largely undeveloped there, that the state owes its entire content to the system of private ownership and exchange.[8]

How does Hegel treat the fact in question, however? Well, as indicated, he *derives* it: he does not analyse its conditions, he 'demonstrates' *its necessity*. And from what exactly does he demonstrate the necessity of the monarch? Well, he demonstrates it from the very characteristic of the monarch, viz. of the individual who so happens to be monarch, which makes that individual precisely a monarch: viz. the enjoyment of sovereignty. He derives the *existence* of the monarch from the *concept* of sovereignty. But, *nota bene*, in other sorts of constitution, which is to say, in other forms of the state, sovereignty could be invested in other sorts of subject. It is the peculiarity, the specific difference, of monarchy as a state-form that sovereignty is invested in a biological individual. But sovereignty could just as well, for instance, be retained in principle by the citizens of the state and expressed through the assembly of their elected representatives, viz. parliament. So, this social attribute, sovereignty, could be exhibited by (at least) two different kinds of real subject depending on the particular form of the state: either by an empirical individual, the monarch, or by a collectivity, 'the people'.

Hegel can hardly be supposed to be ignorant of this fact. Indeed, he remarks – sardonically – upon it: noting that the sovereignty of 'the people' considered in opposition to that of the monarch 'belongs to the confused thoughts based on the *disorderly* conception of the "*people*". Taken without its monarch . . . *the* people is a formless mass and no longer a state' (*Ph.R*, §279).[9] By way of response to the evidence that states founded on this principle, viz. democratic republics, have nonetheless existed, he adds tersely and cryptically: 'in face of the achieved idea there can no longer be any talk of such a conception'. And indeed Hegel does not talk anymore of it.

In light of the heterogeneity of empirical state-forms, how is it that Hegel can derive the singular incarnation of sovereignty, the monarch, from the concept of sovereignty in general? Well, in the first place and as we can infer from our earlier lessons in 'dialectic', the 'mere' *existence* of state-forms other than constitutional monarchy will not pose *for Hegel* any obstacle to his proving that *just* constitutional monarchy embodies the rationality inherent in the very concept of state. While the former may indeed 'exist', only the latter is '*actual*': viz. because it alone exists in conformity with its concept. The rationality of the concept of the state must in turn be preserved in the rationality of the concept of its sovereignty. So, in order to understand how the latter could entail the existence of the monarch, we need to ask whence 'derives' the rationality of the state. Needless to say, it derives from the rationality of the *concept as such*. Inspection of Hegel's paragraph §279 reveals that for the 'necessity' of the monarch as the biological incarnation of sovereignty Hegel offers no more compelling grounds than the alleged 'need' for the moment of 'individuality' inherent to the concept of sovereignty *qua* . . . 'concept' to gain explicit and independent form: to exist 'for itself'. It is clear that in this way Hegel transforms the biological individuality of the monarch, the very *body* of the monarch (cf. *Ph.R*, §280), into a characteristic – a 'predicate', as Marx would say – of sovereignty.

But, as far as Hegel's 'derivation' goes, this is also not all. It is, symptomatically, precisely in his remark to paragraph §279 that Hegel pauses to remind his readers that it belongs to the nature of a 'philosophical science' to 'derive its entire content' from the concept which forms its point of departure.[10] As Hegel likewise reiterates in his remark, at the stage of development proper to the *Philosophy of Right*, this concept or, more precisely, this form of manifestation of '*the* concept' is that of *the will*, which has already gotten speculatively defined in paragraph §4 as that which is in essence 'free'. So, in the final analysis, the biological individuality of the monarch turns out to be a necessary characteristic, a form of existence, of nothing less than '*freedom*'. Lest there be any doubt of this, Hegel concludes his remark to paragraph §279 with the following observation:

> It is this real freedom of the idea – for such freedom consists precisely in giving to each of the moments of rationality its own present *self-conscious* actuality – which assigns the ultimate self-determining certitude, comprising the pinnacle [*die Spitze*] in the concept of the will, as the function of a consciousness. This ultimate self-determination, however, can fall within the sphere of human freedom only insofar as it has the position of a pinnacle, *which exists for itself as distinct from and raised above all particularization and conditionality*. For only thus is it actual according to its concept.

On Hegel's account, it is not, then, the empirical individual who enjoys unrestricted freedom by virtue of his or her sovereignty. It is rather 'freedom' – the freedom, namely, which, according to Hegel, is self-conscious spirit 'actualized' in the state – which in order to give itself the form of sovereignty enjoys the body of the monarch. Rather than, so to speak, 'descending' to the definite form of social relations obtaining among empirical individuals in order to discover there the basis of the monarch's power, Hegel rather 'ascends' to a juridical concept, 'freedom', in order to discover there . . . *its legitimation.* In the order of exposition, this procedure thus appears as precisely a mystical 'descent' from the concept to its concrete epitomization in the empirical individuality of the monarch.

13 Some Passing Remarks on the 'New' Hegelian Marxism

It will be clear from the foregoing discussion that what Marx calls Hegel's '*Umkehrung*' of subject and predicate is also indeed supposed to be a '**Ver***kehrung*' of the same: a 'reversal' which disturbs the rational content of the subject–predicate relation, hence an 'inversion'. Indeed, in order to lay stress on the point, Marx employs the very metaphor which would later acquire such fame through its occurrence in his 1873 'Afterword'. 'It is self-evident,' he writes, 'The true way is turned upside-down [*wird auf den Kopf gestellt* – literally: 'is put on its head']' (*CHDS*, 99–100/242). The puzzle which Marx's 1843 *Critique* presents for us here, however, is that it is manifestly the very same *Verkehrung* of 'subject' and 'predicate' to which Marx yet again alludes in 'the Value-form'. But in 'the Value-form', it would seem that the '*Verkehrung*' is no longer to be regarded as the spurious product of a mystifying theoretical treatment, but rather as pertaining to the real nature of *the object itself* under consideration. Must we conclude, then, that the mature Marx had come to accept as legitimate the very inversion which he once expended such energies to expose as, so to say, the mystical kernel of all of Hegel's mysticism in his youthful critique?

Fortunately, Marx's discovery of the 'inverted world' of economic value – or rather of the 'inverted' character of the phenomena which this 'world' comprises – does not require us to draw such an improbable conclusion. If only *some* objects exhibit the peculiarity in question, if indeed it is precisely a *peculiarity* of them, then Hegel's metaphysical claim, inasmuch as it was supposed to concern the character of objectivity as such, is thereby shown to be *false*. It is not the case that particulars considered simply per se are in reality subordinated to universals (much less to '*the* universal'), such that the essential being of the former would consist merely in their providing the material for the manifestation of the latter. We are very familiar with the mystical import of this claim in the Hegelian context. To reiterate: since things in their empirical existence, viz. as particulars, necessarily deviate from 'the universal', they are, then, destined to *lose* this empirical embodiment, viz. to perish, 'thus' in their dissolution testifying to the merely illusory quality of their supposed independence and to the real power of 'the universal' over them. It is in this – *esoteric* – sense that Hegel declared the realm of particulars as a whole, viz. sensuous reality, to be the 'world of appearance': with respect to which and precisely *in which* 'the universal', viz. '*Geist*', is able to 'show itself' as the abiding essence.[1]

At the very outset of this work, I commented upon the attraction which Hegel's 'derogation' of the empirical concrete to the status of 'appearance' has had for Marxist economists and the willingness of the latter even to adopt the traditional philosophical companion category of 'appearance', viz. 'essence', as somehow being germane to their own (in fact largely unrequited) attempts at a *Methodenstreit* with the neoclassicals. In lending support to the 'spontaneous' philosophical impulses of the economists in this matter – by expounding upon 'dialectical logic' and the like – I am afraid that their 'Marxist' colleagues from the philosophy departments have only made themselves into the handmaidens of bad science. I do not want to go into any detail here on such philosophical 'aids' to the sciences. Much of the work associated with this tendency is of such an ad hoc sort as not to merit close scrutiny: or if it does merit scrutiny, then only by virtue of its symptomaticity and not on account of any intrinsic intellectual qualities.

In light of the severity of this judgement, it might in fact be better to avoid making any particular citations. But for the benefit of readers not already familiar with the style of discourse I have in mind, let me offer just the following as a representative sample:

> *The intelligibility of the concrete and material can only be grasped through asserting the priority of the thought process over how the concrete and material is given in appearances.* The concrete and material has a depth level underlying its surface level of appearances. The task of thought is first to pierce through the appearances to that depth-level (the level of 'value' as measured by labor-time rather than price . . .) and then to proceed to the mediations that connect the depth level with the given appearances. To fulfill this task it is not sufficient for thought to assert its independence, it must assert its *primacy* over the appearances generated by the real process. A dialectical reconstruction of categories allows for this. In this there is no difference in principle between Hegel and Marx.

> Both assert that it is only in thought, in theorizing, that the intelligibility of the world can be grasped.[2]

One would be hard-pressed to come up with any theorist who did not agree that it is 'only in thought, in theorizing' that the world's intelligibility is to be grasped. Where else?! But what has that to do with some alleged 'priority' *of* thought or, for that matter, with the mysterious 'depth-level' to which allusion is made? (And in exactly what dimension are values 'deeper' than prices? And just what, in any case, is *material* about a price?) It can hardly be seriously expected that appeals to philosophically long since discredited 'surface' versus 'depth' metaphors should help clarify already vague talk of 'appearances' and 'essences'.

Marx himself does, incidentally, sometimes write of events occurring and phenomena appearing on the 'surfaces' of a capitalist economy. To these 'surfaces', however, he does not systematically contrast any 'depth-level' which lies 'beneath' them, but rather spheres of social activity which are concealed *behind* them.[3] This usage has absolutely nothing to do with any metaphysical distinction of 'levels' of reality, much less with the protocols of some 'dialectical logic' which is supposed to be especially well-suited to grasping the connection between the latter. Indeed, Marx's own talk of 'surfaces' barely even deserves to be described as metaphorical. The acts which transpire on the 'surfaces' of capitalist economic life are, quite simply, those which transpire *on the market*, and the objective 'phenomena' which appear associated with the latter are *value*-phenomena: most fundamentally, prices, and most crucially in the contexts in which Marx tends to employ such a rhetoric, profits. What occurs *behind* the 'surfaces' of capitalist economic life is, quite simply, what occurs in the *private domain*: most notably for Marx's theoretical purposes, *consumption*, including the consumption *of labour-power*.

Recall the remark in *Capital* with which Marx motivates the transition from the discussion of the capital/wage-labour exchange to that of the labour-process:

> The consumption of labour-power occurs, like the consumption of every other commodity, outside the market or the sphere of circulation. Let us therefore, in company with the owner of money and the owner of labour-power, leave this noisy sphere of what lies on the surface and in full view of everyone, in order to follow them into the hidden place of production, on whose threshold there hangs the

> notice: 'No admittance except on business'. Here will be seen not only how capital produces, but also how it is itself produced. The secret of profit-making must at last be exposed. (*CI*, 279/189)

Once the utterly mundane character of Marx's distinction is fully appreciated, any grandiose metaphysical interpretation of it appears not just mistaken, but frankly rather comic.

In any case, the philosophers might have done more to assist the academic laity in forming a correct appreciation of the sense which the 'essence–appearance' couplet has in Hegel's usage, and hence in acquiring at least a certain prudence with respect to emulating the latter, by calling attention to a passage such as the following:

> . . . essence does not lie behind or beyond appearance, but it is rather the infinite goodness that releases its show [*Schein*] into immediacy and grants it the joy of existence. The appearance which is thus posited does not stand on its own feet and does not have its being in itself, but rather in another. God as the essence, just as He is the goodness that creates a world by lending existence to the moments of His inward showing-forth [*Scheinen*], proves Himself at the same time to be the power over this world and the righteousness which, inasmuch as the content of this existing world wants to exist on its own, reveals the latter to be mere appearance. (*En.L*, §131, add.)

Be that as it may, it will be an extremely simple matter to demonstrate that Marx's observation to the effect that in the value-relation the sensate-concrete counts as but the 'form of appearance' of the abstract-universal has nothing in common – apart that is from a certain, indeed not even entirely felicitous, 'mode of expression' – with the Hegelian derogation of the sensate-concrete *as such* to the phenomenal form of 'the universal'.

In fairness, it should be noted that some of the more astute representatives of the 'new' Hegelian Marxism have not only recognized, but even placed special emphasis upon the isomorphism between the Hegelian 'concept' and the specific object of Marx's value-analysis.[4] This has not prevented them, however, from continuing to credit Hegel with a distinctive and rational 'method' (at least of 'presentation' if not of inquiry) and to attribute to Marx a particular application of it. Consequently, they have set about discovering conceptual 'transitions' on the Hegelian pattern throughout *Capital* or, worse still, in tacit acknowledgement that such 'transitions' are not in fact there to be found, have taken the initiative of devising them on Marx's behalf. C.J. Arthur writes, for example, that 'as merely implicit, value is a vanishing semblance. To be really of the essence it must become posited for itself; it must gain actuality in its further developed forms of appearance. This is what makes money necessary.'[5] Such a 'derivation' of the necessity of the money-form will be recognized as a fair piece of Hegelian 'explanation'. It does not, however, serve to demonstrate how the coalescence of the money-form is necessitated by certain definite features of commodity exchange as a mechanism of social integration, but only how it is 'necessitated' by certain definite features of Hegel's 'doctrine of essence' as a division of the latter's 'logic'.

In an analogous manner, Jairus Banaji, in a pioneering work within the genre of Hegeloid reinterpretations of Marx's economics, confidently asserts that the expository move in *Capital* from the simple commodity circuit to the circuit of capital represents a 'dialectical-logical derivation'.[6] Turning to the actual text, however, what we find is not any 'dialectical derivation', but rather a humble juxtaposition. 'The direct form of the circulation of commodities,' Marx writes,

> is C-M-C, the transformation of commodities into money and the re-conversion of money into commodities: selling in order to buy. But alongside this form we find a second specifically different form: M-C-M, the transformation of money into commodities and the re-conversion of commodities back into money: buying in order to sell. Money which in its movement describes this latter circulation is transformed into capital, becomes capital, and, according to its determination, already is capital. (*C*I, 247–8/162)

Marx's justification for presenting the circuit of capital as he does lies not in the alleged necessity that value overcome its merely immediate being in the commodity and 'posit itself' as 'essential ground' (sic!), per Banaji's creative suggestion, but rather in the more mundane fact that money actually *does* circulate in the manner described by it. Marx notes the empirical occurrence of such a circuit, and establishes that only a quantitative variation between the values represented by its extremes could motivate the social activity with which it is associated (viz. buying in order to sell). He then sets himself the task of explaining how such an apparent augmentation of value through circulation (a) is possible and (b) is compatible with the basic 'law of value' which governs the simple circulation of commodities (viz. that commodities should exchange in just such quantities as their values are equal). He does not 'derive' the circuit of capital from the 'concept' of value, nor could he, since the circuit of capital is not in fact entailed by said 'concept' (that is, in the ordinary rather than the Hegeloid sense). Indeed, it is precisely the prima facie *inconsistency* between the former and the latter that constitutes the problem which Marx attempts to solve.

Even in a text such as the *Grundrisse*, where Marx's own 'flirtation' with Hegelian styles of argumentation is far more overt and prevalent than in *Capital* (and indeed where, to paraphrase Wal Suchting, this 'flirtation' sometimes does even lead to real indiscretions), and even in the midst of passages where (for precisely those reasons here reviewed) Marx finds himself most severely tested by the Hegelian temptation, he still takes hold of himself long enough to interject: 'It will be necessary later . . . to correct the idealist manner of the presentation, which makes it seem as if it were merely a matter of conceptual determinations and of the dialectic of these concepts' (*Gr.*, 151/85–6). The 'new' Hegelian Marxists have by and large not heeded this warning – with the result that for Marx's explanations of economics forms they have in the name of 'dialectical' sophistication tended to substitute mere pseudo-explanations.[7]

14 The Universal and the Particular in the Constitution of Value

14.1 VALUE-RELATION AND VALUE-FORM

Recall Marx's observation from 'The Value-form': 'This *inversion*, whereby the sensate-concrete counts only as the form of appearance of the abstract-universal, and not, on the contrary, the abstract-universal as a property of the concrete, characterizes the value-expression.' In order to begin to grasp how the idealist connotation of Hegelian formulae gets expelled through their usage by Marx, we have only to pay attention to the manner in which Marx's 'mode of expression' here in fact departs from Hegel's. For the topic of Marx's claim is explicitly *not* the sensate-concrete as such, but only the latter inasmuch as brought '*within the value-relation*'. Now, what Marx calls the 'value-relation' is, in effect, just the ratio at which different categories of marketable goods exchange: so many units of one good being regularly obtainable for so many units of another.[1] This 'value-relation' takes central place in Marx's analysis of the 'value-form', since barring a certain evolution in the power of the state to be touched upon below, it is only inasmuch as it occurs in such a relation that the value of any single category of good can gain expression. The 'value-relation' between two sorts of commodities thus indeed constitutes the elementary 'value-form' of any one of them: as in Marx's didactic example '20 yards of linen = 1 coat', with the equal sign here to be read roughly as 'has the value of'.[2]

It will be self-evident from what has just been written that the value-relation does not pertain to particular things simply in their character as natural objects. Or, in other words, it is not simply *qua* natural objects that things stand in such a relation to one another. '[T]he commodity-form,' Marx writes, 'and the value-relation of products of labour within which it gets represented, has absolutely nothing to do with the physical nature of the latter and the material [*dinglich*] relations arising out of this' (*CI*, 165/86). Rather, physical items are placed in the value-relation by virtue of a certain sort of *social practice*. We could even say, per the Hegelian idiom, that they are 'posited' in such a relation by and through that practice.

The practice in question is, of course, *commodity-exchange. Value*, it will be recalled, was precisely one of the 'practical concepts of exchange' – indeed the most fundamental of them – to which we devoted attention above (see chapter 4, section 4). It will be recalled too that it is precisely a peculiarity of such concepts that in contrast to general empirical concepts, the correctness of their application to physical items does not depend upon any features which the latter exhibit *as* physical items. In this sense, value as a practical concept is not *abstracted from* particulars in their empirical diversity, but rather *projected upon* them. It needs to be stressed, however, that it is projected upon them not by the individuals who engage in commodity-exchange – an option which would result in a conception of value as something purely subjective and, so to speak, 'mental' – but rather by the *practice itself* in which these individuals engage. Consequently, whereas value is, if you like, 'ideal', inasmuch as it does not derive from the physical constitution of commodities, it is, nonetheless, *objective*, inasmuch as it does not depend either upon the conceptions or perceptions of individuals as cognitive subjects.

I hope it will already be appreciated that commodity-exchange is not merely a social practice in the sense that, say, theatre-going or reading or football are all 'social practices': all being activities in which only socialized individuals can engage and only on the condition of the participation, however mediated or remote, of other individuals. Assimilating exchange to such a model would reinforce the temptation to construe value as something subjective or, at best, 'inter-subjective', and could only lead to extremely trivialized interpretations of what is here at issue: for instance, in the manner of currently fashionable phenomenological theories of 'social construction'. But commodity-exchange is a 'social practice' in the sense rather that it is a practice which serves precisely to establish and consolidate *social relations*, with 'social relations' to be understood in the fundamental sense discussed in chapter 5 above: viz. as systematic relations of production upon which individual reproduction is in turn dependent.

Commodity-exchange is a mechanism for integrating the branches of the social division of labour through the redistribution of their products, thus for coordinating the collective appropriation of the natural environment. So, it is certainly not a 'game', which individuals can choose to play or not to play. To belong to a society in which commodity-exchange has become the dominant form of sociality, viz. a capitalist society, is tantamount to participating in the network of exchanges. Conversely, the physical items which are placed in the value relation cannot be arbitrarily decided upon by individual exchangers. They are placed in that relation, rather, by the completed *system* of exchange, comprising the various outputs of all such branches of the division of labour as fall under its dominion.

It follows that the value-relation between products of labour does not come into being just in the empirical occurrence of exchange and merely obtain punctually: that is to say, for no longer than the moment in which transactions are completed and between just those particular goods which figure in such transactions. (This can already be appreciated from the fact that under conditions of commodity exchange it is not in any case the norm for definite quantities of products to exchange directly against one another: as indeed, for reasons which will be gone into below, they typically *cannot* be exchanged in just those proportions which their respective values would require.) On the contrary, actual transactions serve merely to *confirm* the value-relation, the prevalence of which is precisely the condition of the possibility not so much of their occurrence as such (though it is the condition of possibility of this too, insofar as we have in mind *monetary* transactions) but of their *orderly* occurrence – of, in brief, the *coherence* of each exchange in the context of the totality of exchanges.

In this sense, we could say that the value-relation – or, more exactly, the whole complex of value relationships obtaining among the outputs of the diverse branches of social production – has a 'transcendental' status relative to empirical incidents of exchange. It is the 'law' which the latter obey. Hence it is not localized and momentary, but rather generalized and enduring: which is to say that it obtains over longer periods, even in the absence of definite transactions, and between not particular products but rather the sorts of which the latter are specimens. The 'positing' of definite sorts of commodities in the value-relation implies precisely that their specimens will exchange not just in some proportions – for how else could they exchange, even under conditions of the most primitive and intermittent barter? – but in *regular* proportions. These exchange ratios may well change over time, but such changes then affect whole categories of products and hence get exhibited systematically in the entire range of transactions in which those products figure.

This durability of the value-relation attests to its objective character. It does not cease to obtain in the interludes between transactions, in the manner that the relation of being 'offsides' cannot obtain in the absence of a game of football and those subjective or 'inter-subjective' interpretations of events which are constitutive of that game. Our explanation of the sources of such durability confirms, however, that the objectivity to which it attests is not of a physical sort. The objectivity of commodities as values derives from society and the exigencies of social reproduction. The enduring value-relation which obtains between products of labour as the objects of exchange is nothing but an expression and index of social-relations, dependencies, which are continually renewed among individuals precisely through their being exchanged. 'It is only the definite social relationship of human beings themselves', Marx writes, 'which assumes for them here the phantasmagorical form of a relationship among things' (*CI*, 165/86).

I take this last principle as having been sufficiently demonstrated. In any event, it will be recognized as the core proposition of Marx's theory of 'commodity fetishism'. In order not to be misled, in order not precisely to fall victim theoretically to commodity fetishism, it needs, then, to be kept in mind that whenever we speak of the 'value-relation' and the 'value-form', we are also speaking implicitly of the *exchange nexus* in which this relation acquires its practical reality. If such is not kept in mind – and this is precisely what Marx warns against in the passage from the *Grundrisse* cited in the last chapter – it could appear as if the 'value-form' were a 'generative form', like the Hegelian 'concept', which differentiates itself in all sorts of surprising ways, passes through numerous 'transitions', but has no connection to any social practice at all. It is, above all, this occlusion of the (in Franz Petry's apt expression[3]) 'social content' of Marx's value-theory which tends to give to self-consciously Hegeloid treatments of it such an arid scholastic quality.

14.2 THE EXTRINSIC AND INTRINSIC MEASURES OF VALUE

As Marx's observations on 'the value-form' suggest, it is indeed the case that the particular commodity in the value-relation – which is to say, in the relation to other commodities in which it is 'posited' by virtue of the continuity of its absorption into the exchange nexus – counts as merely a 'form of appearance' of the general determination of all commodities as values. It will be understood from the foregoing that by 'particular commodity' has to be understood in this context the particular *sort* of commodity and individual commodities only inasmuch as specimens of a sort. Furthermore, we should say, more precisely, that with respect to the elementary value-relation of any two sorts of commodity, just that particular commodity, in the sense indicated, which occupies what Marx calls the 'equivalent pole' of the relation counts as the 'form of appearance' of value.

The commodity occupying the 'relative pole' does not 'count as' anything. Or, if you prefer, it just 'counts as' that particular sort of thing which it is – viz. as *itself* – even if its particular identity qua commodity does not derive from its physical attributes as such, but rather from the suitability of the latter to satisfying particular human requirements (whether these requirements be those of immediate want-satisfaction or those of production). We are dealing here, in effect, with *three* distinct levels of objectivity: the purely physical objectivity of things, their functional objectivity with respect to conscious subjective purposes, and their functional objectivity with respect to commodity-exchange as an automatic mechanism of social integration. The lattermost of the three is what I propose to call their 'economic objectivity'.

In the elementary value-relation, it is precisely the value of the commodity occupying the 'relative pole' which gains expression in the form of the commodity, as Marx puts it, 'officiating' as equivalent. Since equality is self-evidently a symmetrical relationship, however, Marx's talk of these two 'mutually exclusive' poles of the value-expression (*C*I, 140/63) can seem rather obscure. In fact in the simple value-relation both sorts of commodity occupy both 'poles' – *but always the opposite one with respect to the other sort.* Consider again Marx's didactic example. The value-relation '20 yards linen = 1 coat' gives expression to the value of linen, viz. in units of coat; but it also gives expression to the value of coats, viz. in units of linen. No matter in which direction we read the 'equation', what its consideration makes manifest is that the simple value-relation gives expression to the value of any one commodity in the physical form of *some other* commodity. The physical particularity (more exactly, specificity) of the latter thus gets, so to say, enlisted to serve as the representative of the general social property which is projected upon the former through the continuity of its exchange: viz. the property of being convertible in definite proportions into any and all other commodities. Marx calls this the 'first peculiarity' of the equivalent-form of value: 'use-value becomes the form of appearance of its opposite, exchange-value' (*C*I, 148/70).

The described 'simple' value-relation in principle at least obtains between any two definite sorts of commodity. But while it might be useful for didactic purposes, it does not in fact have any immediate practical reality. Practically considered, as will be recalled from our earlier discussion of exchange and its forms, *every* commodity implicitly occupies the 'equivalent-pole' of the value-relation with respect to *all* others. ('To the owner of a commodity,' Marx writes, 'every alien commodity [that is, every commodity belonging to someone else] counts as particular equivalent of his own commodity, his own commodity, therefore, as universal equivalent of all others' [*CI*, 180/101].) This is to say that inasmuch as it is produced as a commodity and so long as it remains a commodity, every product of labour, in whatever definite amount it is controlled by its owner, represents but a means for acquiring through exchange a set of other products, the sum of whose values is equal to the value of that definite amount of the product owned.

If, for example, I happen to own 20 yards of newly-woven linen, then, supposing a coincidence of supply and demand in all sectors of production, the portion of the remainder of the social product which I will be able to obtain for my linen will have the value of precisely 20 yards of it: whether I take this portion in the concrete useful form of 1 coat or, say, 10 lb. tea or 40 lb. coffee or 2 ounces gold or, say, 1/5 ounce gold, 8 lb. coffee, 2 lb. tea, and 1/2 coat (suppose I used 10 yards linen to make a downpayment) or what have you.[4] The concrete useful form of the product I already control precisely 'counts as' but a value-equivalent for a definite amount of some other product or for some heterogeneous set of other products combined in definite, but various amounts.

Now, for any definite amount of some one sort of commodity, there is always in principle some definite amount of any other sort of commodity which represents an equivalent value in exchange. Hence the physical form of any sort of commodity can in principle provide a homogeneous unit in which to give expression to the values of all the rest: thus serving as the 'general equivalent' form of value. This unit is, namely, just that unit in which amounts of the commodity in question are conventionally measured.

In our example, on account of the physical properties peculiar to linen, the conventional measure happens to be an abstract spatial one: namely, yards. As the other goods cited as potential substitutes for our linen make clear, however, depending on the physical nature of the product, this measure could just as well be one, say, of mass. If the product happens to be functionally delimited and hence countable – this obviously being so, for instance, with coats, of which we can say directly how *many* there are, though not linen, of which we can only say how *much* there is – the most apropos unit of measurement can even be just exemplars of *itself*. In any case, whatever the units in which its amount is conventionally measured in light of the particular sort of physical thing which it is and/or the uses to which it is put, as measured in such units the product provides, in short, the 'form of appearance' of *exchange-value*: its 'natural form', in Marx's words, becomes the 'value-form'.[5]

The 'general equivalent' measures the relative degree of convertibility of commodities. It will be noticed, however, that with the establishment of such a measure we have not said anything about what *determines* the degree of their convertibility. But it should be noted too that the issue of what determines exchange-value arises immanently from a consideration of the value-expression. Say, for instance, we know that the value of a coat as expressed in units of linen is 20 yards ('1 coat = 20 yards of linen'), whereas the value of a pound of tea as expressed in units of linen is 2 yards ('1 lb. of tea = 2 yards of linen'). Through comparison of the two expressions we learn that the exchange-value of the coat is ten times as great as that of the tea – a fact of which we could never have become aware by simply comparing the coat and the pound of tea directly.

But the comparison of the 'linen-value' of coat and tea does not merely tell us that with a coat we can obtain ten times more linen than with a pound of tea. The linen here 'counts', after all, as representative of the convertibility of commodities as such. So, the comparison tells us that with a coat we can obtain ten times more commodities of any and every sort than with a pound of tea: that we can, in effect, obtain a portion of the total social product which is ten times greater. Whereas, however, comparisons of different amounts of linen are straightforward, a relevant unit of measurement being ready to hand: how exactly are the 'amounts' of physically *heterogeneous* bundles of commodities to be compared? With respect to *what* does one bundle represent a 'greater' portion of the social product than another?

One might respond, since just a moment ago we were content to speak of the 'linen-values' of coats and tea, that for any two bundles of commodities, no matter what their real constituents, that bundle will represent the greater portion of the social product which requires more yards of linen to obtain. But with such a response we are clearly moving in a circle. Of course, it is true that whatever bundle exchanges against more yards of linen represents a greater portion of the product and greater in exactly that proportion as its 'linen-value' is greater than the 'linen-value' of the other bundle – just as it is true that since a coat, according to our previous stipulations, has a 'linen-value' ten times greater than that of a pound of tea, the coat must not only be a means of *acquiring* a ten times greater portion of the social product, but must itself *represent* a ten times greater portion. The relative 'linen-values' of the respective bundles give expression to this inequality – but they do not *create* it.

The linen, then, in our example merely provides an extrinsic measure of the amount of the social product represented by any given commodity or bundle of commodities and hence of the amount of the product into which it can be converted: in short, it provides an extrinsic measure of *value*. It will be recalled that in discussing what I have called the 'quantitative determination' of the capital/wage-labour relation above, we were in fact content to apply this external measure (even if we recommended estimating total assets in money rather than yards of linen). Our problem in that context was just to find a reliable index of control over the product and this is precisely what the extrinsic measure provides. But there must also be some *intrinsic* measure which gains expression in this extrinsic form. The problem is: measure *of what*?

We have repeatedly commented upon the incommensurability of diverse sorts of product considered simply qua physical things. They become ideally commensurable with respect to their exchange-value, this 'supra-sensate' property, by virtue of the regularity of their exchange against the equivalent, in units of which this property is hence made representable. But what real *physical* property regulates the number of units of the equivalent which correctly represent the exchange-value of any given product? It would seem that there could not be any such property and yet there must be. The solution to this riddle lies in the fact that the property with respect to which diverse products are commensurable is not, after all, an intrinsic property of the products as such, but rather an intrinsic property of an *activity* which is essentially associated with them: namely, the labour requisite for their production. The property in question is, namely, the time this activity endures or, more exactly, should endure given the reigning norms of labour productivity in each sector of production.

In Part II, we discussed the practical logic of exchange as a mode of social integration, having already determined that social integration is nothing other than the integration of a social division of labour. Hence, the connection of value and labour-time was there manifest from the very outset. The 'law of value' is that commodities should exchange in just such quantities as they represent equal values: as measured, namely, in units of the general equivalent. This same law, as formulated in terms of the 'intrinsic' measure, is that they should exchange in just such quantities as require equal allocations of social labour to produce: as measured, namely, in units of *time*. In effect, the equivalent provides an extrinsic *spatial* representation of what is in itself a *temporal* process: it converts the 'form of activity' into 'the form of being'.

This 'law' is, as I have put it, a kind of 'transcendental' axiom of exchange, apart from which the exchange-system, inasmuch as its essential function is to coordinate social production, would lack coherence. What such an axiom means in a practical sense for exchangers is that product can only be 'purchased' against product – or, more exactly, that the results of an allocation of social labour of a determinate quantity can only be appropriated by purchase on the condition that the results of a commensurate allocation of social labour are alienated by sale. This practical injunction is described by Marx as the 'law of appropriation or the law of private property' (*C*I, 729/609). It clearly rests on the assumption, generally acknowledged in the period of classical political economy, that labour is the basis – or 'original purchasing price' – of all legitimately acquired property.

Since under pure conditions of simple-commodity production no person would be able to appropriate a portion of the social product without having made a contribution to it, under such conditions this principle would be nearly self-evident. Though it continues to apply unaltered under capitalist conditions, it gets obscured by two circumstances in particular: first, the monopolization of non-reproducible conditions of production (and, after a fashion, even money becomes such in a capitalist economy), thus allowing for the collection of incomes independently of any actual exchange; and second, the establishment of private property in other person's capacity to labour, thus allowing owners of labour-power to claim a portion of the product – in fact, in the first instance, all of it – *without* having contributed to its production. It is such circumstances which provide the occasion for the development of 'theories of value' that make no explicit reference to production at all, and it is the same circumstances too, of course, which give to such theories their 'vocation'.

15 Money, or the Real Universality of Commodities

15.1 THE PRINCIPLE OF CONTRADICTION AND THE NECESSITY OF MONEY

Every product of labour inasmuch as it is produced as a commodity and so long as it remains a commodity is a value-equivalent: an exchange-value. As we likewise saw above, however, this is in the first instance only so 'ideally' or in principle.[1] In reality and in fact, the product remains just that particular sort of good which it happens to be. A definite portion of the total social product can be measured and is indeed implicitly measured in units of the particular product, viz. on the assumption that the latter is exchangeable with all other products in regular proportions. But this does not guarantee that some given specimens of the product will in practice be exchangeable for anything at all. The actual exchangeability of the latter can only be confirmed by the 'realization' of the exchange-value they ideally represent: viz. through their *sale*.

Note, however, that with the mention of sale, an element is introduced into our discussion of the 'value-relation' which has hitherto been tacitly assumed, but, apart from the occasional parenthesis, remained unexpressed: namely, the mediation of commodity exchange by the circulation of money. The decomposition of exchange into the mutually complementary acts of sale and purchase – of which we have in fact been talking all along under the general title of 'transactions' – implies, of course, exactly that. The necessity of this mediation has been touched upon in our earlier treatment of the exchange-system. Here it will be shown to follow in a strictly deductive manner from what Marx famously describes as the 'inner opposition' between exchange-value and use-value which is 'contained' in the commodity.

Let us start by making certain stipulations. The theoretical propriety of these stipulations might at first glance be doubted, but they will in fact just be explicit statements of assumptions which are implicit to

Marx's analysis of money, and the assessment of with what justification they are made can be left until after having seen the work which they allow us to accomplish. Let us assume, then, that the economy is a 'closed' one: or, in other words, that we are dealing with a *single* 'self-enclosed' economic 'space'. Within this 'space', all economic agents are free to enter into transactions with one another as they please and under exactly the same legal conditions. But no transactions of any sort are permitted with persons living outside this 'space', supposing there are any. In real world terms, this first stipulation amounts to the assumption that the economic system in question is not affected by international trade.

Let us assume, furthermore, that inasmuch as there is a state which intervenes in certain ways in securing the conditions of the economic life of individuals (at the very least by codifying, certifying and enforcing property rights), whatever else this state might do, it does *not* issue tokens of purchasing power: or, in other words, tokens which are meant to function as purchasing power for their holders. Note that this does not exclude the state's minting of metallic currency. In doing so, however, it would only be acting as the guarantor – whether trustworthy or not – of the metallic content of the latter. As will be explained below, our assumption need not exclude either the state's issuing of paper-currency – so long, namely, as the latter is convertible into metal. In short and simply put, what we are assuming by way of this second stipulation is that in the economic 'space' under consideration there is no 'token money' or 'fiat money' in circulation. Of the two basic assumptions made here, this latter is in fact the essential one: the assumption of the 'closed' character of the economy was only needed in order to assure that such 'token money' could not seep into it by way of foreign issuers.

Under the conditions stipulated, in order for the generalized alienation of the diverse elements of the social product to occur, some one (sort of) product among them must acquire the specialized function of serving as, so to speak, the proximate object of exchange vis-à-vis every other. This is to say that it will be accepted in exchange for any product and in lieu of every other product, so long, namely, as it be provided in the correct amount; and – which is just the converse of the aforesaid – every other product will be obtainable for it, so long, namely, as it be offered in the correct amount. By virtue of the manner in which all other commodities thus relate to it – or, more exactly, *are related* to it, viz. through the common and unavoidable practice of all commodity-owners – this one species of commodity is invested with the character of being the real form of existence of exchange-value: of being, in short, *money*.

We will see below that the product which enjoys this special status can under determinate circumstances be replaced in the immediate practice of exchange by what Marx calls 'valueless symbols of itself' (*CI*, 226/142): viz. paper currency; though as far as banknotes are concerned, inasmuch as they are convertible, which is for the most part Marx's supposition, it would be more accurate to describe them as a peculiar sort of circulating *contract*, rather than as 'symbols'. Such notes do not in fact comprise an independent genre of money at all. They do not represent tokens of purchasing power invested with this status on the pure authority of the state – in other words, 'token-money' – but rather tokens *of* money, of *commodity*-money. The currency enjoyed by its tokens is conditional upon the latter being really present in the state-coffers (or, alternatively, in the bank-vaults of private lending institutions) and obtainable by the holders of said tokens, and in the amounts specified in writing on them, upon their return to the issuer. Simply for ease of presentation, however, we can to begin with assume that there is not either any convertible paper currency in circulation and hence that whatever commodity is called upon to discharge the money-function, this commodity must always do so, as it were, 'in person' and not by proxy. We will abandon this assumption later on.

Other commodities, besides that which is invested with the status of money, are exchange-values in principle. It is, so to say, their ideal economic 'essence' to be such: to differ from one another only *quantitatively*, that is, with respect to the portion of the total product which they represent. Their reality, however, is not adequate to their 'essence'. Every specimen of each sort of commodity is burdened with physical characteristics which make it precisely a specimen of just that sort and not of the others. In fact they differ from one another *qualitatively*, viz. as 'use-values', and indeed they must differ from one another qualitatively, since it is only their qualitative diversity which motivates exchange in the first place. It is with this in mind that Marx writes of the 'opposition' between exchange-value and use-value which is 'immanent' to the commodity.[2] One could even say, and indeed with greater precision, that the said opposition is inherent in 'the concept' of the commodity. It is, furthermore, precisely the contradictory demands associated with these two constitutive aspects of commodities that necessitate the 'reduplication' of the implicit opposition between them as an empirical opposition between commodities and money (cf. *CI*, 199/119).

Now, upon reading this last remark a Hegelian might take heart, sensing a chance for vindication. For what is this if not an example of a 'dialectical' *pattern of argumentation*: one upon which nothing less than Marx's proof of the necessity of the money-form crucially depends, and which demonstrates, furthermore, the rationality of the Hegelian notion of 'real contradiction' that I have hitherto derided as the purest mysticism? Marx himself, after all, explicitly invokes the notion of 'real contradiction' precisely in this context (cf. *CI*, 198/118). But regardless of Marx's allusion, far from providing any vindication for the distinctively Hegelian 'law of contradiction', his deduction of the necessity of the money-form – that is to say, his demonstration that the existence of the latter is entailed by the existence of commodities – in fact crucially depends upon strict adherence to the ordinary law of contradiction.

The requirements of commodity exchange are such that the elements of the social product must be qualitatively *heterogeneous*, since otherwise there would be no reason for their exchange, *and* possess the form of being qualitatively *homogeneous*, since only as such are they quantitatively *commensurable* and hence exchangeable in just those proportions which the 'law of value' demands. Precisely in conformity with the principle of non-contradiction, however, an item of a given sort cannot within a common genus both be specifically different from items of other sorts and of the same sort as them. Hence, the only way in which the generalized exchange of the social product can occur is on the condition that the homogeneity of all commodities as values comes to be represented by some particular species of alienable thing. On present assumptions, this means some particular species of commodity. In other words, the ideal determination of all commodities as values must gain an independent embodiment in the physical shape of some one sort of commodity.

It is important that we grasp the practical dilemma which is implied by the logical contradiction here at issue. As noted, the 'law of value' requires that products be exchanged in just such quantities as their values are equal. Since, however, products in their physical or 'use-value' form are qualitatively heterogeneous, their equivalence as values can only normally be established with respect to *un*equal amounts of their own material substance, as expressed, moreover, in incommensurable units. This is to say that it could only exceptionally be the case that, say, 1 yard of linen represents the same value as 1 coat or 1 oz. gold or 1 lb. tea. Now, as a theoretical exercise, we can (using a method to be discussed below) from empirical data, nonetheless, deduce the current exchange ratios of any two commodities we please. We might be able to ascertain, for instance, that the exchange ratio of packs of chewing gum to Cadillac sedans is, say, 60,000:1 or, alternatively expressed, roughly 1:0.0000167. This ratio would, as we learned above, constitute the 'simple' value-relation of the two commodities. Since, however, supposing we could agree on some real part of a sedan which represents 0.0000167 percent of it, a sedan thus disarticulated would not be likely to preserve its value, and since no Cadillac dealer is likely to accept payment in 60,000 packs of chewing gum, the abstract 'value-relation' of these goods would seem to preclude their being exchanged at all.

What the example illustrates is that if goods had to be exchanged directly against one another in precisely those proportions or even just roughly those proportions dictated by their respective values, then the very characteristic of them which motivates exchange, viz. their qualitative diversity, would pose an obstacle to the fulfillment of exchange. The strict upholding of the law of value under conditions of direct exchange would entail that I could only exchange my product on the condition of finding some particular taker for it who wants just as much of it as has a value equal to some amount of his or her product which I want in return. Clearly, subject to such a condition, exchange would be restricted within extremely narrow bounds. This is precisely why the notion of a generalized barter economy is so preposterous. If, however, the law of value was abrogated in the interest of facilitating individual exchanges, then the exchange system would lack any regularity and quickly break down. The assignment of one sort of commodity to the money-function provides, so to speak, the 'spontaneous' solution to this dilemma.

The specific physical forms of commodities as 'use-values' thus create definite obstacles to their functioning as exchange-values. It is in this sense that the 'particularity' of the commodity (that is to say, more exactly, its 'specificity' as a sample of a particular sort) can be said to 'contradict' its general economic determination as a value-equivalent. We could even say, with a Hegelian accent, that a commodity in the determinate form it has as use-value is not yet what it 'ought to be' as a purely economic object: it ought to be universally exchangeable – but in fact it is not. Through its 'realization' in the money-form, however, the value ideally represented by any given commodity (a) is *confirmed* and (b) acquires a form of existence in which it can really function *as* value. This is to say that such value, having gained an 'independent' existence in the money-form, can henceforward be transmuted in turn into any product or fraction of a product[3] or set of products which represents a value of the same amount.

15.2 FROM MEDIUM OF EXCHANGE TO MEASURE OF VALUE

As per the rule stated above, the money-commodity is both the immediate objective of sale and the immediate means of purchase. It is the one inasmuch as it is the other, and any commodity which takes on these attributes is thereby money and functions as the universal medium of the circulation of commodities or, in other words, the medium of exchange. Now, by serving as the medium of exchange of other commodities, the physical form of the particular commodity assigned to the money-function comes also to provide the standard unit of measurement in which the values of all the rest get expressed and are made comparable.

We demonstrated in the previous chapter that in principle any sort of commodity could provide the material in which a definite value is given expression: it was in this sense that we declared them all to be 'value-equivalents'. What is required is only that the commodity (a) itself have a value, viz. be exchangeable in regular proportions with all others, and (b) allow of measurement in some unit, whether the latter, as we have seen, be simply its own physical form, inasmuch as particularizable, or some conventional unit applied to its physical form. Since all commodities by definition satisfy these conditions, any of them can serve as the equivalent form of value.[4] This is indeed true in principle.

In *practice*, however, each sort of commodity does not exchange regularly and directly against every other sort of commodity. Indeed, as we have seen, it would not be usual for them to exchange directly against *any* other sort of commodity – *except* precisely, under the conditions here stipulated, that one sort assigned to the money-function. Hence the regular proportion in which some commodity *x* exchanges against, say, a single unit of some other commodity *y* cannot even *be known* as such. This is to say that it cannot be known from simple observation of empirical transactions among commodity-owners, nor indeed from appeal to any practical 'user's knowledge' possessed by a participant in exchange. This is for the simple reason that if by 'exchange' we understand here *direct* exchange, the two commodities do not 'exchange' against one another *at all*. Rather, both *x* and *y*, so long as they remain saleable, exchange regularly and directly against the money-commodity (or, at a more advanced stage, contractual surrogates for the money-commodity), and only via the mediation of the latter against one another. More exactly, via the mediation of money they each exchange indiscriminately against any and every other sort of commodity, and hence by implication and in principle – if not necessarily, as we will see just below, in fact – against one another as well.

What I mean by this 'indiscriminate' character of commodity exchange will become clearer if we understand why its more commonly recognized indirectness is not in fact sufficient to specify its essential nature. If commodity-exchange were merely indirect, it might imply a scenario such as the following. Act 1: agent A, who is the owner of an exemplar of commodity *x* – let us say a loaf of bread – sells the latter to agent B for £1. Act 2: agent B, who is the owner of an exemplar of commodity *y* – say, a gallon of milk – sells the latter to agent A for £1. Were this the model for commodity-exchange in general, it is self-evident that the mediation of exchange by money would be superfluous. Agents A and B could just as well have exchanged their goods directly. Under the circumstances, the fact that they do not do so, instead resorting to the artifice of exchanging each in turn for the monetary intermediary, suggests not purposive-rational, but rather ritualistic behaviour. Indeed, by reason of the superfluousness of the mediation it provides, the good serving as intermediary ought not properly to be regarded as money at all, since, whatever other functions it might discharge, it does not in fact discharge the money-function. Its circulation among individuals might well promote social cohesion or solidarity in some manner, but its circulation is in no way an intrinsic technical requirement of the very organization of social production.

Direct exchange or barter is a bilateral social act with definite termini, viz. the owners between whom goods exchange qua elements of their respective property domains. The sort of indirect exchange just described would in substance be no different. In fact, however, the process of commodity-exchange is *multi*lateral and indeterminate. Even if we supposed that the 'agent A' of our example, the bread-seller, was peculiar enough always to sell just one loaf at a time, and that s/he always purchased in turn just exactly that amount of some one other sort of good which could be obtained with the proceeds – both of these being quite extraordinary assumptions to make as regards actual commodity-exchange – still it could only exceptionally be the case that agent A should spend a pound in purchasing a good from precisely the person from whom s/he had got just that pound in selling a loaf.

Even on the supposition that agent A behaves in the bizarre manner described, in the normal course of commodity-exchange agent A's exchanging of bread for milk would entail the intervention of not one, but *two* other economic agents – an agent B *and* an agent *C*.[5] One of these – let us say agent B – would have to purchase bread from A in order that the latter obtain the pound, and the other, agent C, would have to sell the milk to A for the pound thus obtained. Whereas the outcome of these successive transactions as far as A, our bread-seller, is concerned will be that s/he has exchanged bread for milk – let us say again, in line with our previous assumptions, one loaf of the former for one gallon of the latter – it need not be true conversely for C, the milk-seller, that s/he exchange the particular gallon of milk in question (or indeed *any* gallon of milk) for bread.

Let us suppose now that agents B and C also behave in the odd manner in which we have supposed agent A to behave. Let us say, furthermore, that B sells eggs and sold a dozen of them to earn the pound with which s/he purchases the bread from A; and let us say, as chance would have it and for the sake of providing closure to our little exchange system, that with this same pound, having received it from A in selling the milk, C buys . . . a dozen eggs – and does so indeed from none other than B. This gives us, then, a very simple and graphic illustration of the 'multilateralism' or 'polyvalence' of commodity-exchange. Each of our three agents exchanges his or her own product for some other good, though no one exchanges that other good for his or her own product.

It might, of course, happen under conditions of commodity-exchange that bilateral exchange relations will accidentally coalesce. But thanks precisely to the circulation of money among exchangers and in contrast to barter, it is not a *requirement* that they do so. Freeing exchange from the necessity of bilateralism, or what we might also call the condition of 'immediate reciprocity', is indeed the fundamental contribution which money makes to the generalization of exchange.[6] The characteristic motion of each specimen of the money-commodity is not, then, to bounce back and forth between exchangers, but rather, as Marx puts it, 'to move constantly away from its point of origin' (*CI*, 211/129) – or, more exactly, to move away from its proximate point of origin, only perhaps cutting back across the latter at random in the course of some later transaction and with greater or lesser likelihood depending on the density of exchanges and the amount of currency in circulation. It is, moreover and as we have already seen, precisely a consequence of their being released from the constraints of bilateral trade that economic agents do not in fact have to behave in the peculiar manner in which we supposed our 'agents A, B and C' to behave. On the contrary, they are able to distribute the proceeds of any single sale over a range of purchases and to aggregate the proceeds of several sales toward a single purchase. Hence, as will be easily appreciated, both the polyvalence of exchange and, as a result, its indiscriminateness – for given the abstract homogeneity of money, how can we determine the exact provenance of the sum of it expended in any given transaction and what would even be the point of trying to do so? – are under conditions of commodity-production in fact far greater than our little schematic example would suggest.

Whereas, for the reasons discussed, the exchange-ratio of any two sorts of commodity, x and y, cannot be known in an immediate fashion, it can, nonetheless, be ascertained. Indeed, it follows from what has just been written that this ratio can be ascertained even, *nota bene*, if sellers of 'xs' never in fact purchase 'ys' – nor, for that matter, sellers of 'ys', 'xs'! (That this is possible clearly confirms the 'transcendental' character of the value-relation upon which I have insisted.) We need only compare the regular proportions in which each of the sorts of commodity in question exchange against the *money*-commodity.

If p_x/p_y represents the ratio of the number of units of the money-commodity regularly exchangeable for single units of commodities x and y respectively, we need only take the inverse of this expression, p_y/p_x, to derive an index of the exchange-ratio of x to y. In other words, the exchange-ratio of x to y is just the inverse of the ratio of the unit 'money-values' or, in more common parlance, the unit-*prices* of x and y respectively. Treating p_y/p_x as a fraction and dividing through, we obtain a figure which represents the number of units of commodity x regularly exchangeable for a single unit of commodity y: or, in other words, the unit 'x-value' of y. (Thus if the unit-price of loaves of bread is £0.5 and the price of a computer is £1000, then the 'bread-value' of the computer is 2000 loaves.)

We could now go on to apply this same procedure in order to derive the exchange-ratios of commodity x to every other sort of commodity as well – except, of course, its ratio of exchange to the money-commodity, which we must already know. By converting the ratios in the manner suggested, we would obtain a set of figures representing, in effect, the values of all other commodities – except, that is, the money-commodity – as expressed in units of commodity x. Adding the x-value of the money-commodity to our set of x-values would be a simple enough matter. We have only to take the exchange-ratio of commodity x to the money-commodity which was previously given, viz. in the form of the unit-price of x, and reformulate it with the number of units of the money-commodity set to 1. (Thus if the unit-value of bread as expressed in sterling is £0.5, the unit-value of a pound sterling as expressed in bread is two loaves.) In this way, we would finally have succeeded in deriving the values of all commodities, but that of commodity x itself, as expressed in units of commodity x. Thus commodity x would, for the purposes of our theoretical exercise at any rate, count as the general equivalent-form of value.

The artificiality and superfluousness of such an exercise is, however, evident at first glance. For in order to have carried it out, we had *already* to know the values of all commodities, including commodity x: viz. as expressed in units of the money-commodity. This demonstrates both in what sense the money-commodity is the general equivalent-form of value – it is so in exactly that sense in which commodity x could theoretically have been so as well – and *why* it is the general-equivalent: it is so because in fact, that is in the *practice* of commodity exchange, it functions as the universal medium of circulation. As Marx puts it: 'gold serves as ideal measure of value only because it already circulates as the money commodity in the process of exchange. Hard cash lurks within the ideal measure of value' (*C*I, 198/118).[7]

15.3 THE MONEY-COMMODITY AND ITS PROXIES

Now, except under the most elementary conditions, the functioning of the money-commodity as universal medium of circulation does not entail that it serve as the actual means of purchase in every possible transaction. Even before the advent of paper currencies, the increasing diversity of exchanges – above all, the division between wholesale and retail trade – provides occasion for the replacement of the recognized equivalent in many petty transactions by less valuable surrogates: for instance, of gold or silver pieces by copper ones. This is to say that the copper coins are accepted in payment in lieu of quantities of gold or silver far greater than the actual rates of exchange between copper and the precious metals, viz. in unminted condition, would justify. Thus the copper coins already serve to circulate commodities not in proportion to their own value, but rather in proportion to the value of definite quantities of gold or silver which they represent. But note that they are only able in this way to 'represent' quantities of gold or silver inasmuch as there are in fact gold or silver coins in circulation with a real metallic content (at least at time of issue) comprising some multiple of the quantities ideally represented by the copper coins. What the copper pieces represent are precisely subdivisions of the gold or silver ones, and the essential condition for their doing so is the actual interlacing of the circulations of the one and the other.

The character of such coins is not quite, then, 'purely symbolic', as Marx somewhat misleadingly puts it (*CI*, 224/140), since a symbol is not ordinarily interchangeable with that which it symbolizes. It needs to be stressed, moreover, that even if we were to continue speaking of them as 'symbols', they are not as such symbols *of value*, but rather of definite quantities of *some one particular sort of thing* which *is valuable*. It is this really existing thing which the coins represent, and the regular acceptance as payment of its surrogates, just as surely as the regular acceptance of the thing itself, confirms that the latter in turn represents the real form of existence or 'epitomization' of the value abstraction.

What has just been said as regards metallic tokens of the money-commodity applies equally well to paper ones. Paper currencies, so long as they are practically convertible into gold or silver, merely perfect the representative function pioneered by copper coins and the like. In comparison with the latter, paper notes offer the advantage of providing more nearly valueless surrogates for the general equivalent. As a consequence, indeed, their surrogate character is all the more clearly revealed.[8] The introduction of paper notes thus completes the process of what Marx calls the 'separation' of the 'nominal content' of the monetary token – Marx in fact writes of 'coinage' (*Münze*), though in this case so-called 'paper-money' must also count as such – from its 'real content' or 'metallic content'.[9] More to the point, this same process, at least in its advanced stages, entails a second sort of 'separation': what Marx describes as that of the 'coined existence of gold [*des Goldes*] . . . from its value-substance' (*CI*, 223/140). The former – and presumably Marx ought to have written here of *Geld*, *money*, and not *Gold* – is the material designated to execute the circulatory function of the money-commodity and the latter is the money-commodity itself.

Furthermore, the paper notes are able fully to discharge a much broader range of transactions – including large-scale commercial transactions – than could be settled with 'small change' alone. Thus, in contrast to the latter, the paper notes nearly saturate the channels of exchange, at least within the internal market of a given national economy, rather than merely filling them out or flowing through their most insignificant subsidiaries (as remains indeed the special assignment of metallic tokens even after the introduction of paper notes). This is the case at least for full-fledged paper currencies issued by the state. On the internal market, such notes are delegated the power to execute all the circulatory functions of the money-commodity itself, thus allowing the latter to withdraw from the circulation sphere and exercise its influence over the latter *in absentia*. The metallic tokens, by contrast, merely served as the money-commodity's occasional adjutants.

This second improvement which paper notes bring to the task of representing the money-commodity in the immediate practice of exchange is not, of course, merely the consequence of the substitution of one material for another, of paper for metal. It requires rather a change in institutional framework: viz. the evolution of the economic power of the state to the point that, through a central bank as its organ, it will be capable of guaranteeing the currency of such paper notes as it issues. On present assumptions, this implies a 'guarantee' in the strict sense and not merely a successful regulatory policy: that is to say, the state agrees (and must be able to fulfil this agreement) to exchange the paper notes on demand for the quantities of the money-commodity indicated upon them.

Convertibility at the central bank thus fulfills much the same condition with regard to the representative function discharged by the paper notes as did interchangeability in circulation vis-à-vis the representational character of the metallic tokens. As already suggested, the paper surrogates are only able to 'represent' definite sums of the money-commodity, that is in the capacity of circulating other commodities, inasmuch as they are, in effect, transferable claims upon such sums. The paper notes are thus able to serve in the place of the money-commodity as, so to say, the immediate *instrument of exchange*. But even if the claims they represent are never called in and the central bank's reserves of the money-commodity remain serenely at rest in its vaults, still it is the money-commodity itself, and not its surrogates, which is the effective *medium of exchange*.

15.4 THE STANDARD OF PRICE

The functioning of the money-commodity as medium of exchange only entails that it be *capable* of being extracted from its deposits and repeatedly returned to circulation, even if the frequency with which it is actually called upon to enter circulation is not great or even if, as in the case just depicted, it is not for the purposes of the home market required to do so at all. The physical property which crucially qualifies some good to discharge this function, and hence to acquire in turn the mantle of general equivalent, is thus that it be highly durable, since only a highly durable good will be able to retain its value intact over long periods.[10]

Gold or silver quite obviously satisfy the criterion in question, whereas bread or eggs, say, self-evidently do not. Direct ownership of the money-commodity and the mobilization of the latter as instrument of exchange can be left to the province of just the major actors of the exchange economy: the merchants of the emergent capitalism of the late Middle Ages or the central banks and large commercial banks of a more mature global capitalist system. For the minor players – the peasants and proletarians or, more recently, even capitalist enterprises controlling quite considerable assets – the surrogates are perfectly serviceable. Once this functional partition has acquired stability, it is only a very small step to the introduction of *non*-convertible paper currencies. Even after their introduction, gold remains in fact the 'valuable thing' (*Wertding*) *par excellence* and hence, so to speak, the 'money of last resort', but now only by virtue of the behaviour of financial institutions in buying and selling it.[11]

Because under the circumstances here assumed all other commodities must in fact exchange regularly against the money-commodity or its surrogates, the regular proportions in which the money-commodity, whether actually or virtually, exchanges against a single unit of each of them can be immediately known. Thus for any given commodity – apart, that is, from the money-commodity itself – the quantity of value it represents can be immediately known in the form of the quantity of the money-commodity which can be obtained for it (or, alternatively, for which it can be obtained). Indeed, the quantity of value which any given commodity represents *must* be immediately known in this fashion in order for the transactions which mediate the exchange of the social product even to occur. The completion of a sale/purchase entails that the participants to the transaction have come to an agreement on precisely this: which is to say, in more familiar language, they have agreed on a price. It is in this way that the value-relation, as what I have called above a 'transcendental condition' of exchange, concretely imposes itself in the actions of economic agents. Of course, under monopolistic conditions, the buyer's agreement can be coerced. Nonetheless, agreement on a price remains, so to say, the juridically imposed presupposition of every such transaction. Where it has not been reached, if but formally, and goods or money change hands, then either we are confronted with a charitable act or a criminal one.

The exchange of every sort of commodity is placed under this same condition: except again the money-commodity, which, precisely as a correlate to the condition under which the exchange of the others is placed, has itself the unique power among commodities of being immediately exchangeable against every other sort. The values of all of the latter thus acquire a general and uniform mode of expression allowing for their immediate comparison. Hence, no special ex-post theoretical effort has to be undertaken in order to select a value-equivalent and express the values of commodities in it. It is, as Marx puts it, the 'social action of all other commodities' – or, more exactly, the action of their owners, who give to commodities their mode of 'behaviour' – which elevates the bodily-form of one sort of commodity to the status of the 'socially recognized equivalent form'.[12] Thereupon, units in which quantities of this commodity are measured serve, in effect, as the *proxy*-units in which value in general gets expressed. These units provide, as Marx calls it, the 'standard of price'.

Especially after what has just been written as regards monetary surrogates (that is, surrogates *for* the money-commodity), it needs to be stressed, however, that value cannot *otherwise* get expressed than through some such proxy. For inasmuch as value is not a directly perceptible property of commodities considered in isolation, but rather the socially-imparted capacity they have to attract one another on the market (their social 'specific gravity'), it can only be known through its effects – and its effects are precisely the regular proportions in which commodities exchange. Thus, under present assumptions, for any given commodity the value it represents can only be expressed in the form of some other commodity by which it is in fact replaceable in exchange. Its 'value-objectivity' (*Wertgegenständlichkeit*) gains expression in the form of some other (sort of) object, an object which in strictly *physical* respects is qualitatively distinct from it, but which qua value is interchangeable with it: viz. in some definite amount.

That value cannot otherwise get expressed than through some proxy remains true, incidentally, even when the circumstances here assumed no longer obtain: that is to say, when the proxy-units need no longer be identical with a definite physical measure of some one commodity, but can be arbitrarily devised by the state. On the world market, the value of a good priced in dollars is no different from the value of the same good priced in yen, but its value cannot be known at all except as expressed in some numerable vehicle which is distinct from it.

Furthermore, even though this vehicle has in itself no real physical form, it being qua measure, in effect, just an arbitrary index of relative values, it must, nonetheless, be provided by the state with at least *some* physical embodiment, however eviscerated. This is because in fulfilling its basic function as the independent form of value, money is, in effect and as I have put it above, also the general form of *property*,[13] and, needless to say, it can only be such inasmuch as itself *appropriable*.

Of course, even long before the emergence of 'fiat monies' created an ideal standard of price wholly unrelated to any real physical measure, quantities of the money-commodity representing in fact just a fraction of its conventional unit continued, nonetheless, to bear the sign of the latter in their capacity as medium of circulation. Consequently, the amount of the good which serves as the unit for the measurement of value ceased to be identical with its own conventional physical unit of measurement, even though both the former and the latter continued to be called by the same name. As expression of value, 'a pound sterling', for example, came to mean something quite different from an actual pound of sterling (indeed it came to mean a far lesser amount of gold), just as all the various silver 'pounds' which served as monies of account in early modern Europe came quickly to mean somewhat less than a physical pound of silver. Such a divergence of the meaning of monetary denominations from the meaning of the same words when used in their primordial sense as the signs for physical measures, does not, however, change anything essential in the matter.[14]

15.5 THE CHRIST OF COMMODITIES

Let us pause, finally, to resume our findings concerning the nature of money, keeping in mind the special set of assumptions under which our analysis has been conducted. In 'spirit', so to say, all sorts of commodity are exchange-values. But under the conditions here assumed, their 'spirit' is only known to the extent that it is represented in the form of their equivalence with the money-commodity, and their 'spirit' is only 'released' from its bodily enclosure to the extent that the latter is replaced in exchange by, so to say, the body of this 'spirit': viz. the money-commodity. The latter is also just one particular sort of commodity among others. But in the manner outlined above its peculiar physical form comes to represent the common 'spiritual' substance of all commodities and indeed in practice to 'be' that substance: its 'natural form', in short, becomes the socially-recognized 'value-form', hence the *real* form of value. It is for this reason that the money-commodity can be described as the 'Christ' of commodities.

Now, in light of the developments characteristic of modern currency systems, the foregoing account cannot stand as an analysis of money as such: that is to say, one with fully general validity. Nonetheless, though just an analysis of specifically commodity-money, it provides many of the elements essential to the explanation of 'fiat money' too. (As for so-called 'credit money', I would argue that it is not in fact an independent genre of money at all, but merely an instrument of payment, akin to the monetary surrogates discussed above, and hence always presupposes the existence of a monetary system based on some sort of, so to speak, embodied currency, whether commodity or not.) For 'fiat money' is assigned the task of accomplishing exactly the same functions as commodity-money, though by other – preferably less cumbersome and less costly – means. Whatever the sort of monetary device, the essential character of every sort of money is dictated by the functional requirements of commodity exchange: which is to say that it is the 'spirit' of commodities as exchange-values to which they are called upon precisely to give – appropriable – form.

In any case, the above account, though not presented in the manner of exegesis, provides, I think, a fair resumé of Marx's theory of money, which thus reveals itself to be an essential component, even indeed the most fundamental component, of his theory of value. Where I have at certain junctures, prompted by the logic of the subject-matter, ventured considerations which do not have any exact parallel in Marx, they are at least consistent with Marx's theory and should be understood just as elaborations of the latter. At any rate, they are understood as such by the author. The task of demonstrating how Marx's theory can be generalized to cover the case of 'fiat' money, is one which lies beyond the scope of the present work. This is not, incidentally, a task which has received much attention from contemporary Marxist economists, absorbed, as they tend to be, by the problem of price-formation or, in other words, the 'quantitative' value problem. In fact, however, the demonstration of the continuing relevance of much of what gets called Marx's 'value theory' depends crucially upon its fulfillment.

Our account is, then, fully serviceable for present purposes, since it affords us insight into that peculiar 'objectivity' of value-phenomena which provides, I am suggesting, the rational basis for Marx's famous 'coquetting' with Hegelian formulae. Starting from an examination of the 'elementary' form of value, we have been able to reconstruct how the very practical exigencies of commodity exchange create the requirement for some particular (sort of) commodity, a 'sensate-concrete' thing, to be assigned to the function of representing the universal value-form of all commodities. Thus we have learned both that and how the money-commodity is precisely an 'empirical universality': not just a sensuous thing which exhibits some 'universal' characteristic in common with other sensuous things, but a sort of thing whose sensuous reality counts in practice *as* the universal 'substance' of a definite range of others. So, it will be evident just how much the money-commodity, as the actuality of economic value, is like the existent 'idea' which, according to Hegelian 'logic', is supposed to represent the actuality of 'the concept'. Earlier we remarked upon the curiosity of Hegel's presenting the sun as the empirical universality of its satellites, and we have commented at length on the mystification wrought by his 'derivation' of the monarch as the empirical universality of the citizens of the state. Yet the proposition that money is the empirical universality of commodities, is neither curiosity nor mystification. It is correct.

16 The Metaphysics of Value: On Second-Order Objectivity

> Not an atom of matter enters into the value-objectivity of commodities. In this it is the direct opposite of the coarsely sensuous objectivity of commodities as physical objects. We may twist and turn a single commodity as we wish; it remains impossible to grasp it as a thing of value. (Marx, *Capital*)[1]

As in Hegel's exposition of 'the concept', so too in Marx's analysis of the value-form, it is 'the universal' which is substantial and 'particulars' which are its accidents. It should, however, be abundantly clear from the foregoing that this formulation loses all its idealist force with the restriction of its scope to just 'particulars' (in the sense specified above) *placed within the value-relation.* We have seen that for any given specimens of some sort of product their universal value-character remains latent and indeed indefinite – so to say, 'imputed' – until such time as those specimens are sold: at which point, this latent universality of commodities is 'realized'. Note that this implies that particular products only definitively exist as values, hence as commodities, precisely in the moment of their *ceasing-to-exist* as values – which by no means, however, entails their ceasing to exist altogether.

Now, for the previous owner of some good who has alienated it, the value which that good potentially represented prior to sale has not, of course, been lost. Far from it – the owner would never have parted with the good were this to be the case. This value has merely been endowed with a new form of existence and one indeed more adequate to its 'concept': whereas it was previously confined to the qualitatively specific form of whatever kind of good the owner happens to have offered for sale, it has now acquired the general-equivalent or 'really universal' form. In this sense, we could say that the value – which is to say, the *quantity* of value – controlled by commodity-owners in the form of commodities is not relinquished when the latter are sold, but, on the contrary, this value is liberated from its particular enclosure, in order to be revealed as but a particularization of the universal value 'substance' of all commodities.

Since, as has been discussed, a definite quantum of exchange-value cannot function as such in the particular form of commodities, it is not hyperbolic or merely poetic to describe this event as a 'liberation'. It is precise: the particular form of commodities represents a limitation which must be overcome in order for their value-character to be actualized. All of this will be recognized as a properly Hegelian reunification of the particular with the universal: a properly Christian 'transubstantiation'. And indeed, as far as the portion of the social product controlled by the owner is concerned – which now appears as qualitatively specific, now again as lacking all qualitative specificity and hence as quantitatively determinate[2] – what has transpired is just that.

But as far as *the commodities themselves* are concerned, considered precisely in their mundane physical existence, no such miracle has occurred. The owner who sold them has retained the same (quantity of) value which the commodities previously represented precisely because the condition under which the latter have been alienated is the receipt in return of a sum of *money* representing the same quantity of value. So the famous 'first metamorphosis' of commodities which sale is supposed to constitute (cf. *C*I, 200/120), is not in fact a 'metamorphosis' of the value represented by just those commodities, much less of the commodities as such in their physical self-identity.[3] The latter simply get *exchanged* not 'metamorphosized'. The 'first metamorphosis' is rather a metamorphosis of the exchange-value at the owner's disposal.

As for the value represented by the commodities themselves, this, so to say, *goes with them* and must ultimately get destroyed: whether through the consumption of the commodities or the subsequent consumption of 'final' commodities whose means of production they are – or supposing the consumption of either the former or the latter does not ensue in a timely fashion, then through the natural erosion of the one or the other. (In a dynamic setting, moreover, commodities may, of course, be instantaneously devalorized through shifting patterns of demand or technological obsolescence, thus suffering 'moral depreciation', as Marx puts it; though this variant need not concern us here.) With the monetary proceeds from the sale of commodities, their previous owners will under 'normal' circumstances purchase in turn other commodities: and the value of the latter must likewise expire in exactly the same way.

As a general rule, inasmuch as and to the same degree as the physical qualities which constitute the specific usefulness of produced goods get depleted, whether through actual use or desuetude, so too does the quantity of value potentially represented by them diminish: until such time, namely, as both are exhausted. This rule holds true for all particular sorts of commodity, whether 'final' goods or 'intermediary' ones, though only in the case of the former does it imply the destruction of value as such. In the case of means of production, assuming the full realization of the commodity product or, in other words, market-clearing conditions, in the same measure as the value which they represent is decreased through their consumption, that represented by the products which they are used to produce is increased. Hence, on the same assumption, the value of the *total* commodity product is destroyed just through the consumption and/or erosion of '*final*' commodities.[4]

Even before their very potential for representing value gets definitively, if gradually, destroyed in the process of their physical destruction, commodities are already in principle stripped of their value-character in the social act of sale/purchase. Of course, so long as its real deterioration has not progressed too far, it is not impossible following the initial sale of some commodity that at some later time its character as exchange-value will be *re*-actualized: either with the quantity of its value reduced in the interim, as in the case of 'used' goods, or with it augmented, as in that of commercially 're-sold' ones. But if one considers the totality of commercial transactions, their basic social function is precisely to transfer commodities, in Marx's words, 'from the hands in which they are non-use-values into the hands in which they are use-values' (*C*I, 198/119). Hence, the 'normal' outcome of the alienation of commodities, however many intermediary transactions may intervene prior to its arrival, is that they *cease* to be commodities and embark upon their respective careers as use-values pure and simple. Abstracting from derivative and merely intermediary transactions, sale/purchase thus results in what might be called a sort of 'desacralization' of the social product.

That the mysterious 'metamorphosis' of value is, nonetheless, possible, is, as we have seen, explicable on the postulate of commodity-money by the assignment of some species of commodity of exceptional durability to the function of continually returning to circulation in order to mediate the exchange of all others.[5] As for specimens of this money-commodity, supposing there is one, they alone do not lose any of their social 'aura', so to say, by virtue of being included in transactions. Indeed, the contrary is the case: it is precisely through the continual recurrence of their 'sale' against other sorts of commodity that they acquire this aura. Only thus does the money-commodity prove itself to be the sacred 'substance' of all other commodities, and only so long as it retains its currency, does it continue to be such. But this again has nothing at all to do with the character of that commodity as physical thing. The fact that its physical specimens, through their economic instrumentalization, come to serve as the 'form of appearance' of the value character of commodities in general, certainly does not provide us with any reason to conclude that per se, in their physical particularity, these specimens are pure 'illusion'!

This is because the 'value-objectivity' of commodities is, in the manner discussed in chapter 13, just *projected upon* the brute physical objectivity of the same, without in any way affecting the latter and without, then, per the Hegelian talk of 'real universality', implying any infringement of the principle of the thought-independence of the physical world. The 'value-objectivity' of commodities is thus what I would propose to call a 'second-order objectivity'. Now, neither commodities in general nor the money-commodity in particular are unique in being 'second-order objects'. *Every* physical thing or constellation or event which is assigned a representational function through a definite social practice becomes thereby the material – 'first-order' – incarnation of a 'second-order object': for example, a particular acoustic vibration which in the context of speech 'counts as' a phoneme to the properly trained human ear. The phoneme is a 'second-order object', a general type; the particular acoustical event is a 'first-order object' which serves as the momentary physical existence of the former, viz. its token. Taken together they too comprise a 'sensate supra-sensate thing'.

The special peculiarity of commodities and money, however, is that (a) as for the former, they can only be possessed of the 'second-order' objectivity of being values to the extent that this general determination in fact acquires a 'first-order' objectification *independent of them* and (b) as for the latter, its 'first-order' objective form is called upon precisely to fulfil this requirement and thus, in the manner outlined, to 'be' in practice the 'second-order' objectivity of all commodities – or, as in the case of specifically commodity-money, of all *other* commodities. This is what makes the 'isomorphism' of the money-commodity with the Hegelian 'empirical universal' so perfect and what makes money qua economic object in fact *sui generis*.[6] For a phonological system to exhibit an analogous peculiarity, for example, it would have to include a single phoneme which represented the linguistic value of all the other phonemes of which it consists: a circumstance which is manifestly impossible, as it belongs to the very nature of linguistic 'value' to be *qualitatively* differential and not, as in the case of economic value, merely quantitatively so.

If money is, then, a 'symbol', as has been frequently remarked, this fact alone does not go very far toward clarifying its specific nature. Marx himself, while drawing attention to the symbolic aspect of money (and, as we have seen, to the functional autonomization of the latter in the form of monetary surrogates), never claimed that money *as such* could be adequately grasped as a symbol and indeed persistently warned against the confusions inherent in such a position.[7] For money does not only 'signify', it also exhibits the quite extraordinary power among 'signs' of being a means for acquiring *real instances* of *that which* it signifies: that is, goods constituting a definite portion of the social product. We would all be very rich and have no need of money if the ordinary run of signs were similar to money in this respect.

In the case of commodity-money, as we have seen, the (first-order) object which discharges the money-function is only able to take on this special economic character inasmuch as it is in fact *itself* an instance of what it 'signifies'. It can only represent the result of a definite allocation of social labour by in fact being such (just as, in Marx's famous example, iron can only represent a certain weight by in fact being heavy). It is because of this that the 'first peculiarity' of the equivalent-form of value is supposed to entail, on the postulate of commodity-money, what Marx calls its 'second peculiarity': viz. that 'concrete labour becomes the form of appearance of its opposite, abstract human labour'.

Marx does not make a very explicit argument on behalf of this claim, but presumably the argument should run somewhat as follows. As we have seen, the 'natural form' of the particular commodity serving as money becomes the general 'value form' inasmuch as commodity-owners continually equate definite amounts of it – first ideally in the positing of a price and then really in the act of sale – with definite amounts of their own products. Inasmuch as the former and the latter should in principle and under 'normal' conditions exchange in just such proportions as require equal labour-time to produce, by acting thus exchangers in effect treat all the diverse forms of labour devoted to the production of the commodities they alienate as interchangeable with the labour devoted to the production of the money-commodity and thereby as homogeneous with one another. This is what exchangers 'do without knowing it': they reduce the various forms of 'concrete labour' comprising the branches of social production to but so many qualitatively homogeneous and hence quantitatively comparable allocations of the total social labour.

Of course, this 'second peculiarity' of the 'value-form', like indeed the first, clearly cannot any longer obtain when the general equivalent has ceased to be a product of labour at all. (Indeed, even on the assumption of commodity-money, Marx's comments on the 'second peculiarity' represent a simplification, since presumably the total labour devoted to the production of the equivalent will itself be distributed among a diverse set of labour-functions.) Nonetheless, the reduction of 'concrete labour' to 'abstract labour' – or what also might be called the conceptual *homogenization* of labour – continues to be brought about through the very practice of exchange, regardless of whether the monetary vehicle of this reduction is a product of labour or not. The 'reality' of the concept of labour as such is thus not in fact dependent upon the formal peculiarities of specifically commodity-money, as Marx's analysis could be taken to suggest, but rather upon the peculiarity of exchange as a mode of social integration.

Since the money-commodity can only represent a definite allocation of social-labour by in fact being such, its material cannot be so widely available in the natural environment as not to require any special exertion for it to be appropriated to human ends. Consequently, precisely what makes air, for instance, a suitable physical vehicle for linguistic signs, absolutely disqualifies it from serving as the material of economic value. Furthermore, and again quite unlike the material of linguistic signs, money – whether commodity or 'fiat' money – must have not only a 'first-order' objective form, but an *isolable* and *enduring* objective form: since only thus is it capable of being *owned and alienated.* The basic function of money, as we have seen, is not merely to 'represent' a measure of control over the social product, but to *be* such for its owners. To ignore all this through an excess of fascination for the symbolic character of money, provides a very convenient way of obfuscating the entire system of private property and exchange which gives to the monetary 'token' its social meaning.[8]

It is, incidentally, precisely in commenting upon the *second* 'peculiarity' of the 'value-form' in his 1867 text, viz. upon the inversion of the 'abstract' and 'concrete' aspects of the labour represented in the value-expression, that Marx pauses to reflect upon the distinctive metaphysics of value. In his revised 1873 presentation Marx repeats in effect his observation from the earlier version – 'in the value-expression of the commodity,' he now says, 'the matter gets turned around [*verdreht*]' (*CI*, 150/72–3) – but without venturing any speculations on 'the' abstract-universal or 'the' sensate-concrete as such and omitting the heuristic allusion to forms of law.

The changes are, I would suggest, symptomatic of an effort precisely to avoid giving the appearance of an endorsement of Hegelian 'logic'. This is why the purging of the allusion to '*the* law' and particular systems of law is so significant. For were I indeed to say that '*the* law, this abstraction, *realizes itself* in Roman law and German law, these concrete systems of law', I would be indulging in a characteristically Hegelian way of writing or speaking, and I would run the risk – especially if I was then to try to say anything more specific on legal matters in line with this first impressive pronouncement – of performing a characteristically Hegelian mystification. How, after all, could my statement be true, unless 'the law' is nothing other than 'reason' itself as present in the domain of 'objective spirit', with regard to which particular systems of law could only, then, be greater or lesser approximations – and so on and so forth? Without any further commentary, Marx's use of such an illustration is thus thoroughly equivocal. Though it should now at least be understandable how he would have been tempted to use it.

Notes

1 'RIGMAROLE' OR 'METHOD'?

1. Cited in Roman Rosdolsky, *The Making of Marx's Capital* (London: Pluto Press, 1977), p. 531. This remark, incidentally, considering its source, underscores the appurtenance of Keynesian economic theory to the neoclassical tradition.
2. For a characteristic example, see Robert Paul Wolff, *Understanding Marx: a Reconstruction and Critique of Capital* (Princeton: Princeton University Press, 1984), pp. 107–9. Böhm-Bawerk himself, incidentally, does not ignore the fact that Marx claimed explicitly to be justified in abstracting from the utility of commodities. Whereas he acknowledges Marx's procedure, however, his dismay over it is so great that, having apparently exhausted the tools of theoretical critique, he is finally led to engage in psychological speculations concerning the motivations which could have compelled a fellow as smart as Marx ('an intellectual force of the very highest order') to have made such a foolish proposal. See Eugen von Böhm-Bawerk, *Karl Marx and the Close of his System* (New York: Augustus M. Kelly, 1966), pp. 73–80. We will be inclined to share Böhm-Bawerk's incredulity only if we share too his conviction – for which no argument is given – that the subjective usefulness of goods is as susceptible of measurement and quantitative comparison as the labour expenditures requisite for their production.
3. Cf. *SL*, 154–5/I, 172: 'The proposition that the finite is ideal constitutes idealism. The idealism of philosophy consists in nothing else than in recognizing that the finite has no veritable being. Every philosophy is essentially an idealism or at least has idealism for its principle. . . . A philosophy which ascribed veritable, ultimate, absolute being to finite existence as such, would not deserve the name of philosophy; the principles of ancient or modern philosophies, water, or matter, or atoms are *thoughts*, universals, ideal entities, not things as they immediately present themselves to us, that is, in their sensuous individuality. . . .' For the connection between this 'constitutive proposition' of idealism and the essence/appearance couplet, cf., for instance, *SL*, 588/II, 259.
4. For two rather self-conscious examples, see Ernst Mandel's 'Introduction' to *CI*, pp. 19–20, and Paul Boccara, *Sur la mise en mouvement du 'Capital'* (Paris: Éditions sociales, 1978), pp. 298 ff. Anwar Shaikh's more casual remark, made in criticizing the 'neo-Ricardian' Ian Steedman, can serve as representative for the genre: 'Steedman goes on to say that because the value rate of profit is "unknown to capitalists," . . . it is "*not* a significant rate of profit in a capitalist economy." How extraordinary it is to claim that only what "the capitalists know" is significant, in other words, that appearances are significant but essences are not! In one stroke Steedman throws out all science' (Shaikh, 'Neo-Ricardian Economics: a Wealth of

Algebra, a Poverty of Theory', *Review of Radical Political Economics*, vol. 14, no. 2 [1982], p. 76). Needless to say, such observations derive their quality of self-evidence from a number of scattered remarks to be found in Marx's own corpus. Cf., for instance, *C*III, 956/825 and, for a more subtle and interesting use of the same sort of formula (Marx's point is that it is 'contrary to appearances' to expect that profit should be explicable on the basis of the exchange of equivalents), *Value, Price and Profit* (collected in *Wage-labour and Capital / Value, Price and Profit* [New York: International, 1976]), p. 37.

5. Marx first makes this assumption explicit in elaborating upon what is arguably the core programmatic proposition of *Capital*, vol. I: namely, that 'the transformation of money into capital is to be developed on the basis of the immanent laws of commodity exchange, in such a way that the starting-point is the exchange of equivalents' (*C*I, 269/180). In a footnote to this sentence, Marx continues: '. . . the formation of capital must be possible even though the price and value of a commodity be the same, for it cannot be explained by referring to any divergence between price and value. If prices actually differ from values, we must first reduce the former to the latter, i.e. disregard this circumstance as an accidental one, in order to have before us the phenomenon of the formation of capital on the basis of the exchange of commodities in its purity and not to be misled in its observation by interfering incidental circumstances which are alien to the genuine development.' (Cf. also *C*II, 109/32, where Marx reaffirms the need for this simplifying assumption.) Having introduced the assumption of commodities exchanging 'at values' and justified it on methodological grounds, Marx does then go on to assert that not only in theory, but in economic practice itself prices are in fact continually being reduced to an 'average price' as their 'inherent norm' (*inneren Regel*) and, furthermore, that these 'average prices' are regulated 'in the last instance' by the value of commodities. But he does not treat the dynamics of this process until volume III.
6. The work of Anwar Shaikh represents just such an attempt at preserving 'orthodoxy' in Marxian economics. See, for example, the article cited in note 4 above.

2 MARX ON THE 'MARX–HEGEL RELATION'

1. Marx's reference to his having avowed himself a 'pupil' of Hegel is particularly intriguing in this connection. The avowal in question is duly noted by Marx in the 1873 'Afterword'. It is not, however, exactly repeated: namely, *in the present tense*, which is, of course, the only tense in which performative utterances in fact function as performatives.
2. Though these too have had their echoes in the subsequent Marxist tradition, albeit in other sorts of discourse-contexts than those with which we are immediately concerned. I have even heard 'the dialectic' defined by way of the alleged fact that however bleak the present conjuncture may seem (here again the unreliable 'appearances'!), the working class will triumph 'in the end'. In such assurances, apparent defeat 'turns into its opposite' – namely, certain victory!

3. On the empiricist tendency of Engels's version of 'dialectics', cf. Althusser's 'The Object of *Capital*' in Louis Althusser and Etienne Balibar, *Reading Capital* (London: New Left Books, 1970), pp. 81–2 and 113–14.
4. Perhaps it could still be claimed that a 'dialectical' idiom is more suitable to grasping reality by virtue of avoiding, for instance, the assumption of ('fixed') substances which simply undergo processes and emphasizing instead the 'fluidity' of those processes themselves. If this is so, however, the peculiarity of a 'dialectical' idiom as opposed to any other will have to consist in certain features of its *syntax* and not, as has sometimes been suggested, in some special 'fluidity' of its 'concepts'. For *any* concept must imply boundary conditions limiting its application. Otherwise, it would not be the concept *of* anything.
5. *Reading Capital*, p. 107.
6. To my knowledge and recollection, the earliest formulation of the 'fetters' hypothesis occurs in *The German Ideology*, which was composed in 1845–6 and to the unpublished manuscript of which Marx alludes in the 1859 'Preface'. Cf. *GI*, 87/72. The hypothesis is stated again (though here without any mention of 'fetters') in *The Poverty of Philosophy* (*PP*, 122–3/130–1), originally published in 1847; and once more in a famous passage from *The Communist Manifesto* (New York: International, 1948; original edition, 1848), pp. 14–15/*MEW*, vol. 4, p. 467.
7. See Cohen's *Karl Marx's Theory of History: A Defence* (Princeton: Princeton University Press, 1978).

3 'DIALECTICS', HISTORICITY AND THE LOGIC OF *CAPITAL*

1. Jindřich Zelený, *Die Wissenschaftslogik bei Marx und 'Das Kapital'* (Wien: Europa Verlag, 1968), p. 62.
2. Zeleny, p. 71.
3. Zeleny, p. 75.
4. Georg Lukács, *History and Class Consciousness* (Cambridge, Mass.: MIT Press, 1971), p. 34.
5. Lukács, p. 14.
6. Lukács, p. 145.
7. Lukács, p. 11.
8. Jean-Joseph Goux, *Freud, Marx: Économie et Symbolique* (Paris: Editions du Seuil, 1973), p. 19. The groping use of the adjectives 'historical' and 'dialectical' as complements is highly characteristic of the style of discourse here at issue. Goux, incidentally, is not wrong in indicating Marx's genetic derivation of the money-form (there is, though, no analogous 'genesis' of capital itself in *Capital*) as a crucial theoretical *locus* for considering the relation of Marx's value analysis to Hegelian logic. He is, however, wrong – and, I am suggesting, in a symptomatic manner – in proposing that there is anything 'historical' about the said 'genesis'.
9. Goux, p. 20.
10. As recorded in note 8 above, the cited passages come from a book first published in 1973 in France. It would seem, however, that above all the most dubious products of French 'Theory' remain in high demand in US

academia long after the disappearance of their domestic market. Thus the programme for the 1995 Allied Social Science Association meetings included a talk by the cited author on the apparently still vital issue of 'The Phallus and Economics'.

11. On such passages as are typically adduced as evidence, cf. section 3.4 below.
12. Maurice Godelier, *Rationality and Irrationality in Economics* (London: New Left Books, 1972), p. 88.
13. Godelier, pp. 83–4.
14. For Marx's presentation of the centralization of capital as precondition for the transition to socialism, cf. *CI*, ch. 25 (ch. 24, section 7 in the *MEW* edition), on 'The Historical Tendency of Capital Accumulation', and especially *CIII*, ch. 27, on 'The Role of Credit in Capitalist Production', where the argument is made in greater detail. In the *CI* discussion, Marx himself insists upon the necessity of the transition. Indeed the latter is supposed to take place 'with the inexorability of a natural process' (929/791). It is interesting to note too that precisely in this context Marx employs a distinctly Hegelian idiom, foretelling the expropriation of capitalist property by the direct producers as the 'negation of the negation' (the 'first negation' having been the expropriation of the original property *of* the direct producers). Marx's assurances in this regard are, however, conspicuously free of any logical connection to the analysis which precedes them. Indeed, much of what Marx says here is merely a rehearsal of the earlier schematic presentations of the 'fetters' hypothesis from the 1859 'Preface' and the *Manifesto* (which Marx then quotes directly in a note attached to the very end of the chapter). The *CIII* discussion is, by contrast, significantly more restrained.
15. Godelier, p. 187.
16. G.W.F. Hegel, *Die Vernunft in der Geschichte: Einleiting in der Philosophie der Weltgeschichte*, ed. Georg Lasson, 2nd edition (Leipzig: Verlag von Felix Meiner, 1920), p. 149. Cf. also p. 44 of the same text.
17. For readers who are inclined to this macabre sort of inquiry, let me, however, simply refer them to paragraphs §347 and §351 of Hegel's *Philosophy of Right*, where Hegel spells out in unmistakable detail some of the more unpleasant consequences of his doctrine of 'national principles'.
18. Cf. *Reading Capital*, pp. 186–7.
19. Michel Foucault, *The Order of Things* (New York: Random House, 1970), p. 252.
20. Cf. *Reading Capital*, pp. 194–8.
21. See especially his discussion of what he calls 'differential' historical times, in *Reading Capital*, pp. 99–105.
22. It should be noted that Althusser also makes some very relevant and telling criticisms of genetic historicism (which he refers to simply as 'geneticism'). But it is a weakness of his account that he fails clearly to distinguish genetic historicism from epochal historicism, and associates both indiscriminately with Hegelian residues in Marxist discourse.
23. It is this sort of historicism which is the main target of Nietzsche's *On the Genealogy of Morals*. 'For all sorts of historical investigation,' he writes, 'there is no more important proposition . . . *viz*., that the cause of

the emergence of a thing and its eventual usefulness, its actual employment and ordering within a system of aims, lie *toto coelo* outside one another . . .' (Friedrich Nietzsche, *Zur Genealogie der Moral*, essay II, section 12).

24. This is especially obvious in the current of 'Marxist' or *marxisant* discourse inspired specifically by Gramsci. A close examination of Gramsci's own writings reveals a marked tendency to attribute the existence of some allegedly 'superstructural' phenomenon directly to the requirements of the *forces of production*, with the 'ruling classes' organized into the state presented as something like the conscious proxies of the latter. Such a contraction of the 'economic base' into its purely technical aspect results in another sort of 'inclusive' historicism: what might be called a 'continuous static' one, since 'superstructural' conditions are here calibrated to the degree of development of the productive forces (which are, after all, supposed to be continually developing) rather than the fundamental structure of the relations of production (which change only intermittently, viz. per the 'fetters' hypothesis at certain crucial plateaus in the development of the former). This tendency in Gramsci is especially conspicuous in the various observations assembled under the title of 'Americanism and Fordism'. See Antonio Gramsci, *Selections from The Prison Notebooks* (New York: International, 1971), pp. 277–318. It is, incidentally, a little strange that Gramsci should be so much invoked by self-styled opponents of 'economism', given how unequivocal the subordination of the 'superstructures' to the 'needs' of the 'base' is in so many of his writings and given too his technicist foreshortening of the concept of the 'base'. Indeed, it would seem more plausible to treat him precisely as a textbook case *of* 'economism'. I suspect that what earns him the opposite reputation in our present circumstances is simply the fact that his 'economism' is not joined with much real interest in economics.
25. Albeit in Popper's reconstruction, perhaps indeed reflecting some bad habits of the tradition against which he was polemicizing, strangely joined with elements of 'epochal' historicism. For reasons which will become immediately clear, I will not consider Popper's critique of 'historicism' in any detail here. For a valuable discussion, which provides a wealth of textual evidence that Marx did not in general hold the position which Popper attributes to him, see W.A. Suchting, 'Marx, Popper, and "Historicism"', in *Inquiry*, 15 (1972), pp. 235–66.
26. Karl Popper, *The Poverty of Historicism* (New York: Harper & Row, 1964), p. vi.
27. From the dedication to *The Poverty of Historicism*.
28. Cf. note 14 above.
29. In the *Grundrisse*, for example, while Marx sharply criticizes Ricardo for the exogenous manner in which the latter derives the necessity of the profit rate's decline, he nonetheless continues to endorse Ricardo's contention that this decline entails an eventual decline in the mass of profits as well. Cf. *Gr*. 756/648–9. It is, of course, entirely another question whether Marx himself does in fact succeed in demonstrating the necessity of the profit rate's decline. But what I am suggesting is that far less hinges on this point than is almost universally supposed. I have developed an argu-

ment to this effect in 'Forget FROP!', an unpublished paper presented to the Conference of Socialist Economists at Newcastle upon Tyne in 1995.

30. Cf. *CI*, 928/789.
31. In the *Encyclopedia*, Hegel introduces the category of negation precisely in the sub-section of the 'Doctrine of Being' entitled '*Dasein*' or 'Determinate Being'. Cf. as well the corresponding '*Dasein*' chapter of *SL*, where Hegel writes, 'Reality is quality, determinate being; consequently it contains the moment of the negative and is through this alone the determinate being that it is' (112/I, 119).
32. Thus, prior to his hyperbolic appeal to the living and the dead, Hegel's examples are all of 'determinates' which at best 'pass into one another' only in a strictly logical sense: a meadow, as opposed to a pond or a wood, the moon as opposed to the sun. If the moon is 'implicitly the other of itself', as Hegel insists, this can only be in the sense that the *concept* of the moon acquires its determinacy in being opposed to that of the sun. But *the moon itself* certainly does not 'pass into' the sun!
33. In a 1922 essay on 'The Significance of Militant Materialism', Lenin recommended the formation of a 'society of materialist friends of Hegelian dialectics'. Cf. V.I. Lenin, *Collected Works*, vol. 33 (Moscow: Foreign Language Press, 1966), p. 234.
34. In more sophisticated versions, such 'movement' is specified as a 'movement through contradictions'. Though this specification creates its own problems, relating as it does an aspect of observable experience to a logical category. Stalin's *Dialectical and Historical Materialism* provides a classically convoluted statement of the figurative conception of 'dialectics': '[The] dialectical method of thought, later extended to the phenomena of nature, developed into the dialectical method of apprehending nature, which regards the phenomena of nature as being in constant movement and undergoing constant change . . .' (J. Stalin, *Dialectical and Historical Materialism* [Moscow: Foreign Languages Press, 1941], pp. 4–5).
35. The second chapter of Smith's *The Wealth of Nations*, where he attributes the development of the division of labour to 'a certain propensity in human nature . . . to truck, barter, and exchange', has become the locus classicus for this sort of move.
36. Cf. Marx's own comments to this effect in *PP*, 120–1/129.
37. Cf. *Reading Capital*, pp. 158–93.
38. For a presentation which is especially rich in historical and ethnological details, see, for instance, Karl Polanyi, *The Great Transformation* (Boston: Beacon, 1957), chapters 4 and 5.
39. Foucault's alleged 'archaeological' discovery that 'nineteenth-century bourgeois economics' and 'Marxism' belong to a common epistemic formation founded on an 'anthropology of natural finitude' is very impressive (cf. *The Order of Things*, p. 262). Not surprisingly, however, this 'discovery' remains completely unsubstantiated. It does not take much knowledge of Marx's economics to realize how little they depend upon any notion of scarcity as an attribute of some supposed *condition humaine*, per Foucault's creative suggestion. Still more spectacular pronouncements à la Baudrillard concerning alleged anthropological prejudices in Marx are even less deserving of serious consideration.

40. For an excellent discussion, cf. Simon Clarke, *Marx, Marginalism, and Modern Sociology* (London and Basingstoke: Macmillan, 1982), especially ch. 6.
41. Cf. Marx's *Marginal Notes on Adolph Wagner's 'Lehrbuch der politischen Ökonomie'* (published in English in Karl Marx, *Texts on Method* [Oxford: Blackwell, 1975]/in the original German in *MEW*, vol. 19).

4 CONCEPTS AND OBJECTS

1. *PP*, 105/115.
2. Cf. Lukács, *History and Class Consciousness*, pp. 27 and 33.
3. *PP*, 104/114.
4. *PP*, 110/119; quoted in *Reading Capital*, p. 92.
5. This makes Lukács's suggestion that Marx criticizes Proudhon from a *Hegelian* standpoint and, above all, for having misunderstood Hegel, all the more remarkable (cf. Lukács, p. 33). Indeed, the very 'observation' in which the cited passage appears contains a sustained critique of Hegel's *own* conception of 'method', quite apart from the trivialization suffered by the latter in Proudhon's application. By the same token, Marx leaves no doubt concerning his judgement of Proudhon's grasp of Hegelian philosophy. In this connection, see Marx's letter to J. B. Schweitzer of 24 January 1865, where he offers some typically caustic reminiscences on his personal association with Proudhon and even takes responsibility for having 'infected him, much to his detriment, with Hegelianism'.
6. Cf. *Reading Capital*, p. 92.
7. *PP*, 109/118.
8. Cf. G.W. Leibniz, *New Essays on Human Understanding* (Cambridge: Cambridge University Press, 1981), p. 308: 'One can understand "species" mathematically or else physically. In mathematical strictness the tiniest difference which stops two things from being alike in all respects makes them "of different species". It is in that sense that in geometry all circles are of a single species, because they are all perfectly alike. . . .'
9. Or, if one prefers, we could say, following Meinong, that they 'subsist' (*bestehen*), and reserve the term 'existence' for empirical things.
10. As Marx would later acknowledge, however, classical political economy was not in fact especially prone to this particular confusion, which has more to do with the theoretical deficiencies of mercantilism. The dehistoricizing blind spot of classical political economy is rather *capital*, which, symptomatic of the immaturity of his thought at this stage, Marx does not even include in his enumeration of 'relations of bourgeois production' in *PP*.
11. Cf. *GI*, 52/32. Just why Marx would, nonetheless, identify the division of labour as a specifically *bourgeois* relation of production in *The Poverty of Philosophy* (begun in the same year – 1846 – that *The German Ideology* was completed) becomes less mysterious when we consider that in both texts Marx for the most part employs what we could call an *emphatic* concept of the division of labour. He distinguishes this from the division of labour as it 'originally' or 'naturally' exists in the family. (In a truly bizarre and perplexing remark elsewhere in *The German Ideology*, Marx

and Engels actually locate this 'original' division of labour not in the structure of the family at all, but rather 'in the sexual act' [51/31]!) Marx's stated criterion for a fully-developed 'true' division of labour is the separation of 'mental' and 'bodily' labour: presumably because inasmuch as such comes to characterize a capitalist mode of production at the level of the individual enterprise – more precisely, in the form of a division of *executive* and *executory* labour – it is associated with an increasingly complex differentiation of branches of production at the level of social production as a whole. This latter *social* division of labour is in turn subject to no conscious regulation whatsoever (at any rate, this is the case in, so to speak, the 'pure form' of capitalist relations). When in *The German Ideology*, Marx and Engels rail against the division of labour and even go so far as to demand its 'supersession' (*Aufhebung*) (cf. 83/74) – or even the '*Aufhebung*' of 'labour' itself! (cf. 85/77) – it is surely this lack of *conscious regulation* of the division of labour that they have in mind.

12. I write here of a '*functional strata* of non-workers' in order to distinguish these from persons who either are potentially workers, though at a given time unemployed, or, as a result of physical or mental condition, are either not yet or no longer deemed able to work (the young, the aged, the disabled, etc.).
13. Cf. the opening lines, under the sub-heading 'Production', of Marx's methodological 'Introduction' to the *Grundrisse* manuscript: 'The object before us, to begin with, *material production*. Individuals producing in society – hence socially determined production by individuals – is, of course, the point of departure' (83/19).
14. Cf. *CI*, 184/104: 'Only a material whose every sample possesses the same uniform quality can be an adequate form of appearance of value, that is a material embodiment of abstract and therefore equal human labour. On the other hand, since the difference between the magnitudes of value is purely quantitative, the money commodity must be capable of purely quantitative differentiation, it must therefore be divisible at will, and it must also be possible to assemble it again from its component parts. Gold and silver possess these properties by nature'. Cf. also *Gr.*, 166/99 and *CPE*, 49/35; and, on an at least equally essential property which Marx in these passages ignores, cf. chapter 15, note 10 below.
15. Cf. *CI*, 226/142.
16. For occasionally confusing indications from Marx himself on the subject of socially-necessary labour-time and price-value deviations, see *CI*, 202/121–2, *CIII*, 287–9/195–7, and *Res.*, 967/108– 9. On the functionality of price-value deviations under conditions of generalized commodity exchange, see especially Marx's observation at *CI*, 196/117: 'The possibility... of a quantitative incongruity between price and the magnitude of value, i.e. the possibility that the price may diverge from the magnitude of value, is inherent in the price-form itself. This is not a defect, but, on the contrary, it makes this form the adequate one for a mode of production whose laws can only assert themselves as blindly operating averages between constant irregularities'. Marx's critique of 'time-chit' utopias of Proudhonist inspiration is based precisely on this fact (cf., for example, *Gr.*, 153/87ff) – making it all the more remarkable that he could be accused of having

held that in general prices should be directly proportional to 'labour-values'.

17. Cf. *CI*, 179/100: 'All commodities are non-use-values for their owners, and use-values for their non-owners.'
18. In saying this, I do not mean to suggest that it is anything other than typical for the ideological legitimation of a social order to consist of its dehistoricization or 'naturalization'. In pre-capitalist societies, however, this naturalization is normally accomplished through an appeal to an instance transcendent to the social order itself. Thus the ideologists of the feudal order invoked a *divine* sanction for earthly hierarchy. A capitalist order is peculiar in that the categories proper to it, by virtue of the duality of reference discussed, create the possibility of a pseudo-scientific naturalization of its constitutive social relations.
19. Cf. *CI*, 166/88: 'People do not . . . bring the products of their labour into relation with each other as values because these things count for them as merely the material receptacles of homogenous human labour. The reverse is true: by equating their different products to each other in exchange as values, they equate their different kinds of labour as human labour. They are not aware of this, but they do it.' The practical nature of the value abstraction serves as the point of departure for Alfred Sohn-Rethel's eccentric and insightful critique of traditional epistemology in *Intellectual and Manual Labour* (New Jersey: Humanities Press, 1978).
20. Cf. *For Marx* (New York: Random House, 1969), pp. 182–93; and *Reading Capital*, pp. 86–90.

5 PROPERTY AND PERSON (OR THE BIRTH OF THE JURIDICAL SUBJECT)

1. For a characteristically mystifying treatment of this same subject matter by one of the leading West German Hegel-interpreters of the post-war period, compare Joachim Ritter, 'Person and Property: On Hegel's *Philosophy of Right*, Paragraphs 34–81' (in Ritter, *Hegel and the French Revolution: Essays on 'The Philosophy of Right'* [Cambridge and London: MIT, 1982]). Following Marx, especially indications to be found in the *Grundrisse*, I try in this chapter to clarify the specific character of the social relations of production which gain expression in the basic concepts of bourgeois law. Ritter, on the contrary, takes those concepts as fundamental, as constitutive indeed of the very 'idea' of right as such, and treats the definite sort of social formation in question – a social formation apart from which those concepts are utterly devoid of meaning – as merely their empirical 'realization'. Hence, the property relations peculiar to a society of generalized commodity production – viz. a *capitalist* society, though in Ritter's vocabulary simply a 'modern' one – are identified by him as the 'determinate being', variously, of 'the freedom of man', 'the freedom of humanness' (sic.) and even 'Christian freedom' (sic!). Ritter's pseudo-derivation cum explanation of the attributes of civil law and 'civil society' (*bürgerliches Recht* and *bürgerliche Gesellschaft*) thus functions as a kind of idealist apotheosis of private property. The ideological serviceability of such an accomplishment in the context of a West German state whose very geo-

political raison d'être was anti-Communism is not difficult to appreciate. (Interestingly, Ritter's 'Person and Property' was originally published in 1961, at the height of the 'east–west conflict'.) It should be added that while Ritter follows Hegel, he does so in fact only up to a point, and in certain crucial respects indeed is only able to sustain his interpretation at the cost of an extreme distortion of Hegel's text. For more on this, see note 5 below.

As so happens, Ritter – whose influence has recently been extended to English-language discussions through the writings of his translator Richard Dien Winfield – had a long and curious history of philosophical service to the state. Before reinventing himself (and reinventing Hegel) as a liberal following the war, Ritter, a Nazi party member since 1937, was a contributor to the 'philosophical workgroup' organized by Nazi ideology chief Alfred Rosenberg. In publications from that period, he presented the 'German' '*Geisteswissenschaften*' or 'sciences of spirit' (in a manner in some ways reminiscent of Heidegger) as a bulwark against the alleged 'technicist' excesses of the physical sciences. Symptomatically, a contribution by Ritter appears in a collective volume from a series devoted to examining (or constituting?) the 'military deployment of the sciences of spirit'. For these and other details from Ritter's career and writings under the Third Reich, see Thomas Weber, 'Joachim Ritter und die "metaphysische Wendung"', in W.F. Haug, ed., *Deutsche Philosophen 1933* (Hamburg: Argument-Verlag, 1989).

2. Though obviously no substitute – as one might be led to believe by all sorts of fashionably extravagant 'post-Marxist' 'theories'.
3. On the difference between Marx's socio-historical 'materialism' and his philosophical 'materialism', see chapter 10, note 16 below.
4. This de facto functioning of political, ecclesiastical or kinship relations as the economic structure of society in pre-capitalist social formations is the principal theme of Maurice Godelier's *The Mental and the Material* (London: Verso, 1986), to which the following discussion is greatly indebted. See too Polanyi, *The Great Transformation*, especially ch. 4 on 'Societies and Economic Systems'.
5. Hegel, incidentally, takes this to be not a requirement of one specific principle of social integration, but – needless to say – a requirement of 'the concept'. See *Ph.R*, §40 ff. Having once 'shown' that property-ownership is the 'immediate embodiment' which 'the concept', viz. here as the concept of the free will, 'gives itself', he then goes on to argue that the entering of property-owners into contractual relations, i.e. exchange-relations, is a further phase necessary to the 'realization' of the said 'concept'. 'Reason', he writes, 'makes it just as necessary for men to enter into contractual relations – gift, exchange, trade, etc., – as to possess property. While all they are conscious of is that they are led to make contracts by need in general, by benevolence, advantage, etc., the fact remains that they are led to do this by reason implicit within them, i.e. by the Idea of the real existence of free personality' (*Ph.R.*, §71). Hegel thus presents the system of commodity exchange – apart from which property qua juridical form would be otiose and 'freedom' as the common attribute of legal persons, meaningless – as the result of its own consequences, as

an attribute, so to speak, of its attributes. (Note too his awkward references to 'gift' and 'benevolence' in this context, which show just how weak Hegel's grasp of the nature of contractually-regulated exchange remained, despite his oft-mentioned readings in political economy.)

It is this sort of procedure to which Marx devoted page after page of detailed critical commentary in his very early text known as the *Critique of Hegel's Doctrine of the State*, which is discussed in chapter 12 below. 'The crux of the matter', Marx writes, 'is that Hegel everywhere makes the Idea into the subject, while the genuine, real subject . . . is turned into the predicate' (*CHDS*, 65/209). Thus, the 'freedom' which characterizes the legal condition of individuals insofar as they practically relate to one another via the mediation of the exchange nexus – this 'freedom' becomes in Hegel's usage the abiding subject which reappears in property, exchange, the developed 'system of need', etc. as so many forms of its own existence.

It is likewise this sort of 'twisting of empirical facts into metaphysical axioms' (*CHDS*, 82/226) which, as indicated above (see note 1), Joachim Ritter emulates in his efforts to present bourgeois property as the very realization of 'human freedom'. But in Hegel's account, property, exchange, indeed the entirety of the relations pertaining to so-called 'civil society', are all but *partial phases* – 'moments' – of the realization of 'freedom', and indeed the completed 'realization' of the latter depends precisely on the exposure of their partiality or '*Einseitigkeit*' and their transcendence. In this regard, it is symptomatic that Ritter's 'Person and Property' is subtitled 'On Hegel's *Philosophy of Right*, paragraphs 34–81', since precisely with *paragraph 82* Hegel initiates his discussion of *wrong*. As the subsequent course of Hegel's exposition reveals, it is only the *violation* of civil law that provides the occasion for the will which is but abstractly expressed in it to acquire tangible reality in the exercise of state power. Contrary to Ritter's interpretation, then, it is in the form of *the state* that 'freedom' in Hegel's sense is finally 'realized': not as the negatively conceived 'freedom' of the particular individual, but rather as precisely the practical *subordination* of the latter which serves to demonstrate the 'substantive freedom' of '*Geist*' itself. For textual evidence to this effect and a discussion, see my 'Freedom's Devices: the Place of the Individual in Hegel's *Philosophy of Right*', *Radical Philosophy* 59 (Autumn 1991), pp. 27–32.

6. If personal status is or has been linked to certain ascriptive characteristics – as is the case, for instance, with the husband-wife opposition and also, at least under some circumstances, that of citizen to slave – it can continue to form the basis of legal exclusions even in a market-based social formation. But such exclusions are alien to the governing principle of commodity-exchange, and it is this fact that has allowed them to be effectively challenged – non-violently, in the name precisely of respecting the legal norms proper to a market system – by various 'civil rights' movements in the course of capitalist development. The only coherent aim which such movements can have is to guarantee that no one (read: no responsible economic agent) will be discriminated against based upon any special 'identity' that might be attributed to them. The aim is certainly *not* to defend any peculiar 'interests' of some group thus identified,

but, on the contrary, to make 'identities' in this sense legally irrelevant. The recent vogue for 'identity politics' among academic 'leftists' is thus especially puzzling. To associate 'identity politics' with some alleged 'radicalization' of the liberal tradition (as, for instance, is the practice of Ernesto Laclau and Chantal Mouffe) shows, moreover, a complete lack of understanding of the basic nature of a liberal social order.

7. See *The Mental and the Material*, p. 233.
8. As is the case in what Marx termed the 'Asiatic' or 'oriental' form of property: 'any fraction of property belongs to no member for himself, but to him only as immediate member of the commune, i.e. as in direct unity with it, not in distinction from it. The individual is thus only a possessor. There exists only communal property [*Gemeindeeigentum*] and only private possession [*Privatbesitz*]' (*Gr.*, 477/389). Cf. also *GI*, 61/79.
9. See Godelier, 'Politics as a Relation of Production', in *The Mental and the Material*, pp. 208–24.
10. In pre-capitalist social formations, to 'own' something is not necessarily to be able to 'do with it what one wants'. Thus, for example, a right to appropriation in the sense of *use* is not always accompanied by a right to *alienation*. (For examples from the ethnological literature, see Godelier, 'Territory and Property in Some Pre-Capitalist Societies', in *The Mental and the Material*, pp. 71–121.) This last point indicates that, prior to the emergence of bourgeois right, even where private appropriation takes place, this does not imply full-blown private property in the modern sense: since the community as a whole retains *positive* rights to the property in question which are not abrogated by and indeed necessarily accompany the special rights of the individual community member. In contrast, in bourgeois legal systems the property rights of the individual owner cannot be restricted by any positive right to the same item of property on the part of another agency, whether collective or likewise individual. Rather, they are limited only by the *negative* right of every other member of the legal order to dispose as s/he will of his or her property in turn undisturbed by the others. The historical sequence of property forms which Marx describes in the *Grundrisse* can, then, be understood as a tendential movement from communal property unrestricted by private appropriation (that is, the 'Asiatic' form) through hybrid forms wherein communal and private property claims co-exist and mutually condition one another (that is, the 'Classical' and the 'Germanic' forms) to private property unrestricted by communal appropriation (namely – at any rate, in principle – the modern 'bourgeois' form). See *Gr.*, 471–514/383–421.
11. More precisely, each agent represents a juridical-personal barrier for every other. S/he is a personal barrier, because by virtue of his or her personal idiosyncracies s/he might not be willing to exchange the property in question: which is to say, if s/he is viewed as owner of goods, to sell at the offered price or even to sell at all, or, if s/he is viewed as owner of money, to buy at the offered price or to buy at all. S/he is a juridical barrier, because as legitimate title-holder to the property in question s/he is formally free to do with it as s/he pleases, and cannot be forced to alienate it except under the conditions of a contract to which s/he has agreed.
12. See *Gr.*, 243/169: 'Although individual A feels a need for the commodity

of individual B, he does not seize it by force, nor vice-versa, but rather they recognize one another reciprocally as owners, as persons whose will penetrates their commodities. Accordingly the juridical moment of the person enters here . . .' Marx makes much the same point at *CI*, 178–9/99–100.

13. With an eye to its epistemological implications, Sohn-Rethel aptly describes the attitude of the participants in exchange as one of 'practical solipsism'.

6 THE OBJECTIFICATION OF SOCIAL RELATIONS

1. *CI*, 176/97. Marx repeats much the same point in *Res.*, 998/24.
2. That the simpler formulation is not suitable for capitalist conditions is made abundantly clear by consideration of the capital/wage-labour exchange itself. Capitalists purchase from workers their capacity to labour; whereas workers purchase from capitalists in the form of wage-goods a part of the product of the use capitalists make of their capacity to labour. Hence, in effect, workers purchase part of a total social product which they have, considered as a class, *themselves* produced.
3. Cf. *Gr.*, 242/168: 'If individual A had the same need as individual B, and if both had realized their labour in the same object, then no relation whatever would exist between them; considered from the point of view of their production, they would not be different individuals at all. Both have the need to breathe; for both the air exists as atmosphere; this brings them into no social contact; as breathing individuals they relate to one another only as natural bodies, not as persons. Only the differences between their needs and between their production occasions exchange and their social equalization in it. . . .'
4. At this point, the individual can either withdraw from the economic system with whatever personal belongings are already in his or her possession (and typically await their dissipation and hence death), disregard the legal norms of the system (that is, steal or rob what s/he cannot buy) or become a ward of personal charity and/or the state. The real loss of personal rights that ensues for individuals within a capitalist system when they are not able to satisfy their needs through the normal channels of commodity exchange is, I hope, not in need of any great effort of proof here. Both of the preceding parentheses in the main text are, incidentally, intended as reminders that under capitalist conditions the *juridical* agent of production is not necessarily identical with the biological individual or individuals who expend their labour in the production process – hence the ambiguity of reference affecting the term 'producer' when applied to capitalist relations.
5. Cf. *Gr.*, 156–7/90: 'The reciprocal and all-sided dependence of the individuals who are indifferent to one another forms their social connection. This social connection is expressed in *exchange value*, by means of which each individual's own activity or its product first becomes an activity or a product for that individual; the individual must produce a general product – *exchange value*, or, the latter isolated for itself and individualized, *money*'. We will see directly just what Marx means by claiming that the product of the individual must *be* money.

6. The reasons for the applicability of such Hegelianisms specifically in this context will be clarified in Part 4 below. For Marx's systematic use of the distinctions introduced in this paragraph, cf. especially *CI*, 199/119.
7. Which is the reason for Adam Smith's identifying labour as the original purchasing or 'real' price of commodities. If the direct producers are dispossessed of the means of production, the original form of acquisition of use-values remains in fact their labour. Only under such conditions, their labour has the peculiar consequence of 'acquiring' use-values for persons other than themselves.
8. Cf. *CI*, 181/101–2.
9. As against the moralistic legends of classical political economy ('Long, long ago there were two sorts of people: one, the diligent, intelligent and, above all, frugal elite; the other, lazy rascals, squandering everything they have, and more, in riotous living' [*CI*, 873/741]), Marx attempts, in the final chapter of *CI* on 'The so-called Primitive Accumulation', to reconstruct how the initial disproportionality arose historically.
10. The expression comes from Karl Polanyi. I adopt it here, however, with a modified sense, since Polanyi would also describe 'labour' and money as 'fictitious commodities', which from a Marxian perspective is clearly more controversial. On the face of it, Polanyi's account would lend support to the dissenting faction in recent debates over whether Marx was correct to treat labour-power as a commodity. In fact, I think the differences between Polanyi and Marx on this point are more a matter of conceptual economy than substantive disagreement. In any event, Polanyi is unequivocal in stating that 'labour' qua commodity is not any *theoretical* 'fiction', but rather a, so to speak, '*practical*' one, which is necessary to the very existence of a full-fledged market economy. Cf. *The Great Transformation*, ch. 6, especially pp. 72–5.
11. Cf. his *Der soziale Gehalt der Marxschen Werttheorie* (Jena: Verlag von Gustav Fischer, 1916), p. 29 and passim.
12. Cf. *CIII*, 755/630–1, where Marx observes that for the landlord 'land represents nothing but a certain monetary tax that his monopoly enables him to levy upon the industrial capitalist, the farmer'.
13. Cf., for instance, *CIII*, 906/780. Even housing-rents paid by workers can, incidentally, be regarded as a deduction from surplus-value (despite the fact that they do not formally appear as such), since they add a tributary element to the real costs of reproduction of labour-power and hence artificially raise the wage-rate. The parasitic relation of rental incomes to capitalist revenues was, incidentally, already taken as a theme by Marx in the *Economic and Philosophic Manuscripts*. See *EPM*, 125/528.
14. In the *Grundrisse*, Marx even suggests that 'capital' itself strives after a reform of the sort described: 'It thus endeavors to dissolve landed property as private property and to transfer it to the state. . . . Thus to transform the entire domestic society into capitalists and wage-laborers' (*Gr.*, 279/204).
15. *CIII*, 760/636.
16. Cf. *Gr.*, 246/172: 'A worker who buys commodities for 3s. appears to the seller in the same function, in the same equality – in the form of 3s. – as the king who does the same. All distinction between them is extinguished.'
17. Cf. William Townsend's remark: 'The slave must be compelled to work

but the free man should be left to his own judgment, and discretion; should be protected in the full enjoyment of his own, be it much or little; and punished when he invades his neighbor's property.' Cited in Polanyi, *The Great Transformation*, pp. 113–14. This same Townsend, in his *Dissertation on the Poor Laws*, makes it clear by what the judgement of the 'free man' should be informed. Thus, of the compulsion to labour, he also writes: 'Legal constraint is attended with too much trouble, violence and noise . . . whereas hunger is not only a peaceable, silent, unremitted pressure, but as the most natural motive to industry and labour, it calls forth the most powerful exertions.' Cited in *CI*, 800/676.

18. Cf. *CI*, 709–10/589–90, where Marx explicitly introduces and discusses the grounds for this assumption.
19. Marx's claim, which I have done no more than dogmatically reproduce in the text, that the value of labour-power is regulated exclusively by the labour-time socially necessary for the production of its 'means of production' (or, in other words, wage-labourers' purchased means of consumption) has been the topic of extended controversy: most notably, in the context of the so-called 'household labour debates'. Nonetheless, if our interest is in understanding the actual workings of a capitalist system, rather than in moralizing, there are, I think, incontrovertible grounds for following Marx in this regard. The most decisive of these is of a simple logical character and can be explained as follows. The real form taken by the value of labour-power in exchange is *the money wage*. Now, the money wage underwrites the purchases of those commodities which wage-labourers and their dependents use for the purpose of their personal reproduction and (if they are fortunate enough) enjoyment. In other words, the money wage underwrites *the real wage*. That the value of labour-power is equivalent to the value of the purchased means of consumption used by the wage-labourer and dependents is, then, simply a *tautology*. To claim otherwise – to claim that the money wage contains a value-increment in *excess* of the value of those means of consumption – is to assert, however unwittingly, that the money-wage underwrites not only workers' consumption but also *workers' savings*. And, *nota bene*, what is implied here is not just occasional savings or 'life-cycle savings', but, so to speak, *permanent savings*, savings which can never be spent, since the moment they are spent the value they represent is converted into a simple equivalent for the value of the goods which they are used to purchase (and hence the alleged 'excess' disappears). The contradictory of Marx's claim, despite the passions which the latter has aroused, is not only, then, demonstrably false, it is manifestly *absurd*.

7 AN 'IDEALISM OF MATTER'

1. This last claim may well be the most dubious Marx ever made – which probably explains the vastness of its fame in some circles.
2. *En.L*, §194, add. 1.
3. Cf. *En.L*, §161, add., where Hegel remarks that through 'the movement of the concept': 'only that gets posited which is already implicitly present . . .'.

4. Cf. Lucio Colletti, *Marxism and Hegel* (London: New Left Books, 1973), p. 208: 'In substance, it is not man who thinks about reality, but the Spirit or *Logos* which by means of man, establishes a relationship to that which it itself has *posited* as reality, and thereby redeems itself from alienation and attains to a full consciousness of itself.'

8 TWO PRINCIPLES OF CONTRADICTION

1. This is Hegel's own formulation (cf. *SL*, 409/II, 36). Though it is more than a little confusing to represent contradictory predicates by the same symbol as the subject to which they are supposed to be attached, Hegel presumably chooses this convention in order to set in relief the dependence of the principle of non-contradiction upon the maxim of identity, 'A = A'.
2. Cf., for example, among many other passages, *En.L*, §81, add. 2, and *Phen.*, §79 (on 'determinate' versus merely abstract negation). Hegel also distinguishes between the sceptical dialectic of ancient philosophy, which he regards as a necessary but subordinate moment of 'true' philosophy, and modern scepticism, which he rejects as unphilosophic by virtue of its empiricist orientation. For a detailed discussion, see Colletti, pp. 68–85.
3. Throughout my discussion, I will continue to translate *aufheben* by 'sublate': this in deference to a convention which has by now become too firmly entrenched to go to the trouble of challenging here. But even in using 'sublate' to render *aufheben*, I will keep the English term in scare-quotes: this in acknowledgement of what strike me as compelling objections which have been raised against its appropriateness. For these objections, see W.A. Suchting, 'Translating Hegel's *Logic*: Some Minority Comments on Terminology', in G.W.F. Hegel, *The Encyclopedia Logic* (Indianapolis: Hackett, 1991), pp. xxxv–xxxvi.
4. Cf. *En.L*, §16: 'How many of the particular parts is requisite to constitute a particular science is indeterminate to the extent that, in order to be true, the part must not only be an individualized moment but itself a totality.' Thus, for example, the 'immediate' object of investigation of the *Rechtsphilosophie* is abstract right, which in the course of its exposition is supposed to give rise to a series of more concrete determinations (such as property, the family, civil society, and so on), all of which are supposed to be revealed in the end as but so many subordinate moments of the state. The state turns out to be nothing other than '*Geist*' actualized and become conscious of itself as such (as opposed to '*Geist*' still immersed in its otherness – or '*Geist* asleep' – which is rather the object of the philosophy of nature). The state, Hegel remarks in no uncertain terms, '[is] the march of God in the world' (*Ph.R*, §258, add.).
5. Most spectacularly by Althusser (see especially 'Contradiction and Overdetermination', in *For Marx*, pp. 87–128) and with far greater precision concerning the specific character of the appurtenance of Hegel's doctrine of contradiction to his idealism by Colletti. '"Dialectical materialism"', Colletti writes pointedly, 'is merely an idealism unaware of its own nature' (Colletti, p. 61).

9 THE WORD MADE FLESH OR HEGEL'S INCARNATION OF LOGIC

1. Cf. 'With What Must the Science Begin?' in *SL*, 67–78/I, 65–78.
2. Cf. also *Ph.R*, §279: 'The immanent development of a science, the *derivation of its entire content* from the *concept* in its simplicity (otherwise a science at least does not deserve the name of a philosophical science) exhibits this peculiarity, that one and the same concept . . . which begins by being abstract (because it is at the beginning), maintains its identity even while it consolidates its specific determinations, and that too solely by its own activity, and in this way gains a concrete content.'
3. In the *Encyclopedia*, Hegel presents this 'transition' more concisely: 'We began with being, abstract being, and now we have the *idea* as being; but this idea which has being is nature' (*En.L*, §244, add.).
4. The reader should pay close attention to Hegel's word-choice in this passage. The concept 'ascends' (*sich emporhebt*) from out of externality. Note too in the next-quoted passage that the 'idea' is said to be the 'creator' of nature. As will be shown in the following (cf. section 9.3 below), such obviously loaded religious language – too easily dismissed as 'merely' metaphorical by the most recent of Hegel's 'Marxist friends' – is by no means inessential to the course of his exposition.
5. In his earlier pronouncements on the subject, Hegel sometimes presents the *Phenomenology of Spirit* as preliminary to the *Logic*, not only chronologically but also with regard to order of demonstration (cf., for example, *SL*, 49/I, 43). However, in keeping with the standpoint of his later works, which makes rather every other sort of knowledge derivative upon logic, he subsequently revises this judgement. Thus already in the preface to the first edition of volume one of the 'greater' *Logic* (composed after the body of the text), he writes with regard to the *Phenomenology*: 'Consciousness is spirit as concrete knowing, a knowing too, in which externality is involved; but the development of this object, like the development of all natural and spiritual life, rests solely on the nature of the pure essentialities which constitute the content of logic' (*SL*, 28/I, 17). Accordingly, the material of the *Phenomenology* reappears in the *Encyclopedia* relegated to its *third* part. This no doubt accounts for Hegel's bashful reference in the same work to 'my *Phenomenology of Spirit*, which . . . upon its publication was described as the first part of the system' (*En.L*, §25, add.).
6. Hegel repeats this charge of nature's '*Ohnmacht*' often. See, for example, *SL*, 607–8/II, 282, where he gives full vent to his frustration with nature on this account.
7. 'Immediate being' is 'immediate' relative precisely to a certain sort of cognition: viz. *perception* or *sensuous intuition*. Whereas Hegel's *Logic* begins with the simple immediacy of being (or, in other words, being in the form of simple immediacy), the *Phenomenology of Spirit* begins rather with this sort of 'immediate consciousness' which corresponds to it.
8. Cf. *En.*, §245: 'Practically, in comporting himself towards nature as towards something immediate and external, the human being himself acts as an immediate, external and hence sensuous individual. . . .'
9. Cf. *En.L*, §163. And for a 'concrete' example of Hegel's application of

these logical distinctions in the further development of his system, see *Ph.R*, §275 (and ff.), where Hegel analyses the power of the monarch as the individuality which lends unity to the diverse moments of the state. In the addition to this paragraph, Hegel says (here in Knox's not quite literal but elegant translation): 'Prima facie, individuality occurs in nature too, but reality, the opposite of ideality, and reciprocal externality [*das Auseinander*] are not the same as self-enclosed existence [*das Beisichseinde*]. On the contrary, in nature the various things subsist alongside one another. In spirit, on the other hand, variety exists only as something ideal and as a unity.'

10. Cf. *En.*, §391, on the 'natural soul'. Cf. also *Ph.R*, §43: 'As the concept in its *immediacy*, and so as in essence a unit, a person has a *natural* existence. . . .'
11. Cf. *Ph.R*, §29: 'An existent of any sort embodying the free will, this is what right is'; and *En.*, §486: 'This reality in general as the *existence* of the free will is *right*, which is not merely to be understood as limited juridical right, but rather comprehensively as the existence of all determinations of freedom.'
12. The above is a condensation of an interpretation which I have developed in greater detail in my 'Freedom's Devices'. See chapter 5, note 5 for bibliographical details.
13. *Rationality* or reason is, for Hegel, thought to the extent that it has reality or, alternatively, reality to the extent that it is a mode of expression of thought. Reason represents, in short, the famous identity of thought and being. It is, in general, opposed by Hegel to the 'understanding', which represents rather thought insofar as it is conceived as 'merely' a mode of reflection upon a reality which is given independently of thought. 'Thought', 'absolute subjectivity', 'spirit', 'reason' are all in the Hegelian style of discourse speculative equivalents.
14. Cf. *Ph.R*, §97: 'The infringement of right as right is something that happens and has positive existence in the external world, though inherently it is nothing at all. The manifestation of its nullity is the appearance, also in the external world, of the annihilation of the infringement. This is right actualized, the necessity of right mediating itself with itself by annulling what has infringed it.'
15. As Hegel explains in the Introduction to the *Encyclopedia*, this is what is meant by the famous motto from the *Philosophy of Right* to the effect that 'what is rational is actual and what is actual is rational': not that everything that *so happens* to exist is rational, but rather that determinate existence or *Dasein* 'is in part *appearance* and only in part actual' (*En.L*, §6). Hegel elaborates upon this point in the section of the *Encyclopedia* on 'Actuality', where he concludes: 'What is not rational, is precisely therefore not to be regarded as actual' (*En.L*, §142, add.).
16. For other examples, see *En.L*, §24, add. 2; *En.L*, §213; and, especially, *En.*, §375, on 'the death of the individual from out of itself', where Hegel, writing of the biological organism, observes: 'its non-conformity to the generality is its *original sickness* and the inborn *seed of death*'.
17. The 'young Marx' might have ventured an answer to this question. A significant part of his *1844 Manuscripts* is dedicated to demonstrating the

objective reality which the human 'species-being' (*Gattungswesen*) acquires in the course of history and, more specifically, in the form of a developed system of private property. Some few years after the composition of the *Manuscripts*, in reflecting upon published texts from the same period, Marx would openly regret having employed the concept of a 'species' at all in this context, since it was in fact the objective reality for the individual of the *collectivity* to which s/he belongs – and not of the general *concept* under which as 'human' s/he could be subsumed – which was at issue (cf. *GI*, 103/217–18). In any event, Hegel himself has no answer to the question posed here; and he could not have resorted to the one which Marx attempted, since the 'power' of the kind over the individual to which he refers is supposed to apply to *all* species, not just the human species.

18. It is worthy of note – especially in light of recent attempts at interpreting Hegel as a champion of liberalism – that according to Hegel's conception of 'right', the 'merely' particular individual can be *forced* to partake in the 'general will'. Since, furthermore, the 'general will' is supposed to be nothing other than the expression of the rational as such, it follows that the individual ought (viz. if s/he is to behave rationally) even to find in this act of coercion the confirmation of 'substantial freedom'. The punishment of a criminal is then, according to Hegel, even a 'mode of existence' of his or her 'freedom' *qua* rational being – it is, namely, the criminal's *right*! Cf. *Ph.R*, §100.
19. 'Universality' on its own is affected by much the same ambiguity (and especially indeed in philosophical discourse). Hence the usual practice of Hegel translators to render *Allgemeinheit*, *das Allgemein*, etc., by 'universality', 'the universal', etc., is entirely appropriate, precisely because it preserves the ambiguity of the original text.
20. It is, incidentally, not at all necessary to go back to Hegel's early works to 'discover' the theological motivation of his system. The theological appeal is everywhere present in the completed system itself. Hegel even attaches theological significance to the triadic structure of the 'syllogism' which organizes his entire exposition. 'The logical categories in general,' he writes, 'can be seen as definitions of the absolute, as the *metaphysical definitions of God . . .*' (*En.L*, §85). I do not want to multiply examples here simply for the sake of doing so. But readers are encouraged to consult especially Hegel's logical interpretation of 'original sin' (*En.L*, §24, add. 3) for abundant confirmation of the importance which he himself attaches to the affinity of his presentation with Christian doctrine.

10 THE 'REALITY' OF CONTRADICTION

1. Cf. *En.L*, §83, add.: 'The relation between the three stages of the logical idea mentioned here appears in real and concrete shape in the following way: God, who is the truth, is known by us in His truth, that is, as absolute spirit, only in so far as we at the same time recognize that the world which He created, nature and finite spirit, are, in their difference from Him, untrue.'

2. In the customary logical usage, 'truth' is just the property of being true and only propositions can exhibit this property. Hence, there is no 'truth' as such, but only true (and false) propositions. For Hegel, however, 'truth' has a substantial being in its own right. It is '*the*' truth. Everything is precisely *un*true to the degree that it does not form part of this one substantial 'truth': which is, namely, the actuality of thought contained in existence. Again, the theological background to the Hegelian conception of truth is both obvious and openly acknowledged by Hegel himself (cf. *En.L*, §19, add. 1).
3. Hegel, who was fond of etymological arguments, would have found an ally in the English language in this regard, since in fact the *primordial* acceptation of the English 'true' is precisely that which gets disclosed by the example. 'True' and the modern German '*treu*', meaning loyal or faithful, share a common morphological ancestor.
4. In deference to the accepted practice among Hegel translators, I will continue for the most part to render Hegel's '*Schluß*' by 'syllogism'. Though there are in fact good reasons to prefer 'inference'. The use of the latter in sentences such as 'Everything is an inference' or 'The living is the inference' gives a better approximation to the bizarre character of their German originals; whereas through sheer repetition, generations of commentators on 'the Hegelian syllogism' have perhaps finally lulled at least students of philosophy into believing that the same sentences rendered with 'syllogism' are in no way exceptional. 'Inference', moreover, preserves the relation of the substantive *Schluß* to the verb *schließen*, hence to the *logical act* of 'inferring' or drawing a conclusion.
5. Hegel has even less patience for inorganic nature than for organic nature: hence, his tendency to give emphatic form to such points by referring them to 'the living', which is, after all, supposed to be 'the truth' of the non-living just as 'spirit' in general is supposed to be 'the truth' of nature.
6. Even Marx himself occasionally succumbed to temptation. This is especially evident in the *Grundrisse*, where Marx sometimes attempts to organize his material in conformity with the moments of the Hegelian 'syllogism'. This practice reaches its apex (or nadir) in a digression, near the outset of the 'Chapter on Capital', wherein Marx attempts to arrange the contents of the entire ensuing development under the headings of 'Generality', 'Particularity' and 'Individuality' (*Gr.*, 275–6/200). In a last burst of Hegeloid enthusiasm, Marx exclaims, 'the form of the syllogism can also be grasped in another way: as wage-labour – capital – ground rent; but capital must always appear as the active middle term' (276/200). Thereafter, in actually carrying out his analyses, Marx makes no further reference to the 'syllogism', nor any use of it. The terms of the 'syllogism' do reappear together once in *Capital*, though in a strictly taxonomic usage and in a passage which is remarkable only for its blandness (cf. *CI*, 471/371), and they also merit a perfunctory allusion in the 1859 *Critique* (*CPE*, 94/76).
7. It is unfortunate that Marx expressed admiration for Hegel's interpretation of judgement (and even worse that he expressed admiration for the latter's interpretation of the syllogism) in a laconic footnote to the first (1867) edition of *Capital*. Cf. *MEGA* II, 5, p. 32, note 20. But it is fortunate at least that he removed the allusion from the second edition.

8. Consider Frege's 'the morning star is the evening star'. As Frege insists, such a statement is not simply definitional, it does not simply tell us that what is *called* 'the morning star' is identical to what is *called* 'the evening star'. Nonetheless, the extensions of the expression in the subject and that in the predicate in fact coincide: subject and predicate exactly 'cover one another', just as Hegel says they should. What differs between subject and predicate is rather what I would call the context of involvements *via which* the extension of the expressions is determined (or, since the expressions are in this case both 'singular terms', we can say rather via which the *referent* is determined). Frege calls this 'the mode of presentation of the thing designated'.
9. Cf., for instance, *SL*, 595/II, 268; *En.L*, §31; and Hegel's remarks on the 'speculative' proposition in the 'Preface' to the *Phenomenology*, §62.
10. I have been greatly aided in the discussion which follows by consulting William and Martha Kneale's *The Development of Logic* (Oxford: Oxford University Press, 1962), where what Hegel called variously the 'pedantic', 'boring' and 'worthless' study of the formal syllogism is presented with great clarity.
11. Cf. *SL*, 721–4/II, 423–6 and *En.L*, §198.
12. In light of Hegel's 'general schema', readers who have been following the discussion carefully up to this point might be surprised to find here the '*universal*' in the position of the middle term. As we have seen, however, Hegel argues that the first figure of the syllogism, which provides this 'general schema', is inherently unstable. Hence, it 'passes over' into the second figure, where (so Hegel alleges) individuality mediates the connection of particularity and universality, and finally the third figure, where now universality mediates the connection of individuality and particularity. According to Hegel, each of the terms of the syllogism is supposed to take the position of the middle in turn: thus making 'everything' not only *a* syllogism, but indeed a system of three syllogisms! What Hegel has to say about the second figure is evident nonsense, since the second figure does not serve to assert a connection at all, but rather to *deny* one (and, in any case, even if we ignore the negative quality of the conclusion, there is simply no reason why the middle term in any of the moods of the second figure should have the character of individuality with respect to the extremes). What he says about the third is equally incoherent, since the conclusion in the third figure is always particular (viz. *in scope*, not in Hegel's sense); hence, even in those moods where it is positive, it does not operate by demonstrating the *subsumption* of one set by another, but merely by showing their *intersection*. Presumably, Hegel has in mind the first mood of the third figure, in which 'major' and 'minor' term get connected by way of their both being predicated of some third subject term which is universal *in scope*, that is to say, which applies to everything which possesses the determination in question (as in 'All A is B, and all A is C, therefore some B is C'). Apart from its universal quantification, however, the subject term is certainly *not* of greater extension than the terms it relates: i.e. 'universal' or general with respect *to them*. In fact, were the third figure as Hegel suggests it ought to be, it would specify the structure of an *in*valid inference: as in, for instance, 'All men

are mortal, Caius is mortal, Therefore Caius is a man'.

13. In the world of commodities too, there is a universality, viz. their value, which takes shape, not exactly as some one *particular*, but rather as some *specific* exchangeable thing among them: viz. the universal equivalent or, in other words, money. I will suggest below that Marx's penchant to 'coquette' with Hegel has everything to do with this.
14. Hegel does not even have the excuse of etymology in this instance. Both the Latinate *contradiction* and the Germanic *Widerspruch* clearly disclose the meta-discursive character of their primordial acceptations.
15. It might be better to say: no proposition can be both true and false – thus allowing for the possibility of propositions which are neither. Leibniz in fact denies that there is any such possibility – as does Russell after him. But, as Strawson has suggested, a sentence can be propositional in form and yet not be suitable to asserting anything about anything, viz. if it has a non-referring expression as its grammatical subject (or, more precisely, an expression which has no reference on the specific occasion of its use). Nonetheless, if we wanted to preserve Leibniz's original formulation, we could do so, for instance, by distinguishing propositions as strictly *logical* entities, from declarative sentences, which are the linguistic means used to express propositions, and 'statements', which are the result of this use of declarative sentences on specific occasions. Keeping these distinctions in mind, we could say, then, that in cases such as those in question certain *statements* might be neither true nor false, but *not* any proposition; and the statements would be neither true nor false precisely *to the degree that*, there not being anything which they are about, they are unsuitable for expressing any proposition.
16. There are in fact two quite distinct forms of socio-historical materialism to be found in the Marxian corpus: what we might call a *scientific* form (the general bases of which are developed in the *Grundrisse* and *Capital*, but which also guides in a certain manner the vast array of Marx's writings on more concrete historical problems and conjunctures) and a *speculative* form (which acquires its most developed expression in *The German Ideology*). On the distinctive principle of the former, cf. Chapter 5 above; and on the mystifying (and relative to Hegel's idealism, mimetic) quality of the latter, Chapter 7. I have borrowed the generic expression 'philosophical materialism' from W.A. Suchting, who likewise contrasts the latter to Marx's socio-historical materialism. See Suchting's 'Marx, Lenin and the Concept of Materialism', in W.A. Suchting, *Marx and Philosophy* (New York: New York University Press, 1986), pp. 53–80. 'Philosophical' materialism involves both an 'ontological' and an 'epistemological' aspect, which can be summarized by the claims that there is a world independent of thought and that knowledge is nothing if not knowledge of this world (or, in other words, that only as such does thought acquire, in Kant's phrase, 'objective validity'). The question as to whether this package of claims or some variant thereof – for instance, the hypothetical formulation of the epistemological principle could be supplemented by the categorical claim that knowledge is indeed possible – ought to be understood as merely outlining a 'policy', per Suchting's suggestion, or as being demonstrable will not occupy us here.

17. See Kant's *Critique of Pure Reason*, Bxl, note *a*. In his 'Refutation of Idealism' (cf. A367–A380 and B274–B279), Kant presents 'transcendental idealism' – roughly, the doctrine that space and time are necessary forms of intuition (rather than attributes of things-in-themselves) apart from which no perception is possible – and 'empirical realism' – roughly, the doctrine that matter, qua object of perception, has an independent and certain existence – as complementary with one another. Hegel had no doubts regarding the materialist character of Kant's epistemology, and indeed many of his own most strident declarations of the principle of idealism are formulated as polemical rejoinders to the latter. Cf., for an example, the following note 18.
18. His polemic against Kant is obviously a privileged topos in much of what Hegel has to say concerning contradiction. The following passage, with which Hegel concludes his criticism of the Kantian antinomies, is typical: 'It shows an excessive tenderness for the world to remove contradiction from it and then to transfer the contradiction to spirit, to reason, where it is allowed to remain unresolved. In point of fact it is spirit which is so strong that it can endure contradiction, but it is spirit, too, that knows how to resolve it. But the so-called world . . . is never and nowhere without contradiction, but it is unable to endure it and is therefore, subject to coming-to-be and ceasing-to-be' (*SL*, 237–8/I, 276). Colletti has assembled many other passages highlighting the connection between Hegel's doctrine of contradiction and his idealism. See especially chapter 1 of *Marxism and Hegel*.
19. I say 'for example', since, despite Hegel's obvious preference for patrilineal forms of descent – 'father is the other of son,' he writes, 'and son the other of father, and each only *is* as this other of the other' (*SL*, 441/II, 77) – reality, as Hegel only begrudgingly concedes (cf. *En.* §220 and §370), is burdened with *two* biological sexes. Clearly, a father can still be a father, even if his 'other' happens to be a daughter, and a son cannot be a son without another 'other' besides his father.
20. Cf. Marx's oft-cited letter to Engels of 14 January 1858.
21. Cf. *CI*, 256/169–70.
22. Cf. Chapter 9, section 9.1.
23. The same structure is apparent in the 'transition' to *wrong* in the *Philosophy of Right*: 'The transition to wrong is made by the logical higher necessity that the moments of the concept – here the principle of rightness or the will as universal, and right in its real existence, which is just the particularity of the will – should be posited as explicitly different . . .' (*Ph.R*, §81, add.). Despite Hegel's insistence on calling this a 'logical necessity' – and logical necessities are not normally susceptible to being judged 'higher' or 'lower' – he has nowhere shown that there is anything about the categories which precede *wrong* in his exposition which, considered independently of the demands of 'absolute subjectivity', in fact necessitates this 'transition'. For the discussion of an analogous example from the 'Essence' section of the Encyclopedia *Logic*, cf. Suchting, *Marx and Philosophy*, pp. 87–90.
24. As for empirical-relational opposites, although they do indeed have extensions, nonetheless they do not have extensions in exactly the same

way as general empirical concepts. Consider, for example, the general empirical concept *zinc*. The extension of the concept is exclusive of the extensions of each of the concepts which are contrastable with it within a common genus (for instance, *platinum*, *bronze*, *silver*, and so on), though the summation of the extensions of each of the specific concepts constitutes in turn the extension of the *genus*, viz. *metal*, to which they all belong. Now consider, for example, the empirical-relational opposite concepts *father* and *son*. On the one hand, neither of the concepts belongs to any *genus*; on the other hand, their extensions are not mutually exclusive.

25. The conflation of *particularity* and *specificity*, such as we have already remarked upon in connection with the 'syllogism', is also to be detected in Hegel's argument here.
26. That is, *when* contradiction is included in this series. In the *Encyclopedia* variant of Hegel's argument, the category into which the opposition of *identity* and *difference* gets resolved is not contradiction (which is in fact just barely alluded to in the passage cited) but rather *ground* (*Grund*), in the sense of a reason or basis. (Thus Hegel cites here Leibniz's 'principle of the sufficient reason' or '*Satz des Grundes*'.) *Ground* is, then, presented as the 'unity of identity and difference' – even though in the 'greater' *Logic* Hegel confers this honour rather upon *opposition* (*SL*, 424/II, 55).
27. '*Es zugrunde geht*', Hegel would say. The semantic polyvalency of the German word *Grund* and its cognate forms (cf. the previous note) is yet another fertile source of slippages in Hegel's argument.
28. Cf. *SL*, 143–4/I, 157–8 and *En.L*, §28.
29. Cf. *SL*, 606–7/II, 281.

11 A FORTUITOUS THEORETICAL ISOMORPHISM

1. Marx in fact employs this simile in analysing the 'simple' value-form, which he does by way of his well-known example: the value of so many yards of linen being expressed in a coat serving as 'value-equivalent'. He writes of the linen in this relation that: 'as a value it is "the same as a coat" [*Rockgleiches*] and therefore looks like a coat. Thus the linen acquires a value-form different from its natural-form. Its being as value [*ihr Wertsein*] is manifest in its similarity to [*Gleichheit mit*] the coat, just as the sheep's nature of the Christian is manifest in his similarity to the Lamb of God'. As we shall see below, however, Marx's analysis is designed precisely to demonstrate that this 'simple' value-form is nothing other than the implicit basis of the fully developed money-form, and that the consideration of the former plainly reveals the very same content which is but obscurely represented in the latter.

   As Colletti has pointed out (*Marxism and Hegel*, p. 272), the comparison between the money-commodity and the Christ as 'God-man' is already central to Marx's very earliest attempts at theorizing the former as general equivalent, viz. in his commentary, composed in 1844, on James Mill's *Elements of Political Economy*. Cf. Karl Marx, *Early Writings* (New York: Vintage, 1975), pp. 260–1/*MEW*, Ergänzungsband, Erster Teil, pp. 445–6.

2. Colletti has brought out the character of these, so to speak, interlocking similitudes with great clarity in the concluding chapter of *Marxism and Hegel* on 'The Idea of "Bourgeois-Christian" Society'.
3. Cf. Marx's 'Theses on Feuerbach' (in *MEW*, vol. 3), especially Thesis IV and Theses VI–VIII.
4. Wal Suchting has coined the apt expression 'cognitive psequdomorphs' to describe such cases of formal similitudes between theories which are substantively quite unrelated. Though I am not sure he would endorse the application of his coinage in the present context, nonetheless his explication of it is worth quoting for the light it throws on the sort of affinity I am suggesting obtains between value theory and Hegelian 'logic'. Whereas I have lifted the distinctions employed in my discussion from biology, Suchting takes his cue rather from mineralogy and geology. Thus he writes: 'These sciences are familiar with the phenomenon of minerals that have the crystal form of one species but the chemical composition of another. . . . The one is called a "pseudomorph" of the other, and the two are obviously easily confused in the absence of deeper, chemical analysis. The analogous situation, where the same or very similar *words* are attached to different concepts (and similar *sentences* to different *propositions*), leading to confusion between the one and the other, I propose to call "cognitive pseudomorphs".' See W.A. Suchting, 'Constructivism Deconstructed', *Science and Education* 1 (1992), p. 259 (note 39).
5. Marx does write in *Capital* of an 'identity of sale and purchase' or, in other words, that 'sale is purchase' (*CI*, 203/123). Such a usage is hardly remarkable, however, and it certainly does not require initiation into the mysteries of Hegelian 'logic' to understand its import. Indeed, a Hegelian devotee might be better prepared to misunderstand the latter. As we have seen, there is nothing mysterious in the fact that a single object, in this case a single social act, can bear either of two relational-opposite determinations or even – as in the case under consideration, since the nature of this act is precisely constituted by a certain relation – must bear both. Any polar relation which is not perfectly symmetrical will have an opposed character with respect to each of the poles related in it. Thus the relation of '*x* being to the left of *y*' will at once have the character of '*y* being to the right of *x*', the relation of lordship with respect to the lord will at once be the relation of bondage with respect to the bondsman, and a sale, with respect to the party who alienates a commodity in exchange for money, will at once be a purchase, with respect to the party who alienates money in exchange for a commodity. As already noted, such banalities do not have the consequence of making that which is to the left 'identical' with that which is to the right of it, nor the lord 'identical' with the bondsman, nor the seller 'identical' with the purchaser. Marx is completely clear about the relational basis of the 'identity of opposites' here at issue (though this clarity, it must be said, is somewhat obscured by the standard English translations). 'Sale and purchase', he writes, 'are one identical act as mutual interrelation [*Wechselbeziehung*] between two persons who stand in polar opposition to each other, the commodity-owner and the money-owner. They constitute two acts which stand in polar opposition to each other as the actions of one and the same person' (*CI*,

208/127). Indeed, the platitude that every sale is a purchase, far from representing any distinctive insight of Marx, provides rather the alibi for the apologetic denial of the possibility of economic crises – most notably, in the form of 'Say's Law' – which is in fact precisely what Marx is *criticizing* in the paragraph from which the cited passage is taken.

6. 'The logical truth', Hegel writes, 'must be the *pure truth* itself' (*SL*, 594/II, 267).
7. Cf. *SL*, 630/II, 310 and *SL*, 668–9/II, 357–9. The latter passage – in which Hegel comments at length on the circumstance that the 'syllogism' in the usual logical sense is, after all, composed of judgements – brings out especially clearly the metaphorical or, to borrow Marx's apt description (cf. *CHDS*, 149/287), '*allegorical*' character of Hegel's talk of 'syllogisms'. Thus Hegel concludes: 'All things are the *syllogism*: a universal that through particularity is united with individuality. But they are certainly not a whole consisting of *three propositions*.' For further references, see chapter 10, note 9 above.
8. As we have seen throughout Part III, opposites are described by Hegel as 'identical' to the extent that they are supposed to 'pass into one another', whereas their 'unity' is rather the putatively more concrete determination in which the abstract opposition gets 'sublated'.
9. See chapter 10, section 10.6 and section 10.8 above.
10. See chapter 9, section 9.2 and section 9.3 above, and chapter 10, section 10.5. Perhaps the most picturesque expression of Hegel's disdain for particulars comes precisely from the 'Sense-Certainty' chapter of the *Phenomenology*. Having praised the 'wisdom' of the 'ancient Eleusinian Mysteries of Ceres and Bacchus', Hegel goes on to remark: 'Even the animals are not shut out from this wisdom but, on the contrary, show themselves to be the most profoundly initiated into it; for they do not stand idly in front of sensuous things as if these possessed intrinsic being, but, despairing of their reality, and completely assured of their nothingness, they fall to without ceremony and eat them up. And all nature, like the animals, celebrates these open mysteries which teach the truth about sensuous things' (*Phen.*, §109).
11. Cf. *EPM*, 191/587: 'to talk in human language, the abstract thinker learns in his intuition of nature that the entities which he thought to create from nothing, from pure abstraction – the entities he believed he was producing in the divine dialectic as pure products of the labour of thought . . . – are nothing else but *abstractions* from *characteristics of nature*'. It is astonishing that prosaic observations such as this one could be taken for the innovative core of Marx's 'materialist' overturning of Hegel – even more so since Hegel does, after all, raise many pertinent objections against empiricism. What is made especially clear from such remarks, incidentally, is just how thoroughly the young Marx's intellectual formation was indeed Hegelian in character – no one otherwise would so readily go to such precarious extremes in order to combat Hegel – and just how little it was affected by any knowledge of, say, Kant's first *Critique*. (On the sparse references to Kant in Marx's writings, see chapter 12, note 6 below.) There is no evidence to suggest that this deficit was ever made up in Marx's subsequent development. Though there is also no reason to conclude that

it had any deleterious effects upon the latter once Marx abandoned the enterprise of generalizing philosophical speculation (which is conceived of in his early works rather as *anti*-philosophical speculation – and even *this* shows how completely Marx identified philosophy *tout court* with specifically Hegelian philosophy) and devoted his attentions to the economic, political and historical studies which comprise by far the greater part of his corpus. The ignorance of Kantian epistemology has, however, continued to haunt so-called 'Marxist philosophy' – which, leaving aside the dogmatic and institutionalized form it acquired in the Soviet Union and the other countries of 'real existing socialism', has tended to have the character of a 'spontaneous' philosophy of Marxist social scientists and political activists. This is evident precisely in the manner in which empiricist commonplaces are able to pass for 'materialist' insights. Such naivety does not disappear all at once from Marx's own writings either: traces of it are still to be detected in *The German Ideology*, with its seemingly straightforward appeal to presuppositions which 'are verifiable in a purely empirical way' (*GI*, 42/20), and, as noted above (see chapter 4), in *The Poverty of Philosophy*. Nonetheless, the, so to say, 'common-sense' materialism of Marx's early works is increasingly absorbed by a more ambitious programmatic 'materialism' in his so-called 'works of the break'. The relation of this programmatic 'materialism' to the prior epistemological tradition is already a much more complicated issue – on which, see the following note.

12. See chapter 7 above. The 'historical materialism' which is the most celebrated legacy of Marx's efforts at 'overturning' Hegel is, as noted, a strangely hybrid sort of historical/epistemological theory: an 'absolute historicism' – which is to say, an absolute historicization of knowledge. Though in the very same texts, sometimes in the very same passages, in which this 'historical materialism' acquires its canonical statements, there is also another tendency to be detected which bears a more unambiguous and explicit relation to the epistemological problematic as such. This philosophically 'materialist' tendency of the 'works of the break' acquires its own independent and programmatic statement in the 'Theses on Feuerbach'. Now, what has been aptly baptized by W.A. Suchting as the 'practical materialism' of the 'Theses' (cf. *Marx and Philosophy*, p. 56), unlike what I have called the 'common-sense' materialism which predominates in the *1844 Manuscripts*, is certainly not to be confused with any simple empiricism. It is, after all, expressly formulated by Marx in opposition to what he himself describes as the merely 'contemplative' character of Feuerbach's materialism – or indeed, as Marx puts it in Thesis I, of 'all hitherto existing materialism (that of Feuerbach included)'. Consequently, there is no room in Marx's 'new' materialism (Thesis X) for any subject of cognition peeling away layers of particularity in order to disengage the general 'predicates' of objects which only first confront it in the epistemological situation. Instead, human subjectivity is treated as 'always already' itself bound up with the material world as its context of practical involvements – it is treated as an *objective* subjectivity, in effect – and, correlatively, the objective reality of which subjects of this sort could acquire knowledge is regarded as 'always already' constituted in relation

to subjective practices. This structure is in fact strongly reminiscent of Heidegger's 'being-in-the-world'. Whereas the '*Dasein*' of the latter, however, is presented by Heidegger as essentially individualized and the contexts in which Heidegger places it are of the most banal 'everyday' variety, Marx's practical subjectivity is clearly collective in character and its objective field of action is given by the totality of the social relations in which its (as Heidegger would say) 'comportment toward the world' acquires historically determinate form. For confirmation of this last point, see Theses VI–X.

13. *MEGA*, Zweite Abteilung, Band 5, p. 634. Colletti also attaches decisive importance to this passage. He discusses it, briefly, though in terms largely consonant with my own treatment, at the very conclusion of *Marxism and Hegel*, pp. 281–2.
14. The passages come from the second of a series of sections on four 'peculiarities' of the equivalent-form of value. The content of three of these is reprised, though more succinctly, in the section on the equivalent-form in the first chapter of the later editions of *Capital*.

12 THE 'SUBJECT–PREDICATE REVERSAL': AN EXCURSUS ON MARX'S *CRITIQUE OF HEGEL'S DOCTRINE OF THE STATE*

1. For a contemporary example of Hegelian apologetics, see chapter 5, note 1 above. For Hegel's own remarks on the philosophy of history as 'theodicy', see *En.L*, §147, add.
2. Cf. *CHDS*, 105/246: 'What Hegel says about the powers of government does not deserve the name of philosophical development. Most of these paragraphs could stand word for word in the Prussian Legal Code.' See too Marx's comments on Hegel's 'derivation' of the alleged necessity of civil service entry exams at *CHDS*, 113/253.
3. So as not to provoke the rebukes of the Hegel enthusiasts, it should be noted that Marx is not suggesting in this passage that empirical reality *as such* is 'accepted as it is' and 'declared to be rational' by Hegel. We know very well that this sort of commonplace interpretation of Hegel is not accurate. (Cf. chapter 9, note 15 above.) Marx's point is rather that Hegel, in accordance with the procedure I have outlined in the previous paragraph, adopts *some* existing state of affairs or institutional arrangement – simply put, as I have said above, a *matter of fact*, though in the specific case a matter of *social* fact – and endows it with the significance of being a form of existence of 'the idea'. Thus, the matter of fact in question is 'shown' to be 'rational' (cf. chapter 9, note 13), but its own *intrinsic* rationality or logic – in the sense, that we could speak of the 'logic', say, of the market as opposed to the 'logic' of economic planning – not only remains unclarified, it ***does not even get broached.***
4. For further comments of much the same tenor, cf. *CHDS*, 64–5/209; 69/213; 71/214; 72/215; 73/216; 73–4/217; 74/217; 75/218; 92/235; 159/296. Marx's final word – elicited by Hegel's 'explanation' of the houses into which the Estates get divided by reference to the alleged necessity that the moment of mediation in them 'acquire a separate existence' – is simply

'O Jerum!': 'Oh Jesus!' (198/333). Thereafter, his commentary breaks off. Marx returns, incidentally, to his critique of the substantialized 'concept' in his discussion of ground-rent in *CIII* (752–3/628–9, n. 26).

5. The phrase appears as such at *CHDS*, 66/210. For similar formulations in Feuerbach, see his *Vorläufige Thesen zur Reform der Philosophie*.
6. *Critique of Pure Reason*, A242–3/B300–1. For a discussion of the grounds for Kant's 'logical definition' and for further citations, see my 'A Transcendental Deduction of the Categories without the Categories', *International Philosophical Quarterly*, vol. XXXIII, no. 4 (December 1993), p. 461 and the attached note 16. Given what I have written in the present context (see chapter 11, note 11), it will be clear that I do not think the affinity between Marx's pronouncements concerning the 'subject–predicate reversal' and Kant's 'logical definition' indicates any direct influence of Kant on Marx. Of the scattered allusions to Kant to be found in Marx's early writings, almost all of them refer to Kant's moral philosophy, not his epistemology. In an appendix to Marx's doctoral dissertation, there is one mention of the famous 'hundred Thalers' from Kant's treatment of the ontological proof of God's existence (cf. *MEW*, *Ergänzungsband*, Erster Teil, p. 371). But since the 'hundred Thalers' had no doubt already become a locus classicus by 1841 and are, in any case, discussed by Hegel (cf. *En.L*, §51), this is no proof of any special familiarity with the first *Critique* on Marx's part.
7. The confusion of these two senses is especially plain and especially disconcerting in the segment of the passage which I have, for just this reason, excised.
8. Cf. *CHDS*, 90/233: 'It is understood that the political constitution as such is only formed where the private spheres have achieved an independent existence. Where commerce and landed property are unfree, where they have not yet become independent, there can also not yet be a political constitution. . . . The abstraction of the *state as such* is first proper to modernity, because the abstraction of private life is first proper to modernity. The abstraction of the *political state* is a modern product.'
9. It should be stressed that what Hegel is objecting to here is just the 'disorderly conception' of '*the* people' [*das Volk* – and it is significant that the emphasis on the definite article in the cited passage is Hegel's own]: which is to say, the *republican* conception of the same. With regard to the idea of *a* people [*ein Volk*] – in other words, the principle of nationalism – it must be said that Hegel, as already noted (cf. chapter 3, section 3.2), is the *völkisch* philosopher *par excellence*. For further evidence to this effect in the *Philosophy of Right*, see §§340–360.
10. Cf. chapter 9, note 2 above.

13 SOME PASSING REMARKS ON THE 'NEW' HEGELIAN MARXISM

1. Cf. *En.L*, §131, add.: 'Merely to be appearance, this is the proper nature of the immediate objective world itself, and insofar as we know it to be so, we recognize at the same time the essence which remains neither be-

hind nor beyond appearance, but rather precisely manifests itself as essence in that it derogates this world to pure appearance.' Cf. too *En.L*, §50, add.: '. . .it lies in the very fact that the world is *contingent* that it is merely something *transitory*, phenomenal and in and for itself *null*'.

2. Tony Smith, *The Logic of Marx's Capital* (Albany: State University of New York Press, 1990), p. 37. Symptomatically, the cited passage occurs in a chapter on 'Dialectical Logic in Marx's Work'.
3. There is one infelicitous passage from the so-called '*Urtext*' of the *Contribution to the Critique of Political Economy*, an 1858 draft of the latter text, in which Marx writes of a 'deeper process' lying behind the 'form of appearance' provided by the sphere of simple circulation (cf. *Grundrisse*, [Berlin: Dietz Verlag, 1953], pp. 922–3) and also another cognate passage in the *Grundrisse* (*Gr.*, 247/173). Such formulations exhibit a distinctly groping quality and what is especially significant about them is only that they disappear from Marx's subsequent finished texts.
4. See, for example, Christopher J. Arthur, 'Hegel's *Logic* and Marx's *Capital*', in Fred Mosely, ed., *Marx's Method in Capital: a Re-examination* (New Jersey: Humanities Press, 1993).
5. Arthur, p. 78.
6. Cf. Jairus Banaji, 'From the Commodity to Capital: Hegel's Dialectic in Marx's *Capital*', in Diane Elson, ed., *Value: the Representation of Labour in Capital*, (London: CSE Books, 1979), p. 28 and passim.
7. Other authors whose work could be cited as representative of what I have here described as 'new' Hegelian Marxism are, for instance, Michael Eldred, Geert Reuten, and Michael Williams. Many of the earliest English-language writings in this vein bear the influence of the West German Hegel–Marx scholar Hans-Georg Backhaus. (For samples of Backhaus's own writings, cf. 'Zur Dialektik der Wertform', in Alfred Schmidt, ed., *Beiträge zur marxschen Erkenntnistheorie* [Frankfurt: Suhrkamp, 1969] and 'Materialen zur Rekonstruktion der Marxschen Werttheorie' in *Gesellschaft. Beiträge zur Marxschen Theorie*, vols. 1, 2 and 11 [Frankfurt: Suhrkamp, 1974, 1975, 1978].) By now it is fair to say, however, that the 'new' Hegelian Marxism, like the 'old', constitutes a full-fledged 'discourse', and scholarly texts drawing upon its norms appear with a certain regularity from diverse sources. The 'new' Hegelian Marxism is, so to speak, 'in the atmosphere' – albeit, of course, only in the quite rarified atmosphere of academic Marxist debates. It should not need to be added that the intellectual quality of individual contributions to this literature varies greatly from case to case.

14 THE UNIVERSAL AND THE PARTICULAR IN THE CONSTITUTION OF VALUE

1. Marx seems to deny this in the first chapter of *Capital*, at one point writing: 'In order to understand how the simple value-expression of a commodity is contained in the value-relation between two commodities, we must, first of all, consider the latter quite independently of its quantitative side. Most often one proceeds the other way around and sees in the value-relation only the proportion in which definite quantities of two sorts of

commodity count as the same [*gleichgelten*]' (*CI*, 140/64). Note, however, that in this passage Marx does not in fact mention the exchange process. If definite quantities of two sorts of commodity 'count as the same', viz. as being of the same value, then clearly this implies that they should, under normal circumstances, be obtainable for one another through the exchange nexus. Since, however, the quantities in question are presumably in most cases *different*, what exactly does it mean to say that they 'count as the same'? What in other words constitutes the value-measure with respect to which *different* quantities of heterogeneous goods 'count as' the *same quantity*?! It is this, as Franz Petry baptized it, 'qualitative' value problem which Marx will continually accuse the classical political economists of having passed over in their eagerness to answer the *empirical* question of what regulates the value of commodities: or, in other words, what determines the quantitative level of the latter. Nonetheless, the 'qualitative' value problem only arises on the assumption that commodities exchange in *some* definite proportions. So, Marx's suggestion in the cited passage is in fact a bit misleading.

2. Marx renders the equal sign in German as 'sind . . . wert', as in '20 Ellen Leinwand sind 1 Rock wert'. The standard English translation 'is worth', as in '20 yards linen is worth 1 coat', has the advantages of being both colloquial and a cognate of the German expression. Its disadvantage, however, is that it effaces the connection between Marx's example and that of which it is supposed to be an example: viz. precisely the '*Wert*form', the '*value*-form'. In fact the translation which best preserves the sense of Marx's *wert sein* is not even 'to have the value [of]' but rather 'to *be* the value [of]'. Since, however, in the given example it is supposed to be the coat which serves to express the value of the linen and not vice-versa, to provide an accurate English rendering of Marx's '20 Ellen Leinwand sind 1 Rock wert' we have precisely to perform a kind of grammatical 'inversion': viz. by bringing the '1 coat' into the position of the subject and shifting the '20 yards linen' into that of the verbal complement which completes the predicate. This gives us in English: '1 coat is the value of 20 yards linen'.
3. See chapter 6, note 11 above, for bibliographical details on Petry's small, now largely forgotten, book *Der sozialen Gehalt der Marxschen Werttheorie*.
4. The exchange-ratios assumed here for heuristic purposes have simply been adopted from the table used by Marx in *Capital* to illustrate the 'general' value-form. Cf. *CI*, 157/79.
5. Cf. *CI*, 148/71: '*Die Naturalform der Ware wird zur Wertform*'. As will be clear from the foregoing, it is a mistake to render '*wird zur Wertform*' here as 'becomes *its* value-form' (as is done in both of the standard English translations of *Capital*). Marx himself emphasizes in the very paragraph which this sentence introduces that a particular (sort of) commodity *cannot* in fact serve to express its *own* value.

15 MONEY, OR THE REAL UNIVERSALITY OF COMMODITIES

1. See chapter 6, section 6.1.
2. Cf. *CI*, 153/75; 181/102; 199/119; 209/128. In the last cited passage, Marx

writes paratactically of both an 'immanent opposition' and an 'immanent contradiction'.

3. Of course, since the specimens of most products will not be divisible into homogeneous parts and, in any case, as with the sedan of our last example, would not retain their value when thus disarticulated, such 'fractions' are more ideal than real. This is to say that to the fraction of the value of some good whose specific use-value derives from its real physical integrity, there does not correspond any real physical fraction of the good itself. Nonetheless, it will be clear what is here implied: viz. that the exchange-value realized in the sale of a specimen of some commodity can function in turn as a fraction of the total exchange-value required to realize the purchase-price of a more valuable commodity.
4. Note that it does not follow from this that anything which just so happens to be exchangeable can serve as value-equivalent. The obstacles to non-reproducible goods serving as equivalent help indeed to elucidate the meaning of the proposition that such goods do not have values, even though they clearly can be given a price. If something has a value or 'is' a value, we should be able to express value in it. But how, for instance, could we express the value of bread in, say, Matisse canvasses? Since the prices which the latter can fetch depend precisely on their uniqueness, their samples cannot be homogeneous with one another – indeed had we chosen some contemporary artists for our example, it would be clear that this is as much a matter of principle in the art-market as a matter of fact. They thus fail to supply any consistent unit of measurement. Furthermore – and this is just a correlate to the requisite singularity of so-called 'fine art' – however often even just a particular canvas is sold, its selling-price cannot be expected to exhibit any regularity. So, even if we insisted on treating just the single canvas as our 'unit', the 'value' which this unit represents would be too erratic for it to provide a suitable mode of expression for value in general. This is to say, in effect, that the single canvas does *not* represent a value, since the regularity assumption is essential to the very concept of value and indeed is what distinguishes the latter from the empirical concept of market price.
5. Cf. *CI*, 206/125: 'The complete metamorphosis of a commodity presupposes, in its simplest form, four extremes and three personae dramatis.'
6. Indeed, for this very reason, it might be thought better to avoid the word 'exchange' altogether: that is, in light of the strong connotation of bilateralism which typically attaches to the latter. Nonetheless, the principle of reciprocity, which is self-evident in barter, is at least formally preserved under conditions of commodity-exchange too. Only in commodity-exchange the reciprocity in question is no longer immediate: the parties between whom it should obtain are no longer particular economic agents, but rather *each* particular economic agent and the *whole* of society. In contrast to the concrete transferral of goods through which reciprocity is achieved in barter, the principle thus becomes abstract: requiring, as we have seen, that for each economic agent, that agent can only appropriate some portion of the total social product (in whatever concrete form) on the condition of alienating an equivalent portion of the total social product (in whatever concrete form). Hence, even if it be 'multi-' rather than

'bilateral', the outcome of the totality of transactions remains best and most simply grasped under the title of 'exchange'. It should be recalled, however, that empirically-existing market systems allow for exceptions to their golden rule – for example, in the case of landed proprietors (see chapter 6, section 6.3 above) – and it should be kept in mind too that with the establishment of private property in other persons' capacity to labour, viz. under specifically capitalist conditions, the formal reciprocity of exchange can serve, in ways already examined, to secure substantive relations of exploitation.

7. Cf. also *CI*, 180–1/101.
8. Of course, paper notes too have regular costs of production. Indeed, given the intricacy of design required to safeguard the authenticity of paper currencies, such costs can become quite high. Paradoxically, it is precisely the cheapness of the material employed that entails the greatness of the expense incurred by the state in order to place upon it an imprint of sufficient ornateness as to deter the illicit reproduction of the monetary tokens. Nonetheless, no matter how great such costs become, that there is no intrinsic connection between them and the circulatory function discharged by the notes is made plain, for instance, by the range of denominations in which the latter get issued. Clearly, the capacity of a £50 note to circulate goods with a value five times greater than those circulated by a £10 note does not depend on the labour-time requisite to the production of the former being 5 times greater than the labour-time requisite to the production of the latter. In fact it merely depends on the number 50 being 5 times greater than the number 10.
9. Cf. *CI*, 222–3/140 and *CPE*, 114/93. As Marx discusses at far greater length in the *Critique* than in *Capital*, the process in question begins simply with the abrasion suffered by actual gold coins through their circulation.
10. This apart from the other properties which any commodity must exhibit in order to provide an adequate practical and theoretical representation of exchange-value – on which, see chapter 4, note 15 above. Marx recognizes the decisiveness of the durability criterion, when he remarks in passing in *Capital* that: '. . .the seller has money, i.e. a commodity which preserves a form capable of circulation, whether it sooner or later appears on the market again' (*CI*, 208/127). Cf. too *Gr.* 231/158, where he observes: 'All commodities are just perishable money; money is the imperishable commodity.' It will be understood that when I say that the money-commodity should be such as to retain its value, this has nothing to do with the classical political economists' search for a so-called 'invariable standard of value'. Indeed, the value represented by the money-commodity *must* be variable, since it is quite simply of the nature of value to be so. This pertains to the *sort* of commodity in question. But, however much the value of the sort of good may vary, in order properly to exercise the functions of the money-commodity, its particular specimens must not too rapidly lose the value which they represent as samples of that sort. Apart from a wholesale and absolute devaluation of the sort and hence all its samples, the way in which individual commodities lose their value is, of course, through their physical destruction: which ensues either as a consequence of their use or simply as a consequence of their exposure over

time to the natural environment. It is clear that metals, in the various configurations they are given through human intervention, are especially well-suited to resist such destructive influences. The further advantage which a more precious metal affords over a less precious one is the capacity to concentrate the greatest possible value in the least possible space.

11. Consider in this context the very curious words of Michel Camdessus, director of the International Monetary Fund, upon the announcement of an IMF proposal to sell 5 percent of its gold reserves: 'This gold will not be abandoned de facto. We will sell it, invest it [sic] and we will only use the revenues.' 'IMF chief backs gold "ringfence"', *Financial Times*, 30 April 1996.
12. Cf. *CI*, 180–1/101.
13. Cf. chapter 6, section 6.2 above.
14. For Marx's comments, see, among other places, *CPE*, 72–3/55–7 and *CI*, 193–5/114–16. The described phenomenon alone certainly does not make the amount of the money-commodity actually represented by some denomination any less 'real' – as Fernand Braudel has, for instance, suggested in discussing the history of the *livre tournois*. (Cf. Fernand Braudel, *L'identité de la France*, seconde partie [Paris: Arthaud-Flammarion, 1986], p. 363.) To pursue Braudel's example: if, due to the gradual diminution of the weight of the *denier* (viz. the coined sub-division of the *livre*), 240 *deniers* come to constitute a monetary '*livre*' which is in fact somewhat less than a pound-weight of silver (*une livre-poids d'argent*), then all that this proves is that the *word* '*livre*' has no necessary connection to what it signifies. It is not *this* development which transforms the *livre* into a so-called 'imaginary money', but rather the de facto inability of the *denier* to establish itself as the uncontested medium of circulation. The device of employing an 'imaginary money' as the customary money of account became necessary under historical circumstances in which *various* currencies – both coins composed of different metals (viz. gold and silver) and coins composed of the same metal but of diverse weights – coexisted and were used interchangeably as means of exchange: circumstances in which *no* particular currency had in fact gained recognition as the uncontested equivalent-form. Under such circumstances, the exchange-system was only able to function by appeal to the artifice of an 'imaginary money' in units of which each of the empirically-existing monies were rated. For some brief indications by Marx touching upon this issue, cf. *CPE*, 73–4/57–8; and for an extensive discussion, see Luigi Einaudi, 'The Theory of Imaginary Money from Charlemagne to the French Revolution', in *Enterprise and Secular Change*, eds. Frederic C. Lane and Jelle C. Riemersma (Illinois: Irwin, 1953).

16 THE METAPHYSICS OF VALUE: ON SECOND-ORDER OBJECTIVITY

1. *CI*, 138/62.
2. Recall our earlier discussion of 'concrete' versus 'abstract' forms of property, in chapter 6, sections 2–4.

3. Marx recognizes this nuance at *Gr.*, 261/185: 'It is not the same exchange-value – precisely because its substance is a particular commodity – which first becomes money and then a commodity again. . . .'
4. For a detailed treatment of the dynamics of devalorization, including an analysis of the concept of 'final' consumption, cf. my 'Value and Consumption: Prolegomena to the Theory of Crisis', *Capital and Class*, Fall 1993, pp. 53–80.
5. This entails, however, that at any given moment there must always be in circulation a sum of value *greater* than the value of those commodities which are in fact required for purposes of consumption – which is why, as alluded to above, commodity-money represents a definite social cost.
6. Cf. the original 1867 version of the first chapter of *Capital* (*MEGA*, Zweite Abteilung, Band 5), where Marx reflects, in almost perplexed tones, on just this peculiarity: 'It is as if next to and apart from lions, tigers, hares and all other really existing animals, which together constitute the various genera, species, sub-species, families, etc. of the animal kingdom, there existed also *the Animal*, the individual incarnation of the animal kingdom in its entirety. Such an individual, which in itself comprises all really existent sorts of the same thing, is a *Universal*: like Animal, God, etc.' (37). Compare *CPE*, 48/34, where Marx describes the money-commodity as 'commodity as such, *the* commodity'.
7. Cf., among other passages, *Gr.*, 154/88, 162– 3/96; *CPE*, 49/34; and, especially, *CI*, 185/105.
8. Whether this be accomplished by way of a dilettantish 'play' of analogies, as is typical of so many ostensibly 'postmodern' treatments of money (see chapter 3, section 1, 'case c' for a characteristic example), or in the apparently more sober and *streng wissenschaftlich* form of Jürgen Habermas's conceptualization of money as a 'symbolically-generalized medium of communication' – the effect is much the same. As regards Habermas's efforts, it is remarkable and more than a little revealing that a man whose international fame has been earned as a theorist of 'communicative action' should so glibly overlook all those respects in which monetary-transactions are quite unfit to be described as instances of 'communication'. Given that according to Habermas's own typology, 'communicative' types of social interaction are supposed to be distinguished precisely by their non-coercive character, one can appreciate the ideological baggage which this description carries in his work. In his *magnum opus*, Habermas in fact claims to take a certain inspiration from Marx's theory of value. He exhibits no awareness at all, however, that the analysis of money has something to do with the latter. On the novelty of Habermas's 'interpretation' of value-theory and on related matters, see my 'What is Life?: a Habermas Critique', in *Social Science Information* 31, no. 1 (March 1992).

Index

Note: entries relating to Hegelian terminology or formulae or to the Hegelian treatment of some subject-matter have been marked with an asterisk.